For Roxana

SURVIVING
POVERTY
IN MEDIEVAL
PARIS

VOLUMES IN THE SERIES
Conjunctions of Religion and Power in the Medieval Past
Edited by Barbara H. Rosenwein

UNJUST SEIZURE
Conflict, Interest, and Authority in Early Medieval Society
by Warren A. Brown

ERMENGARD OF NARBONNE AND THE WORLD OF
THE TROUBADOURS
by Fredric L. Cheyette

SPEAKING OF SLAVERY
Color, Ethnicity, and Human Bondage in Italy
by Steven A. Epstein

SURVIVING POVERTY IN MEDIEVAL PARIS
Gender, Ideology, and the Daily Lives of the Poor
by Sharon Farmer

THE BISHOP'S PALACE
Architecture and Authority in Medieval Italy
by Maureen C. Miller

GENDER, IDEOLOGY,

AND THE DAILY LIVES

OF THE POOR

SURVIVING
POVERTY
IN MEDIEVAL
PARIS

SHARON FARMER

Cornell University Press

Ithaca and London

First published 2002 by Cornell University Press

Printed in the United States of America

Library of Congress Cataloging-in-Publication Data

Farmer, Sharon A.
    Surviving poverty in medieval Paris : gender, ideology, and the daily lives of the poor / Sharon Farmer.
        p.   cm. — (Conjunctions of religion & power in the medieval past)
    Includes bibliographical references (p.   ) and index.
    ISBN 0-8014-3836-5 (cloth)
    1. Poverty—France—Paris—Sex differences—History—To 1500.   2. Poor—Services for—France—Paris—History—To 1500.   3. Cost and standard of living—France—Paris—History—To 1500.   4. Women—France—Paris—Economic conditions.   I. Title.   II. Series.
    HC278.P3 F37 2001
    362.5'8'09443610902—dc21   2001003585

Cornell University Press strives to use environmentally responsible suppliers and materials to the fullest extent possible in the publishing of its books. Such materials include vegetable-based, low-VOC inks and acid-free papers that are recycled, totally chlorine-free, or partly composed of nonwood fibers. For further information, visit our website at www.cornellpress.cornell.edu.

Cloth printing   10 9 8 7 6 5 4 3 2 1

CONTENTS

Illustrations   *ix*
Acknowledgments   *xi*
Abbreviations   *xiii*

Introduction   *1*
Chapter 1
   Wealth, Migration, and Poverty   *11*
Chapter 2
   Adam's Curse   *39*
Chapter 3
   Men in Need   *74*
Chapter 4
   Eve's Curse   *105*
Chapter 5
   Women in Need   *136*
Conclusion   *165*

Appendix
   Parisian Wills, 1200–1348   *171*
Bibliography   *173*
Index   *193*

ILLUSTRATIONS

FIGURES

1. Lorenz, Prior of the Abbey of Chaalis,
   Cured by Saint Louis's Cloak   *54*
2. Dudes, A Canon of Paris, Consults Physicians   *55*
3. Amelot of Chambly   *57*
4. Moriset of Ranton   *58*
5. Louis the Deaf-Mute   *74*
6. Jehanne of Serris   *120*
7. Nicole of Rubercy   *136*

MAPS

1. Paris in the Early Fourteenth Century   *14*
2. Places of Origin of Witnesses and
   Beneficiaries of the Miracles of Saint Louis   *22*
3. The Journeys of Louis the Deaf-Mute
   and Moriset of Ranton   *76*

ACKNOWLEDGMENTS

This project began over a decade ago, when I put together a set of primary sources for a course on women and the family in the Middle Ages. Already familiar with the valuable evidence on familial affection that could be found in collections of saints' miracles, I took a look at the published edition of the *Miracles of Saint Louis*. It was, I soon realized, a treasure trove of information on the private lives of the working and nonworking poor. Only a few years later, when I began to read the work of feminists of color, did I begin to understand the questions that I wanted to pose about the medieval poor: most especially, how differences of social status complicated medieval gender categories. I owe a special debt to the undergraduates who enrolled in Women's Studies 100a in the winter of 1993 for compelling me to consider such issues. Eventually, as I delved further into the project, my own experience as a single mother heightened my awareness that marital status also complicates gender categories.

In the meantime, in order to understand the daily lives of the Parisian poor, I needed to learn a great deal about medieval Paris. The published work of Bronislaw Geremek provided a primer on the sources. Caroline Bourlet, of the Section Diplomatique of the Institut de Recherche et d'Histoire des Textes in Paris, generously shared data from her work on a computerized database of the Parisian tax assessments of the late thirteenth and early fourteenth centuries. She also introduced me to the rich archive of notes and unpublished scholarship left behind by Anne Terroine, and provided me with a microfiche of ms. 5848 of the Archives des Quinze-Vingts, which I had been unable to locate at the Hospital of the Quinze-Vingts. Nicole Bériou allowed me to read her magnificent *thèse* on thirteenth-century sermons and guided me to the most reliable manuscripts of the works of Jacques de Vitry and Gilbert of Tournai. Janice Archer shared a copy of her dissertation.

My present and former graduate students Michael Connally, Deborah Gerish, Nancy McLoughlin, Mark O'Tool, and Tanya Stabler provided skilled research assistance. I am especially thankful to Deb for tabulating data from the Parisian tax assessments and to Mike, who shared some of his research on the Haudriettes. Fellow historians of France, Paul Sonnino and David Troyansky, were kind enough to check references at the Archives Nationales and the Archives de l'Assistance Publique. Roberta Bloom of the University of California, Santa Barbara's Artworks department did a wonderful job producing the maps.

A fellowship from the Office of the President of the University of California provided nine months' sabbatical leave during the 1991–92 academic year and a membership at the School of Historical Studies of the Institute for Advanced Study enabled me to write a substantial portion of the book during the 1997–98 academic year. The Committee on Research and the Interdisciplinary Humanities Center at the University of California, Santa Barbara, supported travel to Paris and research assistance in Santa Barbara.

Finally, a number of colleagues provided valuable comments on earlier versions of this work. I am especially indebted to John Ackerman, Michael Burger, Giles Constable, Paul Freedman, Lisa Kallet, Carol Lansing, Alice O'Connor, Carol Pasternack, Amy Remensnyder, Barbara Rosenwein, Jeffrey Russell, participants in the University of California Medieval History Seminars, participants in the UCSB History Gender Brown Bag discussions, and the anonymous reader for Cornell University Press.

My daughter Roxana has grown up with this book. Ten years ago I gave Roxana her first bottles while reading about artisans in thirteenth-century Paris; in the summer of 2000, we drove to UCSB together so that she could attend "Young Writers' Camp" while I completed the final revisions of this book at my own "adult writer's camp." This book is dedicated to her.

ABBREVIATIONS

AN   Paris, Archives Nationales

PL   *Patriologiae cursus completus, Series latina*. Edited by J.-P. Migne. 221 vols. Paris, 1841–1866.

RHGF *Recueil des historiens des Gaules et de la France*. Edited by M. Bouquet et al. 24 vols. Paris, 1738–1904.

SURVIVING POVERTY IN MEDIEVAL PARIS

INTRODUCTION

This book is about poor men and women in thirteenth- and early fourteenth-century Paris: their daily struggles for survival, the forms of charity that were made available to them, and the cultural values and stereotypes that shaped their experiences. The choice of time and place is, in part, an accident of the sources: rare indeed are those that can open a window onto the daily lives of the poor, but a set of such sources happens to exist for Paris in this period. This accident is a fortunate one, however: because Paris was the largest city in western Europe at the time its poorest inhabitants provide particularly poignant examples of the problems that accompanied the growth of medieval towns. The painful stories recounted here reveal the other side of the "age of the cathedrals," as Georges Duby once called it, in the very place and time where Gothic architecture and Scholastic theology were born.[1]

One of the central themes of this book is that poor men's and poor women's patterns of survival were not the same. Gender—the cultural construction of masculinities and femininities, which differed for rich and poor, Christian and Jew—was an integral part of the hierarchical ideologies that imposed expectations and prejudices upon the poor. Gendered constructs played a major role in shaping both the social networks that poor men and women were able to carve out for themselves and the charitable assistance that was made available to them. Stated so simply, this assertion may seem almost too obvious to deserve our attention. But it is never an easy matter—for those of us who are privileged enough to engage with the social universe conceptually, through the printed word—to understand either the experiences of the destitute or the cultural constructs that shape our understandings of those experiences. It is, in fact, one of the contentions of this book that our understanding of the medieval poor is incomplete in part because

1. Georges Duby, *Le temps des cathédrales: L'art et la société, 980–1420* (Paris, 1976).

modern medievalists have failed to address the multiplicity of medieval gender categories, and thus to understand that poor men and women were gendered differently from elite men and women.

Our picture of medieval poverty is also mediated by the available sources. Because poor people have only a fleeting relationship with possessions, they tend to elude those public records—which predominated in the Middle Ages—that concern the possession, conveyance, and taxation of property. Poor men and women, moreover, are rarely in a position to represent themselves to the larger community, and the professionals whose task it is to shape our understanding of the social world rarely turn their attention to the very bottom of the social hierarchy. Even in the late twentieth and early twenty-first centuries only a few journalists, anthropologists, and sociologists have successfully evoked an empathetic understanding of the daily struggles of the poor.[2] Rarer still have been the makers of policy who have listened to such professionals. Recent dismantlings of the welfare state are illustrative of the fact that policies concerning the poor are as much the product of political ideologies as of firsthand knowledge of poor people; "poverty knowledge" is always mediated knowledge.[3]

In the thirteenth and fourteenth centuries, preachers, teachers of preachers, and theologians were the principal professionals who wrote about the social world in general, and their works also constitute an important source for the understanding of the world of the poor in particular. But their reasons for describing or discussing the social universe were not the same as those of modern social scientists and journalists. When the authors of sermon literature—men like Jacques de Vitry, a secular cleric who wrote at the beginning of the thirteenth century, or Humbert of Romans and Gilbert of Tournai, prominent members of the Dominican and Franciscan orders, who wrote at midcentury—divided the world into social categories, their pur-

2. The enduring importance of Carol B. Stack's *All Our Kin: Strategies for Survival in a Black Community*, which was first published in 1974 (New York), and reprinted in 1997, indicates that few have followed in her footsteps. See also Kathryn Edin and Laura Lein, *Making Ends Meet: How Single Mothers Survive Welfare and Low-Wage Work* (New York, 1997); Edin, *The Myths of Dependence and Self-Sufficiency: Women, Welfare, and Low-Wage Work* (Piscataway, N.J., 1994); Edin, *There's a Lot of Month Left at the End of the Money: How Welfare Recipients Make Ends Meet in Chicago* (New York, 1993).

3. I have borrowed the expression "poverty knowledge" from Alice O'Connor: *Poverty Knowledge: Social Science, Social Policy and the Poor in Twentieth-Century U.S. History* (Princeton, N.J., 2001).

pose was to describe, for the less learned preacher, the vices and temptations that could hinder the moral progress or salvation of individuals within each group. When they wrote about women, the perceptions and representations of these men were shaped by ancient texts—the Bible, the works of the church fathers, and those of Greek and Roman authors, most especially Aristotle. The sexual danger that all women posed to the celibacy of these clerics, a threat that was thought to have increased in the eleventh and twelfth centuries, also shaped their representations of women.[4]

When these male clerics wrote about the poor, they had in mind not only men and women who were so destitute that they had to beg in order to survive, but also those who had no income-producing property and thus performed bodily labor to earn their daily bread, and it is both these groups that are dealt with in this book. The clerics' accounts were shaped by the same texts that influenced their view of women; by the gap between their own comfortable circumstances and those of the poor; and by their identification of themselves—as members of the church hierarchy—as the truly deserving poor. This concept of themselves as the deserving, or voluntary, poor was especially important for the mendicant preaching orders—the Dominicans and Franciscans—who practiced stylized imitations of the manual labor and begging that were the keys to survival for the working and nonworking poor. By the mid–thirteenth century the mendicant orders predominated in the school of theology at the University of Paris, and members of those orders had become the principal theorists and practitioners of the art of preaching.

In part because of the nature of the sources, most of the historiography of the medieval poor has so far consisted of two kinds of studies: those that focus on the perspectives and actions of the wealthier members of society, and those that attempt to analyze standards of living.

Historians who have focused on the actions and perspectives of propertied members of medieval society have produced numerous studies of hospitals and hospices (which, from the thirteenth century on, were usually founded by wealthy urban dwellers); of charitable almsgiving in urban wills;

4. For a general introduction to the sermon literature of Humbert of Romans, Jacques de Vitry, and Gilbert of Tournai that was directed to men and women of different social strata, see D. D'Avray and M. Tausche, "Marriage Sermons in *ad status* Collections of the Central Middle Ages," *Archives d'histoire doctrinale et littéraire du moyen âge* 47 (1980): 71–119. On the intersections of the campaign for clerical celibacy and portrayals of women's sexual danger in the eleventh and twelfth centuries, see especially Dyan Elliott, *Fallen Bodies: Pollution, Sexuality, and Demonology in the Middle Ages* (Philadelphia, 1999).

of the charitable activities of confraternities; and of elite attitudes toward the poor.[5] Occasionally, but not often, studies of hospitals and confraternal charity offer a profile of the recipients of such charity, but the sources left behind by medieval hospitals and confraternities reveal almost nothing about their daily lives.[6]

5. Studies of hospitals and confraternal assistance to the poor include: Michel Mollat, ed., *Etudes sur l'histoire de la pauvreté*, 2 vols. (Paris, 1974); Michel Mollat, *The Poor in the Middle Ages: An Essay in Social History*, trans. Arthur Goldhammer (New Haven, Conn., 1986 [Paris, 1978]); Miri Rubin, *Charity and Community in Medieval Cambridge* (Cambridge, 1987); Nicole Gonthier, *Lyon et ses pauvres au moyen âge (1350–1500)* (Lyon, 1978); Alain Saint-Denis, *L'Hôtel-Dieu de Laon, 1150–1300* (Nancy, 1983); John Henderson, ed., *Charity and the Poor in Medieval and Renaissance Europe, Continuity and Change* 3, no. 2 (1988); John Henderson, *Piety and Charity in Late Medieval Florence* (Oxford, 1994); M. J. Tits-Dieuaide, "Les tables des pauvres dans les anciennes principautés belges au moyen âge," *Tijdschrift voor Geschiedenis* 88 (1975): 562–83. The best general study of French confraternities is Catherine Vincent, *Les confréries médiévales dans la royaume de France: XIIIe–XVe siècle* (Paris, 1994).

Studies of charitable bequests in wills include: Jacques Chiffoleau, *La comptabilité de l'au-delà: Les hommes, la mort et la religion dans la région d'Avignon à la fin du moyen âge (vers 1320–vers 1480)* (Rome, 1980), 302–22; Gonthier, *Lyon et ses pauvres*, 161–166; Dennis Romano, "Charity and Community in Early Renaissance Venice," *Journal of Urban History* 11 (1984): 63–82; Steven A. Epstein, *Wills and Wealth in Medieval Genoa, 1150–1250* (Cambridge, Mass., 1984), 167–200; P. Godding, "La pratique testamentaire en Flandre au XIIIe siècle," *Tijdschrift voor Rechtgeschiedenis* 58 (1990): 281–300.

Studies of attitudes toward the poor include: Mollat, *Etudes*; Mollat, *The Poor*; Bronislaw Geremek, *Poverty: A History*, trans. Agnieszka Kolakowska (Oxford, 1994); Jean-Louis Roch, "Le jeu de l'aumône au moyen âge," *Annales: Economies, sociétés, civilisations* 44 (1989): 505–27; Richard Trexler, "Charity and the Defense of Urban Elites in the Italian Communes," in *The Rich, the Well Born, and the Powerful: Elites and Upper Classes in History*, ed. Frederic Cople Jaher (Urbana, Ill., 1973), 64–109.

6. The confraternity of Orsanmichele in fourteenth-century Florence kept a list of the names and addresses of the recipients of its charity, thus enabling John Henderson to "provide one of the most detailed studies of the recipients of poor relief for medieval Europe": Henderson, *Piety and Charity*, 11, and chaps. 7 and 8. There were similar charitable distributions in the Low Countries, Spain, and southern France, but I have seen no mention of lists of recipients: Tits-Dieuaide, "Les tables des pauvres," 562–63; Mollat, *The Poor*, 139–42. Nor have I seen any mention of patient or inmate records in the monographs on hospitals.

Historians interested in standards of living have employed tax records, account books, price lists, and archeological data in an attempt to depict the wage and unemployment levels, buying power, diets, and housing conditions of the working and nonworking poor in late medieval towns.[7] These studies certainly make clear how widespread urban poverty was, for they point to a high percentage of urban households whose incomes could not support the members of those households. In Florence, whose sources have enabled historians to derive the best statistics, almost one-third of the heads of household were defined, in 1355 and 1378, as destitute, and thus excluded from taxation.[8] Between 1290 and the end of the fourteenth century, moreover, the average Florentine salaried worker was able to meet the most basic needs of a family of four only in the decade of the 1360s when wages were still high because of the labor shortage that had been caused by the first wave of the Black Death (1347–51). Wages were also inadequate in thirteenth-century England and presumably in France as well, where the buying power of wage earners declined throughout the thirteenth century, especially toward its end.[9]

Studies of charitable activities and standards of living give us some idea of who was at risk of falling into dire poverty, and of the types of poor people whom propertied individuals preferred to assist, but they tell us

7. The most extensive study of the relationship between wages, prices, and standards of living is Charles de la Roncière, *Prix et salaires à Florence au XIVe siècle*, 1280–1380 (Rome, 1982). Others include: Christopher Dyer, *Standards of Living in the Later Middle Ages: Social Change in England c. 1200–1520* (Cambridge, 1989), chap. 8; and Gérard Sivéry, *L'économie du royaume de France au siècle de Saint Louis (vers 1180–vers 1315)* (Lille, 1984).

8. Alessandro Stella, *La révolte des Ciompi: Les hommes, les lieux, le travail* (Paris, 1993), 187. For other discussions of the "fiscal poor," see: Gonthier, *Lyon et ses pauvres*, 39, 56–57, 91–127; Henri Dubois, "La pauvreté dans les premières 'cherches de feux' bourguignonnes," in *Horizons marins, itinéraires spirituels (V^e–XVIIIe siècles)*, ed. Henri Dubois, Jean-Claude Hocquet, and André Vauchez, 2 vols. (Paris, 1987), 1:291–301. Unfortunately, many tax assessments, including those of Lyon, Burgundy, and Paris, did not list those who were too poor to pay taxes, so that discussions of "fiscal poverty" that rely on these lists cannot tell us what proportion of the population fell below the working "poverty line." On the problems with various approaches to defining a "poverty line," see John Henderson and Richard Wall, "Introduction," in *Poor Women and Children in the European Past* (London, 1994), 1–4.

9. La Roncière, *Prix et salaires*, 381–461; Dyer, *Standards of Living*, 226–29; Sivéry, *L'économie*, 133–48.

little about how the poor actually lived and survived.[10] We have virtually no comprehensive studies of the total number and collective impact of the formal charitable institutions in a single community. Indeed, such a study would be nearly impossible, given the nature of the records that such institutions kept.[11] Moreover, those historians who have attempted to analyze the economic impact of formal charitable giving generally agree that it was far from adequate, and that those propertyless individuals who were incapable of working for their living must have relied on noninstitutional forms of charity—informal almsgiving, and support from relatives, friends, and neighbors.[12] Because of the limitations of the sources, however, medieval historians have thus far uncovered only fragmentary information about poor people's noninstitutional social networks and forms of support.

Isabelle Chabot has found occasional evidence for women's mutual aid in the Florentine *catasto* of 1427: several widows, in support of claims that they were too poor to pay taxes, indicated that they lived on alms, or received free lodging from friends or fellow widows. Unfortunately, the brief notices in the tax records reveal neither the quality of the relationships between these women and the individuals who assisted them nor how long they were able to rely on such support.[13] P. J. P. Goldberg has identified a pattern of "spinster clustering" in late medieval poll tax records from England. Moreover, through a creative use of court records he has discovered that women often migrated to English towns in clusters and sometimes shared lodgings and even beds. However, his sources offer no direct evidence concerning

10. Brian Tierney, *Medieval Poor Law: A Sketch of Canonical Theory and Its Application in England* (Berkeley, Calif., 1959), 15, 18; Trexler, "Charity," 64–109; Henderson, *Piety and Charity*, 245; Stella, *La révolte*, 188; Charles de la Roncière, "Pauvres et pauvreté à Florence au XIVe siècle," in Mollat, *Etudes*, 2:661–745. La Roncière is especially effective in discussing the ways in which accepted categories of poverty—which were largely biblical—masked the realities of poverty among working men.

11. Surveys of multiple sources of charity in single communities include: Gonthier, *Lyon et ses pauvres*, 135–76; Bronislaw Geremek, *The Margins of Society in Late Medieval Paris*, trans. from the French by Jean Birrell (Cambridge, 1987), 167–92; Rubin, *Charity and Community*, 99–147, 237–88.

12. Dyer, *Standards of Living*, 240–57; John Henderson, "The Parish and the Poor in Florence at the Time of the Black Death: The Case of S. Frediano," in Henderson, *Charity and the Poor*; Tits-Dieuaide, "Les tables des pauvres."

13. Isabelle Chabot, "Widowhood and Poverty in Late Medieval Florence," in Henderson, *Charity and the Poor*, 304 and notes 65, 67, 68, 69.

networks of support, which, as Goldberg suggests, must have developed among these women.[14]

There is, however, one set of sources that does provide a unique window onto this and many other aspects of the daily survival of the poor. These sources concern the posthumous miracles of Saint Louis—King Louis IX of France (1226–70)—who died in Tunis, and was buried in 1271, in the basilica of the Benedictine abbey of St.-Denis just outside of Paris.[15]

The original source for the miracles of Saint Louis was the transcript of an inquest conducted by a panel of papally appointed clerics who investigated the sanctity of the deceased king. Between May of 1282 and March of 1283 the archbishop of Rouen, the bishop of Auxerre and the bishop of Spoleto interviewed around 330 witnesses to sixty-three posthumous miracles.[16] Most of those miracles were cures that had taken place at Louis's tomb between 1271 and 1282.

Inquests such as the one that took place at St.-Denis became standard procedure for canonizations during the thirteenth century. They consti-

14. P. J. P. Goldberg, *Women, Work and Life Cycle in a Medieval Economy* (Oxford, 1992), 305–23. Like Goldberg, C. Klapisch-Zuber sees a rise in female domestic service after the Black Death, "Women Servants in Florence during the Fourteenth and Fifteenth Centuries," in *Women and Work in Preindustrial Europe*, ed. Barbara Hanawalt (Bloomington, Ind., 1986), 56–80. In contrast with their opportunities in domestic service, women's role in the production of ale declined in England after the Black Death; and by the fifteenth century their opportunities in the gilds tended to decline throughout Europe: Judith Bennett, *Ale, Beer, and Brewsters in England: Women's Work in a Changing World, 1300–1600* (New York, 1996); Maryanne Kowaleski and Judith Bennett, "Crafts, Gilds, and Women in the Middle Ages: Fifty Years After Marian K. Dale," *Signs: Journal of Women in Culture and Society* 14 (1989): 486; Martha Howell, "Women, the Family Economy, and the Structures of Market Production during the Late Middle Ages," in Hanawalt, *Women and Work*, 198–222.

15. Guillaume de St.-Pathus, Confesseur de la reine Marguerite, *Les miracles de Saint Louis*, ed. Percival B. Fay (Paris, 1931). I have consulted two of the principle manuscripts upon which Fay based his edition (Paris, Bibliothèque Nationale de France, ms. fr. 4976, and ms. fr. 5716) and I have found Fay's edition and his attention to manuscript variations to be meticulously accurate.

16. A separate panel was probably sent to Parma to interview the witnesses to miracles 64 and 65, which took place in southern Italy. H.-François Delaborde, ed., "Fragments de l'enquête faite à Saint-Denis en 1282 en vue de la canonisation de Saint Louis," *Mémoires de la Société de l'Histoire de Paris et de l'Ile-de- France* 23 (1896): 4; Louis Carolus-Barré, *Le procès de canonisation de Saint Louis (1272–1297): Essai de reconstitution* (Rome, 1994), 20–21. The Vatican archivists were not able to locate for me the original documents that Delaborde consulted.

tuted part of the general development of inquisitorial method, which was elaborated in the thirteenth century. Inquests and inquisitions have yielded some of our richest sources for medieval social and social-cultural history.[17] To date, however, most social historians who have used canonization inquests have examined them for what they reveal about religious belief and practice; few historians, moreover, have examined these sources within the context of a particular place and time. This book employs the Saint Louis sources in conjunction with all other available materials on the working and nonworking poor of thirteenth-century Paris and the town of St.-Denis, here treated as a part of Paris.[18]

17. The best-known work of medieval social history based on inquisitorial materials is Emmanuel Le Roy Ladurie's *Montaillou: The Promised Land of Error*, trans. Barbara Bray (New York, 1978). André Vauchez's *La sainteté en occident aux derniers siècles du moyen âge: D'après les procès de canonisation et les documents hagiographiques* (Rome, 1981) is still the authoritative work on the social history of sanctity, based on the canonization inquests. See Vauchez's comments on pp. 2–3 on the value and similarity of these two kinds of sources; and pp. 39–67 on the evolution of canonization inquests.

18. Works of social history based on canonization inquests, or canonization inquests and other hagiographical sources include: Vauchez, *La sainteté*; Ronald C. Finucane, *Miracles and Pilgrims: Popular Beliefs in Medieval England* (Totowa, New Jersey, 1977); Ronald C. Finucane, *The Rescue of the Innocents: Endangered Children in Medieval Miracles* (New York, 1997); Michael Goodich, *Violence and Miracle in the Fourteenth Century: Private Grief and Public Salvation* (Chicago, 1995); Christian Krötzl, *Pilger, Mirakel und Alltag: Formen des Verhaltens im skandinavischen Mittelalter* (Helsinki, 1994); Claudia Opitz, *Frauenalltag im Mittelalter: Biographien des 13. und 14. Jahrhunderts* (Weinheim, 1985).

Most of the studies of the sources for the miracles of Saint Louis have examined only Guillaume de St.-Pathus's French version, in isolation from other sources, and they have focused on religious or medical *mentalités*: Jacques Le Goff, "Saint de l'église et saint du peuple: Les miracles officiels de Saint Louis entre sa mort et sa canonisation," in *Histoire sociale, sensibilités collectives et mentalités: Mélanges Robert Mandrou* (Paris, 1985), 169–80; Le Goff, *Saint Louis* (Paris, 1996), 844–56; Sharaf Chennaf and Odile Redon, "Les miracles de Saint Louis," in *Les miracles: miroirs des corps*, ed. Jacques Gelis and Odile Redon (Paris, 1983), 53–86. Didier Lett's wonderful study of medieval children is based on ten miracle collections, including Guillaume de St.-Pathus's *Miracles de Saint Louis*. Apparently because he wanted to keep within a particular genre (miracle collections rather than canonization inquests), he looked only at Guillaume de St.-Pathus, and not at the fragment of the inquest or at the Latin versions of the same miracles, which sometimes fill in gaps left by Guillaume. Lett tends to ignore differences of social status, perhaps because his other nine sources do not give sufficient evidence for the backgrounds of the beneficiaries; *L'enfant des miracles: Enfance et société au moyen âge (XIIᵉ–XIIIᵉ siècle)* (Paris, 1997).

Unfortunately, only a fragment of the original transcript of the inquest at St.-Denis has survived.[19] However, Guillaume de St.-Pathus, a Franciscan friar who had been the confessor of Louis's wife, and who wrote his *Life and Miracles of Saint Louis* around 1303 at the behest of the king's daughter Blanche, summarized the evidence from the inquest, and a comparison of his retellings with the surviving fragment of the inquest indicates that he remained quite faithful to the original narratives.[20] Guillaume also retained much of the information that the original transcript contained about the civil status of the beneficiaries of the miracles. At the beginning of each testimony the scribes had recorded, for each witness to or beneficiary of a miracle, that person's name, place of birth, place of current residence (often including the street name), and number of years residing in the current town or village. They also recorded the names of the spouses of female witnesses, and they often recorded male witnesses' occupations. In many cases where occupations were not recorded in the opening section of the testimony, moreover, the witnesses revealed their occupations in the course of their narratives. This rich detail enables us to determine the social status of fifty-two of the beneficiaries of the miracles and the places of origin of thirty-two beneficiaries and witnesses who had moved to Paris or St.-Denis from elsewhere.

Such detail concerning the background of even the poorest witnesses and beneficiaries—which we do not find in most canonization inquests or miracle collections—and the rich quality of the narratives themselves renders the Saint Louis sources extremely valuable for reconstructing the world of the working and nonworking poor. This is especially true for those living in Paris and St.-Denis: thirty-eight of the sixty-five miracles recounted by Guillaume de St.-Pathus concern people from Paris and St.-Denis, most of them from artisanal, laboring, and poor backgrounds.[21]

Though Guillaume de St.-Pathus remained quite faithful to his source, his narratives are not transparent windows into the lives of the poor. It is impor-

---

Raymond Cazelles employed Guillaume de St.-Pathus's miracle stories, but not the Latin fragment, to look at more traditional social-historical issues such as immigration and employment, but he failed to ask questions about social relationships; "Le parisien au temps de Saint Louis," *Septième centenaire de la mort de Saint Louis, Actes des Colloques de Royaumont et de Paris (21–27 mai 1970)* (Paris, 1976), 99. My own discussion of immigration in chapter 2 is much fuller than that of Cazelles.

19. Delaborde, "Fragments de l'enquête."

20. Guillaume de St.-Pathus, *Les miracles*; Carolus-Barré, *Le procès*, 24.

21. Guillaume de St.-Pathus, *Les miracles*, miracles 1–5, 7, 9, 11, 16–20, 22–27, 30, 34–39, 41–44, 46, 48, 49, 51–54, 58. Miracle 18, which concerns a young man who was on his way to Paris when he became disabled, is included in this total.

tant to note, first, that Guillaume had spent most of his career as a mendicant friar serving as spiritual advisor to the family of King Louis IX.[22] Guillaume's retellings are shaped—through selective silences and word choices—by his own prejudices and assumptions and presumably by those of his intended audience as well. Moreover, the prejudices, purposes, and assumptions of the clerics who were responsible for the inquest shaped the questions that were posed at the original inquest and the ways in which the answers were recorded. Finally, the memories, purposes, and prejudices of the witnesses filtered the information that the clerics on the panel managed to collect. In this last case, however, the clerics were able to discourage deliberate distortions and to compensate for faulty memories by interviewing multiple witnesses.

All the sources used in this book—not only sermon and miracle literature but also testaments of propertied Parisians, gild statutes, and records of tax assessments—were shaped in one way or another by cultural assumptions. But these assumptions are themselves valuable evidence. They testify to the construction by male clerical writers of hierarchies of masculinities and femininities and to the intersections between those hierarchies and hierarchies of labor and social status. They reveal, moreover, that while cultural elites divided the poor into those who were deserving of charitable assistance and those who were not, they simultaneously distrusted all of the poor, especially those who were male and unable to work.

Although the assumptions of bureaucrats, clerics and scholars played the predominant role in shaping the written record, the sources also contain fragments of evidence concerning the cultural assumptions of the poor themselves, indicating that they were not only influenced by but also resistant to elite assumptions. And while the cultural assumptions of those who wrote the texts shaped and distorted them, it is still possible to read through the distortions in order to recover valuable information about the daily lives of the poor. The evidence points to important links between poverty and rural to urban migration, and to significant differences between men's and women's patterns of migration to the city. Moreover, it opens a window onto the informal assistance that the nonworking poor received from the working poor, and onto the networks of mutual support that enabled women, especially single women, to survive on the margins of urban society. Through a nuanced reading of the sources, both for what they reveal about cultural stereotypes and for the what they tell us about daily survival, this book attempts to deepen our understanding of the complexities of medieval social categories, of the concrete details of everyday survival among the medieval urban poor, and of the links between the two.

22. Carolus-Barré, *Le procès*, 24.

CHAPTER ONE
WEALTH, MIGRATION, AND POVERTY

Ribaut, or estes vos a point:
Li aubre despoillent lor branches
Et vos n'aveiz de robe point . . .

RUTEBEUF, *"Li diz des ribaux de Grève"*[1]

CITY OF SPLENDOR, CITY OF HOPE

When we think of Paris in the thirteenth and early fourteenth centuries we tend to think not of poverty, but of extravagant, sumptuous wealth. Here, in the mid–thirteenth century, King Louis IX built the Sainte-Chapelle, which was renowned, as Jean de Jandun asserted in 1323, for "the most choice colors of its paintings, the precious gilding of its images, the transparent beauty of the stained glass all around, the most elegant ornaments of its altars . . . [and] the forms of its reliquaries, decorated on the outside with brightly shining gems."[2] Here, too, in the Great Hall of King Philip the Fair (1285–1314), the largest hall in western Europe, the king's notaries and masters of requests exercised the administrative functions of government on a huge table of polished marble, surrounded by statues of all the preceding kings of France, so perfect in representation that "on first inspection one almost judges them to be alive."[3] And here, in June 1313, at the knighting

1. "Vagrant, now you really have nothing. / The trees are disrobing their branches / And you have no garment at all. . . ." Rutebeuf, *Oeuvres complètes*, ed. Michel Zink, vol. 1 (Paris, 1989), 200.

2. Jean de Jandun, *Eloge de Paris, composé en 1323 par un habitant de Senlis, Jean de Jandun*, ed. Taranne and Leroux de Lincy (Paris, 1856), 13.

3. Ibid., 14. On Philip the Fair's Great Hall see: Jean Guerout, "Le palais de la Cité à Paris des origines à 1417: Essai topographique et archéologique," *Mémoires de la Fédération des Sociétés Historiques et Archéologiques de Paris et de l'Ile-de-France* 2 (1950): 23–44; and Michael T. Davis, "Désespoir, Esperance, et Douce France: The New Palace, Paris, and the Royal State," in *Fauvel Studies: Allegory, Chronicle, Music and Image in Paris, Bibliothèque Nationale de France, ms. français 146*, ed. Margaret Bent and Andrew Watley (Oxford, 1998), 187–214.

ceremonies for his three sons and at least 197 other men, Philip the Fair spent 32,000 livres on horses for the new knights, as well as giving 94 oxen, 189 pigs, 380 rams, 200 pike, 160 carp, and 80 barrels of wine to his daughter Isabel and her husband King Edward II of England, who attended the ceremonies.[4] In honor of the same events, the members of the Parisian craft gilds dressed in livery, decorated their city with tapestries, staged more than twenty-four *tableaux vivants*, and provided a fountain decorated with "mermaids, . . . leopards, and many fabulous inventions," which flowed with wine for three days.[5]

The administrative and financial capital of the largest, most populous, and—at the time of Louis IX's death—richest kingdom in Europe, Paris was also the home of Europe's greatest university and a leading center of artistic production. It became, moreover, the second home of some of the most powerful notables in the realm. Lured to the capital by the advantages of proximity to the center of power, some thirty-five archbishops, bishops, abbots, dukes, counts, and powerful members of the royal family built or purchased residences in Paris by the end of the thirteenth century. Another dozen or so joined them in the early decades of the fourteenth.[6] In his laudation of the city Jean de Jandun stated that the Parisian *hôtels* of notables and prelates were "so numerous and so large" that they alone could constitute "a wondrous city."[7]

Noble and royal elites were joined in Paris by numerous Italian bankers. A number of Italian firms established themselves in Paris during the reign of Louis IX, who turned to them for help in financing the Seventh Crusade.[8] By the beginning of the fourteenth century there were more Italian banking firms in Paris than in the towns of the Champagne

---

4. Unless otherwise indicated, monetary values are in livres parisis. There were twelve deniers to one sou, and twenty sous to one livre.

5. Elizabeth A. R. Brown and Nancy Freeman Regalado, "*La grant feste*: Philip the Fair's Celebration of the Knighting of His Sons in Paris at Pentecost in 1313," *City and Spectacle in Medieval Europe*, ed. Barbara Hanawalt and Kathryn L. Reyerson (Minneapolis, 1994), 56–86.

6. Josef Semmler, "Die Residenzen der Fürsten und Prälaten im mittelalterlichen Paris (12.–14. Jahrhundert)," *Mélanges offerts à René Crozet*, ed. Pierre Gallais and Yves-Jean Riou, 2 vols. (Poitiers, 1966), 2:1217–36.

7. Jean de Jandun, *Eloge*, 17.

8. Anne Terroine, "Etudes sur la bourgeoisie parisienne: Gandoufle d'Arcelles et les compagnies placentines à Paris (fin du XIIIe siècle)," *Annales d'histoire sociale* 7(1945): 60–61.

fairs.[9] The Parisian tax assessment of 1292 listed 180 Lombard—that is to say, Italian—taxpaying units. Unlike most Parisian taxpayers, who were assessed as individuals or as heads of household, most Lombard taxpaying units were companies, which might have included several heads of household who were residing temporarily in Paris. The average assessment of Lombard taxpaying units was 7.77 livres, which was over 9 times greater than the average assessment in 1292, and about the same as the total annual income of a salaried mason.[10] Forty-six of the Lombard taxpaying units, or just over a quarter, were assessed for ten livres or more. Most prominent of these, and indeed, of any taxpaying unit in Paris, was the assessment of Gandolfo Arcelli of Piacenza, who resided in Paris from at least 1288 until his death in 1300. Gandolfo was assessed for 114 livres, 10 sous in 1292; 142 livres, 10 sous in 1296; and 120 livres in 1299 and 1300.[11]

Prominent Parisian taxpayers included the Gentiens, Haudrys, Marcels, and Pacys—bourgeois families that earned their wealth not only from commercial activity but also in service to the king. In 1292 Pierre Marcel the Elder, who resided on the Péleterie (see map 1), was assessed for a tax of 58 livres; four of his sons, all of them living on the same street, were assessed for a total of 44 livres. In that same year, Sire Pierre Gentien the Elder was assessed for a tax of 38 livres, another Sire Gentien for 40 livres, and Jacques, the son of the latter, for 10 livres. Etienne Haudry was assessed for a tax of 32 livres in 1292, Raoul de Pacy for 26 livres, and the wife (or, more probably, widow) of Jehan de Pacy for 24 livres.[12] Among 14,936 non-Lombard and non-Jewish taxpaying units in the 1292 tax assessment, 118, or less

9. Gérard Sivéry, *L'économie du royaume de France au siècle de Saint Louis (vers 1180–vers 1315)* (Lille, 1984), 243.

10. I follow Bronislaw Geremek in estimating a salaried mason's annual income at eight livres. Geremek reckoned the income of a salaried mason in 1299 at eight deniers per day, and he estimated around twenty working days per month: *Le salariat dans l'artisanat parisien aux XIIIe–XVe siècles*, trans. from the Polish by Anna Posner and Christiane Klapisch-Zuber (Paris, 1982), 84, 89.

11. Anne Terroine, "Etudes sur la bourgeoisie," 7 (1945): 65, 8 (1945): 53.

12. Hercule Géraud, *Paris sous Philippe-le-Bel d'après des documents originaux et notamment d'après un manuscrit contenant "Le Rôle de la Taille" imposée sur les habitants de Paris en 1292*, reproduction of the 1837 edition with introduction and index by Caroline Bourlet and Lucie Fossier (Tübingen, 1991), 102, 103, 119, 120, 136. On the predominance of widows among those women designated as "the wife of so-and-so" in the Parisian tax assessments, see Janice Archer, "Working Women in Thirteenth-Century Paris" (Diss., University of Arizona, 1995), 129–30.

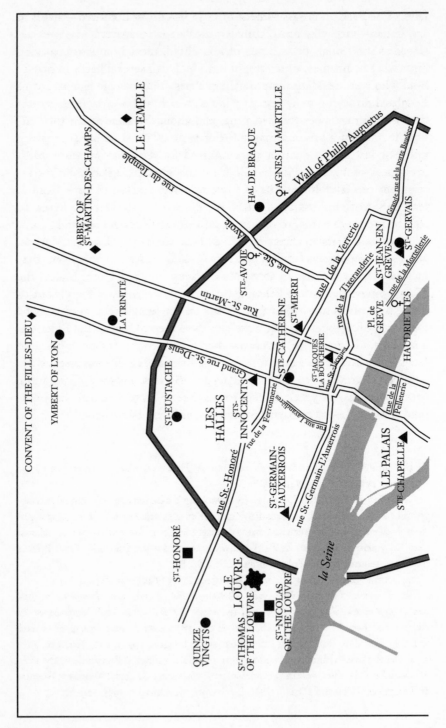

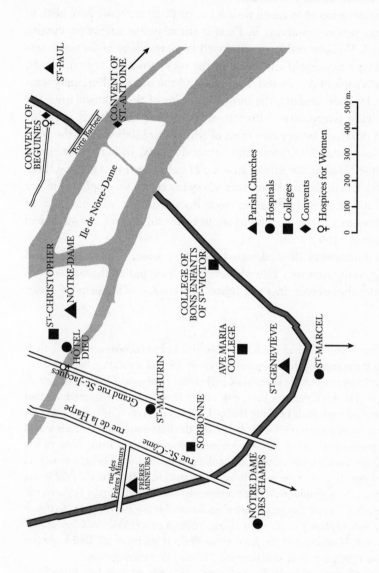

Map 1: Paris in the Early Fourteenth Century

Parish Churches ▲
Hospitals ●
Colleges ■
Convents ◆
Hospices for Women ♀

| 0 | 100 | 200 | 300 | 400 | 500 m. |

ST-PAUL

CONVENT OF
ST-ANTOINE

CONVENT OF
BEGUINES

Porte Barbel

Ile de Nôtre-Dame

ST-CHRISTOPHER

NÔTRE-DAME

COLLEGE OF
BONS ENFANTS
OF ST-VICTOR

HÔTEL
DIEU

Grand rue St.-Jacques

AVE MARIA
COLLEGE

ST-GENEVIÈVE

ST-MARCEL

ST-MATHURIN

rue de la Harpe

SORBONNE

rue St-Côme

rue des Frères Mineurs

FRÈRES
MINEURS

NÔTRE DAME
DES CHAMPS

than 1 percent, were assessed for ten livres or more.[13] Nobles and clerics were not included in the assessment.

The concentration of so much wealth in one place naturally gave birth to an enormous service economy; in Paris it stimulated a sizable productive sector as well. Wealthy residents employed large numbers of domestic servants: the king's household and those of the most powerful regional lords, such as the counts of Artois and Toulouse and the duke of Burgundy, employed hundreds of servants, the most important of them drawn from the nobility or elite bourgeoisie.[14] Prominent bourgeois households probably employed a dozen or so servants, most of whom were drawn from the population of lower-status migrants and urban dwellers. In her testament of 1309, Jehanne Haudry, the wife of Etienne Haudry, bestowed gifts on three male and five female domestic servants who were currently employed in her household, and on several former servants; Robert Evrout, who paid a tax of fourteen livres in 1292, gave gifts to seven male and one female servant in his testament of 1306.[15]

Wealthy consumers desired rich meat, fine wine, exotic spices, and fresh fish from the Atlantic. The wholesalers who supplied these needs became wealthy themselves: in 1313 Jehan le Grand, a wholesaler of ocean

13. Lombards and Jews are not included in this and in subsequent overall averages because the makers of the assessments treated them as separate groups, and because, for differing reasons, they were not permanent residents of Paris. The Jewish community of thirteenth-century Paris was a mere fragment of the community that had been expelled from Paris by King Philip Augustus in 1198. The earlier community had been concentrated on the Ile de la Cité; the later community, which would be expelled permanently in 1306, was concentrated on the right bank. Most of the Italians in Paris were representatives of banking firms in their home towns. See: Géraud Nahon, "La communauté juive de Paris au XIIIᵉ siècle: Problèmes topographiques, démographiques et institutionnels," *Etudes sur l'histoire de Paris et de l'Ile de France: Actes du 100ᵉ Congrès National des Sociétés Savantes, Paris, 1975, Section de philologie et d'histoire jusqu'à 1610*, vol. 2 (Paris, 1978), 143–58; William Chester Jordan, *The French Monarchy and the Jews: From Philip Augustus to the Last Capetians* (Philadelphia, 1989), esp. 8–9; and Terroine, "Etudes sur la bourgeoisie."

14. *Sources d'histoire médiévale IXᵉ–milieu du XIVᵉ siècle*, ed. Ghislain Brunel and Elisabeth Lalou (Paris, 1992), 717–18; Jules-Marie Richard, *Une petite-nièce de Saint Louis: Mahaut, Comtesse d'Artois et de Bourgogne* (Paris, 1887), 48–54; J. Favier, "L'hôtel royal de Philippe le Bel," *L'histoire*, no. 4(1978): 33; R. Fawtier and F. Lot, *Histoire des institutions françaises au moyen âge*, vol. 2, *Institutions royales* (Paris, 1958), 70.

15. See appendix.

fish, was assessed for a tax of 30 livres tournois (or about 24 livres parisis); his fellow fishmongers, Mauger of Cayeux and Guillaume Babille, for 22 livres, 10 sous tournois.[16] In that same year, Girart of Soleret, a spice trader, was assessed for a tax of 90 livres tournois, which placed him among the ten wealthiest taxpaying units in that year. Five other spice traders were assessed for taxes of 20 livres tournois or more in the same year.[17]

Wealthy consumers also required stately homes, fine tableware, ornate tapestries, sumptuous clothing, and illuminated manuscripts. In Paris the breadth of their tastes could be gratified by local architects, artists and artisans. The buildings of Paris were imitated throughout western Europe; its architects were summoned to Germany, Sweden, and Avignon. Wealthy residents could purchase sumptuous cloth, furs, and leather and ivory goods in the workshops of their creators or in Les Halles (see map 1); they could commission golden vessels and ornaments from the goldsmiths on the Grand Pont; and on the Left Bank, on the rue Erembourc-de-Brie, they could find or have made the most prized illuminated manuscripts in all of Europe.[18]

The large numbers and elevated levels of consumption of wealthy Parisians created an enormous labor market, and the laborers came, in droves. Between 1240 and 1328 Paris grew from an estimated 160,000 to somewhere around 210,000, which was at least twice, if not four times, the size of any other town in northern Europe and probably larger than the largest cities in Italy.[19] As was the case with any city, migration was the prin-

16. Karl Michaëlsson, ed., *Le livre de la taille de Paris, l'an de grace 1313* (Göteborg, 1951), 57, 64; François Maillard, "Tarifs des 'Coutumes' pour la vente du poisson de mer à Paris au début du XIVᵉ siècle," *Bulletin philologique et historique* (1966): 248. In the assessment of 1313 taxpayers were assessed in livres tournois. There were about eighty livres parisis to one hundred livres tournois; Michaëlsson, *Le livre de la taille . . . 1313*, xiii.

17. Michaëlsson, *Le livre de la taille . . . 1313*, xvi–xviii. On Girart's location and assessments in the other Parisian tax assessments, see ibid., xvi n. 2.

18. Raymond Cazelles, *Nouvelle histoire de Paris, de la fin du règne de Philippe Auguste à la mort de Charles V, 1223–1380* (Paris, 1972), 399–407; Robert Branner, *Manuscript Painting in Paris during the Reign of Saint Louis* (Berkeley, Calif., 1977), chap. 1; Sivéry, *L'économie*, 256–60. In the Parisian tax assessment of 1292, 12 of the 17 listed illuminators resided on the Rue Erembourc-de-Brie; Branner, *Manuscript Painting in Paris*, 15.

19. Raymond Cazelles, "La population de Paris avant la peste noire," *Académie des Inscriptions et Belles Lettres: Comptes Rendus* (Paris, 1966): 539–54; Cazelles, "Le

cipal cause of Paris's growth. In the sources for the miracles of Saint Louis about 63 percent of the women and 73 percent of the men residing in Paris had migrated from elsewhere. Among those residing in St.-Denis, 50 percent of the women and about 89 percent of the men were immigrants.[20] Although St.-Denis was not technically part of Paris its laboring population

---

parisien au temps de Saint Louis," *Septième centenaire de la mort de Saint Louis, Actes des Colloques de Royaumont et de Paris (21–27 mai 1970)* (Paris, 1976), 98; Cazelles, *Nouvelle histoire*, 131–53; David Herlihy, *Opera Muliebra: Women and Work in Medieval Europe* (New York, 1990), 128–31; Herlihy, "Demography," in *Dictionary of the Middle Ages*; Kathryn Reyerson, "Urbanism, Western European," ibid.

Several decades ago a few historians raised doubts that Paris could have had such a large population, but they did not realize that this number included suburbs that were outside of the walls that had been built by King Philip Augustus. I am satisfied that Cazelles and Herlihy adequately dealt with the objections to these estimates, thereby showing that Paris was the largest city in western Europe. The size of London is now under dispute, with advocates of a population of one hundred thousand arguing against an older estimate of forty thousand: for discussion see William C. Jordan, *The Great Famine: Northern Europe in the Early Fourteenth Century* (Princeton, N.J., 1996), 128.

20. The numbers are: sixteen women residing in Paris, ten of them immigrants; eleven men residing in Paris, eight of them immigrants; twelve women residing in St.-Denis, six of them immigrants; nine men residing in St.-Denis, eight of them immigrants. The sample is drawn from the thirty-four miracles of Saint Louis involving people from Paris or St.-Denis who were cured: Guillaume de St.-Pathus, Confesseur de la Reine Marguerite, *Les miracles de Saint Louis*, ed. Percival B. Fay (Paris, 1931), miracles 1–5, 7, 9, 11, 16–20, 22–25, 30, 34–37, 39, 41–44, 48–49, 51–54, 58. I have left out miracle 38, which involved a cleric, and miracles 26–27, which involved the children of the man cured in miracle 25. For children who received a cure I have counted only the parent who is first mentioned by Guillaume de St.-Pathus. If no place of origin is clearly mentioned, I have counted the individual as a native—even if that person is given a surname that could describe a place of origin. Information for the place of origin for miracle no. 4 comes from Guillaume de Nangis, *Vie de Saint Louis, RHGF* 20:462. Information for the place of residence for miracle 48 is in Guillaume de Chartres, *De vita et actibus regis Francorum Ludovici et de miraculis, RHGF* 20:40. To the sample of thirty-four individuals from Guillaume de St.-Pathus I have added the fourteen nonclerical witnesses in the Latin fragment of the inquest into Saint Louis's miracles who do not overlap with the individuals already counted from Guillaume de St.-Pathus; H.-François Delaborde, ed., "Fragments de l'enquête faite à Saint-Denis en 1282 en vue de la canonisation de Saint Louis," *Mémoires de la Société de l'Histoire de Paris et de l'Ile-de-France* 23 (1896): 1–71.

had migrated from the same general catchment basin and some of its artisans apprenticed with artisans from Paris.[21] Thus, in order to extend the limited Parisian database, cases from St.-Denis are included and discussed throughout this book.

Paris created a level of attraction that was unmatched by other towns. Many surnames in the Parisian tax registers of the late thirteenth century are derived from the place of origin either of the individuals being assessed or of their parents, grandparents, or in-laws; these names indicate that Paris drew a large migrant population not only from a catchment basin that extended sixty miles out from the city, but also from further away, especially from England, Brittany, Normandy, Picardy, and Pas-de-Calais.[22] Most pre-

---

This is, admittedly, a limited sample: forty-eight individuals (twenty-eight female and twenty male) for about a forty-year period (c. 1242–82). However, P. J. P. Goldberg based his discussion of immigration statistics in late fourteenth- and fifteenth-century England on a sample of sixty-three individuals for a 161-year period: "Marriage, Migration and Servanthood: The York Cause Paper Evidence," in Goldberg, ed., *Woman is a Worthy Wight: Women in English Society c. 1200–1500* (Wolfboro Falls, N.H., 1992), 10–12; Goldberg, *Women, Work and Life Cycle in a Medieval Economy* (Oxford, 1992), 282–87.

David Herlihy argued that in the 1292 and 1313 tax assessments four out of ten Parisian males and three out of ten females were "apparently" immigrants; *Opera Muliebra*, 136. The larger proportion of immigrants in my sources reflects immigration rates among those who were too poor to be assessed in the tax rolls. See note 22 for the reasons why we cannot assume that the individuals in the tax assessments with place-name surnames were themselves immigrants.

21. For details of the sample, see note 20. Immigrants to St.-Denis came from Normandy, England, the Beauce (the region around Chartres), and the Ile-de-France; those to Paris came from Normandy, England, the Ile-de-France, the diocese of Thérouanne (Pas-de-Calais), Burgundy, and Brittany. The catchment area in this sample confirms Karl Michaëlsson's assertion that immigrants to Paris tended to come from the area north of the Loire: *Etudes sur les noms de personnes français d'après les rôles de la taille parisiens* (Uppsala, 1927).

On artisans from St.-Denis and Paris apprenticing together, see Delaborde, "Fragments de l'enquête," 44.

22. Cazelles, *Nouvelle histoire*, 143. Janice Archer's appendix 5, concerning the transmission of familial businesses in the Parisian tax assessments of 1296–1300, demonstrates that place-names did not necessarily represent an individual's place of origin. Spouses, children, and spouses of children sometimes took on the place-name surnames of the original business owners; "Working Women," 275–309.

modern towns, by contrast, drew migrants from catchment basins with a radius of about twenty-five miles.[23]

The tax assessments give us a strong sense for those regions that supplied the bulk of immigrants, but they should not be trusted to indicate the exact proportions of immigrants from different regions. The predominance of persons identified as English or Breton—155 and 146 in the 1313 tax assessment, as opposed to 44 Normans—does not necessarily indicate that there were more migrants from England and Brittany than from Normandy. Rather, people with foreign accents were more likely to be identified by their region of origin than were other people.[24]

The tax assessments are even less trustworthy in providing data concerning the gender ratios of people who migrated to Paris. Individuals who were assessed in the tax rolls sometimes bore names identifying the place of origin of a parent, grandparent or in-law, who could have been of the opposite sex. Moreover, many individuals in the tax assessments were not identified by place of origin at all, and the majority of migrants were too poor to appear in the assessments.

Although they constitute a migration database of only thirty-two individuals, the sources for the *Miracles of Saint Louis* provide some corrective for the problems encountered with the Parisian tax assessments. Among the thirty-two migrants to Paris and St.-Denis in the database, thirteen were from Normandy, seven from the diocese of Paris, four from England, and two from Brittany. Certainly, the preponderance of people from Normandy over those from England and Brittany gets us closer to actual proportions of long-distance migrants than do the tax assessments. Similarly, because the Saint Louis sources make it clear that the individuals themselves had migrated, they give us some evidence for gendered patterns among migrants.

23. Goldberg, "Marriage, Migration and Servanthood," 12; Jean-Pierre Poussou, "Mobilité et Migrations," in *Histoire de la population française*, ed. Jacques Dupâquier et al. (Paris, 1988), 2:118–20; Paul M. Hohenberg and Lynn Hollen Lees, *The Making of Urban Europe* (Cambridge, Mass., 1988), 95, citing Alfred Perrenoud, *La population de Genève du seizième au debut du dix-neuvième siècle: Etude démographique* (Geneva, 1979); and J. Patten, "Patterns of Migration and Movement of Labor to Three Pre-Industrial East Anglian Towns," *Journal of Historical Geography* 2 (1976): 111–29.

24. Karl Michaëlsson, "Les noms d'origine dans le rôle de la taille parisien de 1313," *Symbolae Philologicae Gotoburgenses*, Acta universitatis Gotoburgensis 56, no. 3 (1950): 398–99. Adding in those who were identified by town or village of origin, at least 172 individuals were identified by place-names from England and over 135 were identified by place-names from Normandy.

Among sixteen men and sixteen women who migrated to Paris and St.-Denis between 1242 and 1282, thirteen of the men and twelve of the women traveled over twenty-five miles. Of even greater interest are the large and nearly equal proportions of men and women who traveled over one hundred miles: eight out of sixteen women and nine out of sixteen men (see map 2). Indeed, the only significant difference between the men and women immigrants in the sources for the *Miracles of Saint Louis* is that four of the men were from England, while all of the women migrated from within the boundaries of modern France—although two of the women traveled from western Brittany to Paris, a move that involved a change of language.

Historical demographers have sometimes argued that unskilled laborers and women migrated shorter distances than did skilled laborers.[25] The Saint Louis sources suggest that this thesis does not hold for women migrants in late thirteenth-century Paris. Moreover, the evidence in the tax assessments suggests that distance traveled did not necessarily correlate with eventual economic success: among the individuals identified by region of origin in the tax roll of 1292, the English and Scots had the lowest average tax assessments: 7.74 and 7.28 sous, respectively.[26] These averages were well below the average assessment in that year for non-Lombards and non-Jews: 14.62 sous.

Most migrants came to Paris and St.-Denis to find work; many arrived with little more than the clothes on their backs. Some, like Herbert and Adam of Fontenay, cloth dyers who had migrated to Paris around 1256 from the village of Fontenay in the diocese of Paris, entered into formal apprenticeships and were thus able to become part of the laboring elite. By 1282, some twenty years after he completed his apprenticeship, Adam, who had settled in St.-Denis, had accumulated property that was worth forty livres; Herbert, by contrast, who had three children by then, reported that he had no property and lived from his own labor.[27] His inability to save was common among laboring men with children, whose incomes were often inadequate to support a family of four.[28]

It is impossible to determine whether Adam was more successful at saving than was Herbert, or if Adam's earning capacity was supplemented at some point by an inheritance. An individual migrant's share (or lack of it) in

25. See the works cited in note 23 above.
26. Herlihy, *Opera Muliebra*, 139. I have averaged together male and female migrants from Herlihy's chart, since, as I have pointed out, we cannot use these sources to derive statistics on gender and migration.
27. Delaborde, "Fragments de l'enquête," 39, 42, 44, 46.
28. See above, p. 5.

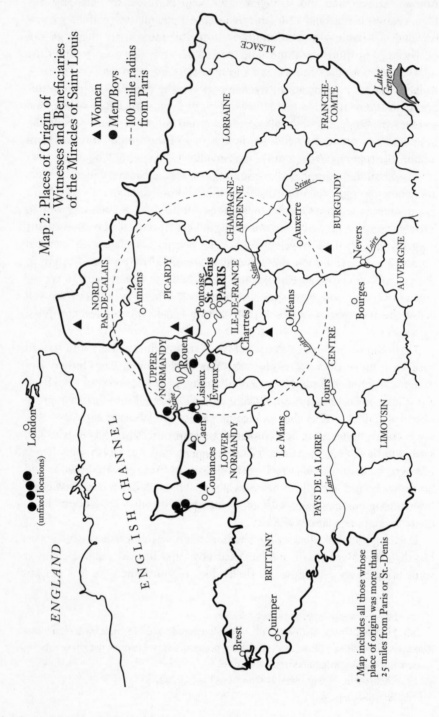

Map 2: Places of Origin of
Witnesses and Beneficiaries
of the Miracles of Saint Louis

▲ Women
● Men/Boys
--- 100 mile radius
from Paris

* Map includes all those whose
place of origin was more than
25 miles from Paris or St.-Denis

(unfixed locations)

a family inheritance could not only determine whether or not he or she was able to accumulate wealth, but also help lead that person to migrate, and, in some cases, to return home. Richard Vaudien, a Parisian cloth dyer from the town of Ely in England, told the clerics of the Saint Louis inquest that his eldest brother had come into the family inheritance at home; thus Richard was apparently compelled to migrate to Paris when he was about sixteen. Twenty years later, at the time of the inquest, he and his family lived "well and courteously" on the income from his labor.[29] Richard of Briqueville, a tailor or tailor's assistant, had migrated to St.-Denis from Normandy, as had his sister. Richard, however, had "a good inheritance" at home and eventually returned there.[30]

Many migrants had to settle for positions as domestic servants or unskilled laborers. This was especially true for women, who tended to work in the lowest-paid sectors of the economy and were paid lower wages than were men.[31] All of the migrant women in the Saint Louis sources whose work can be identified worked in low-level positions. Amelot of Chaumont, who was about twenty-eight when she migrated from her village in the Vexin to St.-Denis (a distance of about thirty miles), ended up working as a domestic servant for a prominent bourgeois; Orenge of Fontenay, who had migrated over a hundred miles from her village in the diocese of Bayeux to Paris, became a wool carder. Nicole of Rubercy, a forty-two-year-old Parisian who had also migrated from the diocese of Bayeux, became a laundress in her widowhood if not before; so did Agnes of Capella, a married woman who had migrated to St.-Denis from the diocese of Beauvais. Luce of Rémilly-sur-Lozon, a married woman who had migrated over a hundred miles from her village in Normandy to St.-Denis, sold pickled fish and other merchandise.[32]

Because women's wages were often not sufficient to support one person, many unattached women—including many laundresses—had to supplement their wages through prostitution.[33] This was especially true for single

29. Delaborde, "Fragments de l'enquête," 42, 44.

30. Guillaume de St.-Pathus, *Les miracles*, miracle 24.

31. Alessandro Stella, *La révolte des Ciompi: Les hommes, les lieux, le travail* (Paris, 1993), 182; Archer, "Working Women," 158, 168–69; Goldberg, *Women, Work and Life Cycle*, 82–202; Geremek, *Le salariat*, 91.

32. Guillaume de St.-Pathus, *Les miracles*, miracles 2, 39, 58; Delaborde, "Fragments de l'enquête," 52, 70.

33. Ruth Karras, *Common Women: Prostitution and Sexuality in Medieval England* (New York, 1996), 48–55; Bronislaw Geremek, *The Margins of Society in Late Medieval Paris*, trans. from the French by Jean Birrell (Cambridge, 1987), 214 n. 12.

women and widows. Tax assessments from late thirteenth-century Paris and from post-1348 Lyon, Burgundy, and Florence indicate that female heads of household were over represented among the "fiscal poor" (those paying the smallest taxes in Paris, Lyon, and Burgundy, and those considered too destitute to pay a tax in Florence).[34] The situation of such female heads of household was probably worse in the pre-1348 period, since the plague opened up parts of the labor market for women. It is even possible that Nicole of Rubercy supplemented, or had once supplemented, her income through prostitution. Laundresses were often associated with prostitution, and Nicole's close friend "Contesse" had the kind of name that prostitutes frequently gave to themselves. We are told, moreover, that when she was at Saint Louis's tomb Nicole implored the saint not to "look at her sins," and that she believed "that he was so powerful that no matter how much of a sinner she was, he could deliver her from the affliction that had held her captive for so long."[35] While all of those seeking cures were encouraged to confess their sins before going on pilgrimage to the saint's tomb, Guillaume's narrative about Nicole goes the furthest in suggesting that the beneficiary may have exceeded the norm in her identity as a sinner. Nevertheless, the purpose of the inquest concerning Saint Louis's miracles would have led Nicole, the witnesses who knew her, the inquisitors who interviewed them, and Guillaume to suppress specific evidence concerning her possibly illicit sexual behavior: persons of ill repute did not make desirable witnesses.

34. Nicole Gonthier, *Lyon et ses pauvres au moyen âge (1350–1500)* (Lyon, 1978), 56–65; Henri Dubois, "La pauvreté dans les premières 'cherches de feux' bourguignonnes," in *Horizons marins, itineraires spirituels (V°–XVIII° siècles≈*, ed. Henri Dubois, Jean-Claude Hocquet, and André Vauchez, 2 vols. (Paris, 1987), 1:296–98; Dubois, "Les feux féminins à Dijon aux XIV° et XV° siècles (1394–1407)," in *La femme au moyen-âge*, ed. Michel Rouche and Jean Heuclin (Maubeuge, 1990), 405; Stella, *La révolte*, 141. In Paris, women constituted 13.7 percent of the total number of people who were assessed in the tax assessment of 1292, but they constituted 19.25 percent of those with the lowest tax liability (twelve deniers). On the percentage of women in the 1292 tax assessment see Caroline Bourlet, "L'anthroponymie à Paris à la fin du XIII° siècle d'après les rôles de la taille du règne de Philippe le Bel," in *Genèse médiévale de l'anthroponymie moderne*, ed. Monique Bourin and Pascal Chareille, vol. 2–2 (Tours, 1992), 11. Bourlet excluded those whose sex could not be determined, the Lombard and Jewish communities, and communities such as the bourgeois of Laon, the Hôtel de Chaalis, and the Hôtel de Clairvaux. I have calculated the percentage of women among those paying the lowest tax (excluding the same groups that Bourlet excluded) from the published edition of the 1292 assessment: Géraud, *Paris sous Philippe-le-Bel*.

35. Guillaume de St.-Pathus, *Les miracles*, 123.

In recent years, historical demographers have argued that the populations of late medieval and early modern northwest European towns were regularly replenished by rural migrants, and that unmarried men and women in their teens and early twenties predominated among those who migrated. Most of the young women migrants, the demographers argue, and indeed many of the young men, took up employment as domestic servants but then gave up these jobs when they married in their late twenties. Historians have labeled this pattern of youthful, celibate servanthood "life-cycle servitude." According to the demographic historians, migration and life-cycle servitude were essential components, in the period after 1348, in "northwest European household formation," which was characterized by a relatively late marriage age (mid- to late twenties) for nonelite men and women, proximity of age of spouses, the formation of new conjugal households upon marriage, and frequent remarriage among widows.

The northwest European household pattern was first described by John Hajnal, who drew on evidence from the early modern period. Richard Smith and P. J. P. Goldberg have added convincing evidence that this type of household existed in England, and probably elsewhere in northwestern Europe, in the period immediately following the Black Death of 1348.[36] According to Hajnal and Smith, the northwest European household differed dramatically from that which predominated in Italy and other parts of southern Europe. In southern Europe, they argue, women rarely left home before marriage; they tended to marry young and not to remarry in widowhood; there was frequently a significant age difference between younger wives and older husbands; and couples did not always form a new household upon marriage.[37] Peter Laslett has argued, moreover, that complex, ex-

36. J. Hajnal, "European Marriage Patterns in Perspective," in *Population in History*, ed. D. V. Glass and D. E. C. Eversley (London, 1965), 101–43; Richard Smith, "Geographical Diversity in the Resort to Marriage in Late Medieval Europe: Work, Reputation, and Unmarried Females in the Household Formation Systems of Northern and Southern Europe," in Goldberg, *Woman is a Worthy Wight*, 16–59; Goldberg, "Marriage, Migration and Servanthood"; Goldberg, *Women, Work and Life Cycle*.

37. Other scholars have pointed to a greater variety of households in southern Europe than that described by Hajnal and Smith, and to contradictory evidence concerning women's early age of marriage in that region. Nevertheless, the evidence still indicates that complex households were more common in southern Europe than in northwestern Europe and that southern European men had a far greater chance of

tended households such as those more commonly found in southern Europe provided a greater safety net for individuals in distress than did the nuclear households of northwest Europe, though this view has been persuasively disputed by Peregrine Horden.[38]

Along with Parisian testaments of the thirteenth and early fourteenth century, the sources for the *Miracles of Saint Louis* suggest that the northwest European household pattern described by Hajnal, Smith, and Goldberg probably existed in the period before the Black Death, in the late thirteenth and early fourteenth centuries. We find unmarried women migrating to find work, women migrating and then marrying, and a number of widows—both propertied and nonelite—remarrying.[39] Moreover, nearly all nonelite households appear to be conjugal rather than extended. It is not clear that nonelite men and women in this period tended to marry at about the same

---

remarrying than did southern European women. Moreover, the scholarship continues to suggest that premodern women in southern Europe rarely migrated away from their natal families before they married, in contrast to the pattern found in England and in parts of France: David Kertzer and Caroline Brettell, "Advances in Italian and Iberian Family History," *Journal of Family History* 12 (1987): 87–120.

38. Peter Laslett, "Family, Kinship and Collectivity as Systems of Support in Pre-Industrial Europe: A Consideration of the 'Nuclear-Hardship' Hypothesis," *Continuity and Change* 3 (1988): 153–75; Peregrine Horden, "Household Care and Informal Networks: Comparisons and Continuities from Antiquity to the Present," in *The Locus of Care: Families, Communities, Institutions, and the Provision of Welfare since Antiquity*, ed. Peregrine Horden and Richard Smith (New York, 1998), 21–67, esp. 45–51.

39. For cases of unmarried women who apparently migrated to find work, see Amelot of Chaumont and Orenge of Fontenay (above, p. 23). Cases of single women migrating and then marrying are found in Delaborde, "Fragments de l'enquête," 46 (Yfame of Lagny migrated to Paris when she was twenty-three or older, and married a year later), and 52 (a probable case—Oliva de Ploumgmel, who was married and about forty-two years old at the time of the inquest, migrated to Paris from Brittany at the age of eighteen). Widows who remarried include Luce of Rémilly-sur-Lozon; Marie of Fresnay-l'Évêque; Marie the Burgundian; Marie, widow of Robert Evrout and wife of Jacques Olier; Jehanne of Malaunay, widow of Jehan le Grand (possibly the father of the Jehan le Grand mentioned below, p. 33) and wife of Laurence of Malaunay; and Emeline wife of Nicolas, minister of the Hôspice des Quinze-Vingts, and widow of Pierre Harent. Delaborde, "Fragments de l'enquête," 64; Guillaume de St.-Pathus, *Les miracles*, 71, 147–48; testaments of Marie, widow of Robert Evrout, Jehanne de Malaunay, and Emeline, wife of Nicolas, minister of the Quinze-Vingts (see appendix).

age; however the limited data do suggest that nonelite women were older than propertied women when they married, as was the case in northwest Europe in the years after 1348. Yfame of Lagny, who had migrated to Paris a year before her marriage, was twenty-four or older when she married her husband, a dyer who was ten years older than she; Ameline, another nonelite woman, and a native of St.-Denis, was already married at the age of twenty-two. Jehanne of Melun, a propertied resident of St.-Denis, was married by the age of eighteen; Gile of St.-Denis, the daughter and wife of bourgeois butchers in St.-Denis, was married at the age of fifteen.[40]

While the sources from late thirteenth- and early fourteenth-century Paris tend to suggest that the northwest European type of household already existed before the Black Death, those sources also point to a more complex pattern than that described by the principal proponents of such a household. First, as we shall see later on, the Parisian sources support the argument articulated by Peregrine Horden that supportive kinship networks could, and did, extend beyond the walls of individual households.[41] Indeed, in thirteenth-century Paris, a number of adults who had migrated considerable distances maintained meaningful ties with their siblings.

Secondly, the Saint Louis sources point to a significant number of individuals for whom celibate servitude was an indefinite arrangement rather than a life-cycle phenomenon that ended with marriage when they reached their mid- or late twenties. Amelot of Chaumont was already twenty-eight when she immigrated from Chaumont to St.-Denis. After a brief illness, she went to work as a domestic servant for a prominent bourgeois, in whose house she remained until she fell ill and died two years later.[42] Agnes of Pontoise worked in several bourgeois households in Pontoise until she was more than thirty years old. Then, in 1271, she fell victim to an eye disease that rendered her blind and compelled her to beg for a living. When she recovered her sight about four years later she took up residence in the house of a bourgeois, for whom she spun wool until she was at least forty-

---

40. Delaborde, "Fragments de l'enquête," 39, 46, 56; Guillaume de St.-Pathus, *Les miracles*, 163, 12. Jehanne's aunt had an image of the Virgin in her house, which suggests that the family had considerably more than a subsistence income; ibid., p. 165. On elite women's younger ages of marriage after the Black Death see: Maryanne Kowaleski, "Singlewomen in Medieval and Early Modern Europe: The Demographic Perspective," in *Singlewomen in the European Past, 1250–1800*, ed. Judith Bennett and Amy Froide (Philadelphia, 1999), 44 and table A1, 326.

41. See below, chapters 3 and 5.

42. Guillaume de St.-Pathus, *Les miracles*, miracle 2.

five.[43] Henry the Englishman was apparently in his mid-twenties when he became a servant in the household of Luce of Rémilly-sur-Lozon, who lived in St.-Denis. Henry continued to work for Luce and her first and second husbands for at least another ten years.[44] Orenge of Fontenay lived for thirty years with the Parisian weaver for whom she carded wool.[45]

These examples of older and long-term domestic servants—individuals who apparently never married, or who went into domestic service in their widowhood—are not anomalies for high and late medieval northern Europe. David Nicholas found a number of such servants in late fourteenth-century Ghent; and Pierre Desportes showed that female servants in their thirties and forties constituted 27 percent of the female servants in two parishes in Reims in 1422.[46] Desportes found, moreover, that the female population in general, and the number of female domestic servants in particular, increased between the ages of thirty-four and forty-four, suggesting that some of the older servants were not lifelong servants but widows who had moved to the city and taken up employment as domestic servants after their husbands' deaths.

Thus, while it is probably true that the predominance of youthful migra-

---

43. Ibid., miracle 59. It is also possible to read the account as indicating that Agnes began working when she was fifteen and was still single and spinning wool when she was thirty. When Guillaume de St.-Pathus gives an individual's age at the beginning of a narrative he is sometimes referring to the age at which that person became ill and sometimes to the age at which he or she appeared before the panel of clerics at Saint Louis's canonization inquest.

44. Delaborde, "Fragments de l'enquête," 64–66.

45. Guillaume de St.-Pathus, Les miracles, miracle 58.

46. David Nicholas, The Domestic Life of a Medieval City: Women, Children, and the Family in Fourteenth-Century Ghent (Lincoln, Neb., 1985), 104–5. In a later article Nicholas asserts that almost all female servants in Ghent were adults, but he seems to be basing this not only on his handful of examples of older and long-term servants, but also on the fact that a number of servants got pregnant—which was certainly possible for teenagers as well as for women in their twenties or thirties. He also mistakenly says that Herlihy had indicated in Opera Muliebra that female servants in Paris were all adults, whereas Herlihy had surmised that they were probably aged between eight and eighteen: "Child and Adolescent Labour in the Late Medieval City: A Flemish Model in Regional Perspective," English Historical Review 110 (1995): 1106.

Pierre Desportes, "La population de Reims au XVe siècle d'après un denombrement de 1422," Le Moyen Âge 72 (1966): 498. Desportes does not actually calculate the percentage of female servants who were in the thirty- and forty-year-old age brackets—I have made my own calculations from his age pyramid.

tion and female domestic service contributed to the formation of the north-west European household, and that this type of household was already present among nonelite people in the thirteenth century, the evidence also points to significant numbers of people whose life cycles differed from that described by Hajnal, Smith, and Goldberg. The evidence reminds us, moreover, that migrants and servants were at the bottom of the economic ladder and many of them stayed at the bottom all their lives. Many people in north-west Europe—including many servants—never married at all.[47] Women who never married were even worse off than widows because they could not draw on the collective means of the conjugal household in order to set themselves up in business and they were often excluded from the technical training and gild participation that were available to wives and widows.[48]

The migration of substantial numbers of widows—in Reims, and most likely in Paris and England as well—also suggests that we need to broaden our understanding of northern European marriage customs, which almost always granted widows use, if not full ownership, of a substantial portion of the conjugal property.[49] Historians have already stressed that among women who had conjugal property to control those customs resulted in a great deal of financial independence. In thirteenth-century Paris, for instance, widows, rather than their children, usually took control of the family business and maintained that control even after their children came of age.[50] Among the laboring poor, however, there was no conjugal property to control.

---

47. On single women in general see the essays in Bennett and Froide, *Single-women in the European Past*. For an analysis of the scholarship and data concerning the northwest European household, with the argument that late marriage went hand in hand with a high proportion of individuals who never married, see Kowaleski, "Singlewomen."

48. Martha Howell, *Women, Production, and Patriarchy in Late Medieval Cities* (Chicago, 1986), 41–43, 76–77, 85–86; Dubois, "Les feux féminins," 405; Judith Bennett, *Ale, Beer and Brewsters in England: Women's Work in a Changing World, 1300–1600* (New York, 1996), chap. 3; Maryanne Kowaleski and Judith Bennett, "Crafts, Gilds, and Women in the Middle Ages: Fifty Years After Marian K. Dale," *Signs: Journal of Women in Culture and Society* 14 (1989): 474–88. The strap makers' gild of Paris did not allow women to have apprentices unless they were wives of strap makers: René de Lespinasse and François Bonnardot, eds., *Le livre des métiers d'Etienne Boileau* (Paris, 1879), no. 87, article 9, p. 189.

49. Martha Howell, "Fixing Movables: Gifts by Testament in Late Medieval Douai," *Past & Present*, no. 150 (February 1996): 3–45; and Howell, *The Marriage Exchange: Property, Social Place, and Gender in Cities of the Low Countries, 1300–1550* (Chicago, 1998).

50. Archer, "Working Women," 128.

Widows were compelled to survive on their own labor, and their own labor often earned them less than they needed to survive. Thus, they took to the road in search of better livelihoods. Such was the case with a woman from the village of Ranton near Loudun, who moved, after her husband's death, to Saumur, which was about twenty miles to the north. In Saumur, she took up work as a domestic servant in the Hôtel Dieu.[51] Such may have been the case as well for Amelot of Chaumont: the fact that she was twenty-eight at the time that she immigrated to St.-Denis suggests that she may have been a widow; the fact that she became a domestic servant after her migration indicates that she was of modest means and in need of employment.

The importance of widow migration points to another migration pattern that historical demographers have tended to overlook: men and women tended to migrate at different ages. Differences in men's and women's ages of migration are important for this study because they contributed to—or were symptomatic of—differences in the kinds of training opportunities that were available to them once they arrived in town, and differences in the kinds of vulnerabilities that they faced both before and after disability forced them into the category of the nonworking poor.

Among individuals who migrated to Paris and St.-Denis between 1242 and 1282 for whom an age of migration can be determined, seven out of thirteen boys or men migrated by the age of eighteen, four of them by the age of fourteen. By contrast, only one of six women migrated at as young an age as eighteen. The others were all older: one in her mid-twenties, two in their late twenties, and two between twenty and forty.[52]

Because of the limited size of the Saint Louis database relative to the overall size of the Parisian population we might be inclined to dismiss this evidence for gendered differences if it stood alone. However, the evidence in the Saint Louis sources is supported by evidence from fifteenth-century Reims and fourteenth- and fifteenth-century England as well. Pierre Desportes found that in the 1422 enumeration of households in Reims' boys who were between the ages of ten and fourteen far outnumbered those who were under ten and significantly outnumbered boys and men between the ages of fifteen and twenty-four, although the older group also outnumbered

51. Guillaume de St.-Pathus, *Les miracles*, 46.

52. Ibid., miracles 2, 7, 17, 18, 20, 49 (this miracle provides approximate ages of migration for a husband and wife), 54; Delaborde, "Fragments de l'enquête," witnesses 5-1, 5-3, 5-6, 41-1, 41-2, 41-3, 41-4, 41-5, 41-6, 51-3, 51-6. The two women for whom I assign a migration age between twenty and forty had already married and had a child when they migrated. One was still married and the child was still young; the other could have migrated much later, perhaps as a widow.

the boys who were under ten. Desportes was not sure how to interpret this aspect of his data, but I would argue that the bulge among ten- to fourteen-year-olds was caused by immigration, and the contraction among fifteen- to twenty-four-year olds was caused by reverse migration, which may have been more prevalent among men than among women.[53] The female population, by contrast, bulged only slightly among the ten- to fourteen-year-olds, with a much larger increase among women between the ages of fifteen and twenty-four.[54]

Among the male and female migrants to fourteenth- and fifteenth-century English towns to whom P. J. P. Goldberg was able to assign an age of migration, ten of the seventeen males were below the age of nineteen, and six or seven of those ten were below the age of fifteen. Among the female migrants, three, or possibly four, out of seven were below the age of nine-

53. I have argued elsewhere that I find the evidence for Goldberg's and Smith's arguments for "female-led" migration to towns problematic, and that the skewed gender ratios between countryside and towns (with higher proportions of women in towns than in the countryside) may have been caused in part by male reverse migration to the countryside; "Gender and Migration in Thirteenth-Century Paris," paper presented to the January 1999 meeting of the American Historical Association.

54. Desportes, "La population de Reims," 498–500. On his age pyramid, the male population increases from 4.5 at age nine to 8.25 at age fourteen, then decreases to 7.1 at age twenty-four; the female population increases from 4.2 at age nine to 5.5 at age fourteen and to 8.5 at age twenty-four. It is not clear what quantities are represented by the numbers. The total number of individuals in his database from the two parishes (out of thirteen) for which the 1422 survey survives was 3,175; ibid., 479.

Desportes did not think that the recorded age differences in the male and female bulges in the population actually reflected a later age of migration for girls and women because there were equal numbers of girl and boy domestic servants in the pre-fourteen-year-old age bracket. Instead, he attempted to explain the discrepancy by offering the tentative hypothesis that girls represented themselves as older than they really were while boys represented themselves as younger than they really were, perhaps to avoid military conscription. This is a confusing hypothesis, since clearly female domestic servants listed as under the age of fourteen were not representing themselves as over fourteen.

My own inclination after reviewing the evidence from Paris and England would be to accept Desporte's data as an indication that girls or women in fifteenth-century Reims really did migrate at an older age than did boys. If this was indeed the case, then about two-thirds of the pre-fourteen-year-old girl servants would have been local girls who started out their working lives close to their natal homes.

teen, but none were younger than fifteen.[55] Goldberg, however, did not discuss this difference when he analyzed ages of migration.

CITY OF THE POOR

Some migrants came to Paris and St.-Denis not because of work opportunities, but in response to the lure of the charitable wealth there; still others came because of the healing reputation of the shrines of the local saints. In 1271 a deaf-mute who was eventually named Louis followed the royal entourage bearing Saint Louis's remains all the way from Lyon to St.-Denis—a distance of about two hundred miles—because the members of the entourage supported him with their alms. When he arrived in St.-Denis he realized that he could live off of the abbey's alms and so he stayed on.[56] Between November 1281 and May 1282 a young swineherd named Moriset, who was suffering from an oozing, crippling ulcer on his left thigh, slowly made his way from Saumur, in the western Loire valley, to the shrine of St.-Sulpice, in the diocese of Paris, where he had been told that he might find a miraculous cure. There, he learned about the cures that Saint Louis had been performing at his burial site in St.-Denis, so he added another 30 miles to the 145 or so that he had already covered between Saumur and St.-Sulpice. If he had not been cured, he probably would have stayed on as a beggar. Indeed, there is every reason to believe that he did stay on in St.-Denis or Paris, since he had very little to return to in his home village of Ranton, which was about 195 miles away, 20 miles south of Saumur.[57]

People such as these—the laboring and the nonlaboring poor—constituted about half the population of Paris. The best evidence for this estimate is the tax assessment of 1292, in which less than 25 percent of the heads of households were included as potential taxpayers. The remaining 75 percent comprised those who did not have to pay this tax—nobles, clerics, and students—but most of the excluded households consisted of the dependent poor, propertyless wage earners, and those whose business inventories and incomes were so insignificant that they were not even considered liable for a modest tax of twelve deniers, or one sou, which was equal to about a day and a half's wages for a hired laborer in the construction business.[58] When ill-

55. Goldberg, "Marriage, Migration and Servanthood," 10–11.
56. Guillaume de St.-Pathus, *Les miracles*, miracle 15.
57. Ibid., miracle 14.
58. Archer, "Working Women," 79, 83–84; Geremek, *Margins*, 68. Archer argues convincingly on pp. 152–53 that the tax assessment was probably based on some combination of business inventory and income; thus individuals with busi-

ness, age, or disability interrupted the work rhythms of these people, they crossed the line from the working to the nonworking poor, joining the masses of beggars who congregated at parish doors, at the gates of monasteries, at the Place de Grève—the major commercial riverport of Paris (see map 1)—and at funerals.[59]

The numbers of individuals attending charitable disbursements could reach well into the thousands. Two early fourteenth-century Parisian testators—Simon Piz-d'Oue (1307) and Jehan de Troyes (1332)—anticipated that up to forty-eight hundred poor people would attend their funerals: each stipulated that twenty livres, or forty-eight hundred deniers, were to be set aside for handouts of one denier to each poor person who was present at the burial or funeral services following their deaths.[60] In 1310 Jehan le Grand, a currier, anticipated a possible nine thousand poor people, setting aside seventy-five livres for handouts of two deniers to each poor person coming to his funeral.[61] The most astonishing example that I have found, however, is that of Jehan Langlais, a furrier and tavernkeeper, who made his testament in 1316, at the height of the Great Famine. Jehan set aside one hundred livres for one-denier handouts at his funeral, thereby anticipating that as many as twenty thousand poor people might show up.[62]

Were these bourgeois testators making realistic estimates, or simply acting out of ostentatious extravagance? Modern historians have estimated that the begging population may have constituted 10 percent or more of the total population of a given city.[63] Thus it is certainly possible that in a city of over two hundred thousand residents, five to nine thousand poor people showed up for a single funeral. And there is no reason to doubt that such numbers swelled to over twenty thousand during the Great Famine. According to Villani, seventeen thousand Florentines showed up for a funeral handout in that town in 1330, and Florence was only half or two-thirds as

---

nesses with the most valuable inventories, such as fur merchants, tended to be assessed at the highest rates. On wage levels, see Geremek, *Le salariat*, 89 (in the summer of 1299 a salaried mason earned eight sous in Paris). In England, according to Judith Bennett, those who moved in and out of a state of poverty constituted between one-third and one-half of the population; "Conviviality and Charity in Medieval and Early Modern England," *Past and Present*, no. 134 (1992): 20.

59. On beggars on the Place de Grève see the poem by Rutebeuf quoted at the beginning of this chapter.

60. See appendix.

61. See appendix.

62. See appendix.

63. Geremek, *Margins*, 194.

populous as Paris.[64] We have anecdotal evidence, moreover, that the press of the crowds at these disbursements could be dangerous. In 1271, Raou the Cobbler was injured in the foot "by the enormous press" during a Christmastide almsgiving at Ourme Gauchier, which was about ten kilometers south of Paris.

Raou's example also tells us something about the inadequacy of working wages: he was employed at the time that he received this injury.[65] As we shall see in the next chapter, the huge crowds of beggars frequently elicited responses of mistrust among propertied Parisians. Raou is a prime example of the kind of beggar whom members of the elite mistrusted the most: since he was not yet disabled when he went to the almsgiving at Ourme Gauchier he did not qualify as one of the "deserving" poor to whom outdoor alms should freely be given. From our perspective, however, Raou's need for alms probably points to the inadequacy of his income, which may have been exacerbated by the structural factors discussed below.

Despite the evidence for huge crowds of beggars at formalized moments of charitable distribution, and despite the impersonal attitude among clerical moralists toward the "undeserving" poor, propertied Parisians did not always experience beggars as members of a faceless crowd. Unlike blind, deaf, and feeble beggars, paralytic and lame beggars often frequented one specific place—usually their own parish church. Hence it is not surprising that Marie, the widow of Robert Evrout, developed some kind of relationship with "a certain lame man" at the Church of St.-Germain l'Auxerrois, to whom she left the relatively large sum of one hundred sous in her testament of 1307.[66] The relationship was not strong enough, however, for Marie to learn the man's name. Such intimacy, as my discussion will reveal, emerged in more horizontal types of charity, between the still laboring and the nonlaboring poor.

Propertied Parisians also turned to parish networks when they wished to find the "deserving" poor. In 1227, for instance, Jehan de Fontenoi and Bauteut his wife designated that any money that was left over after the payment of their debts and disbursement of their various legacies should go to the dowries of poor girls, who were to be identified by the provost of the parish

64. John Henderson, *Piety and Charity in Late Medieval Florence* (Oxford, 1994), 260. After 1348 the number of beggars in Paris would have diminished. According to Geremek, the largest sum set aside for funerary handouts in the testaments of fifteenth-century Paris would have supported thirty-eight hundred beggars: Geremek, *Margins*, 185–6.

65. Guillaume de St.-Pathus, *Les miracles*, 68.

66. See appendix.

of St.-Jacques and by the "counsel of the three most prudent men of the parish."[67]

Individuals usually crossed the boundary from the laboring to the nonlaboring poor as a consequence of bodily disability or old age. Nevertheless, structural factors in the economy also contributed to people's inability to work or to find work. Despite its stunning concentration of wealth, Paris felt the pinch of the sluggish economy that began to affect all of Europe in the second half of the thirteenth century. Already during the reign of Louis IX there were disturbing levels of unemployment, and in 1288 the master dyers of Paris complained that half of the journeymen of their craft frequently experienced unemployment.[68] Salaries, moreover, remained constant while grain prices grew.[69]

In the early fourteenth century the situation worsened. In 1305 and 1309 there were food and grain shortages.[70] In 1306 King Philip the Fair revalued the coinage, and propertied Parisians demanded rents in the new currency, thereby causing them to triple. In January 1307 poor and middling Parisians—weavers, fullers, tavernkeepers and others—responded to the change violently, burning one house of the king's counselor, Etienne Barbette, and sacking another. A number of individuals who participated in the violence were later hanged.[71] Then, between 1315 and 1322 the Great

67. See appendix.

68. The statute of the hosiers' gild in Etienne Boileau's *Livre des métiers* indicates that masters in that craft were being forced to take employment as day laborers: René de Lespinasse and François Bonnardot, eds., *Le livre des métiers* (Paris, 1879), no. 55, p. 115. Raymond Cazelles sees in the *Livre des métiers* attempts on the part of the king and his provost to raise the level of employment by regulating work hours and establishing lengthy apprenticeships: Cazelles, "Le parisien," 103. On unemployment among dyers, see Réné de Lespinasse, *Les métiers et corporations de la ville de Paris*, 3 vols. (Paris, 1886–97), 3:116; cited by Bronislaw Geremek, *Le salariat*, 122.

69. Sivéry, *L'économie*, 75. Between 1256–57 and 1289–90 the price of a standard measure of wheat rose from 5s. 4d. to 6s. 3d. in Paris. In St.-Denis it rose from 3s. 6d. in 1256–57 to 10s. in 1286–87, then went back down to 7s. in 1289–90. On stability of salaries and overall loss of buying power over the course of the thirteenth century, see ibid., 133–48.

70. Elizabeth Hallam, *Capetian France 987–1328* (New York, 1980), 286.

71. Raymond Cazelles, "Quelques reflexions à propos des mutations de la monnaie royale française (1260–1360)," *Le Moyen Âge* 72 (1966): 258; Jean of St.-Victor, *Excerpta e memoriali historiarum auctore Johanne Parisiensi, Sancti Victoris Parisiensis canonico regulari*, RHGF 21:647; A. Hellot, ed., "Chronique Parisienne anonyme de 1316 à 1339, précédée d'additions à la chronique française dite de Guillaume de

Famine ravaged Paris along with the rest of northern Europe. In 1315 poor people died in the streets.[72] In 1316, the price of wheat, barley and oats skyrocketed. A number of bakers responded to the price rise by adulterating their bread; they were exiled from the kingdom.[73] In the summer of 1323 an epidemic struck the weakened population, "throughout the realm, and especially in Paris," killing a great number of people.[74]

Other factors served to exacerbate an individual's vulnerability during times of personal or collective hardship. For those whose disabilities struck soon after, or even during, their migration to Paris and St.-Denis, the distance they had traveled could serve as a formidable obstacle to finding help: too far from home to turn to their families, many had not yet formed new networks of support in the metropolis. Such people had to survive on informal alms, as was the case not only with Louis the deaf-mute, but also with Jehan of La Haye. At the age of eighteen Jehan left his home in the forest of Lyon in the diocese of Rouen in order to seek employment in Paris, which was about seventy-five miles away. Somewhere on the road between Pontoise and St.-Denis, however, he began to suffer from dizziness and some kind of muscular failure, which caused him to fall repeatedly and left him without any strength in his hands. Several groups of travelers who were making their way from Pontoise to the Lendit fair, which was held each year between June 11 and June 24 on the plain between St.-Denis and Paris, were willing to help Jehan. Suspecting that he was drunk, however, most of them eventually became annoyed, leaving him behind. Finally, two men helped him to the church of St.-Denis where he begged alms and slept on the exterior porch for three weeks.[75]

Unlike Jehan, Amelot of Chaumont seems to have had a network to tap into when she fell ill soon after her arrival in St.-Denis. When Amelot and two companions from her home village arrived in St.-Denis in 1277 they went first to the home of Marguerite of Rocigny to seek lodging; Marguerite had no room at the time, but she told the women that a neighbor

Nangis," *Mémoires de la Société de l'Histoire de Paris et de l'Ile-de-France* 11 (1884): 18–20. For general context see E. Lalou, "Les révoltes contre le pouvoir à la fin du XIIIᵉ siècle et au début du XIVᵉ," *Violence et contestation au Moyen Age* (Paris, 1989), 159–84.

72. Jordan, *The Great Famine*, 142.

73. Ibid., 135, 162.

74. "Chronique parisienne anonyme," 90, cited by Cazelles, "Quelques reflexions," 147.

75. Guillaume de St.-Pathus, *Les miracles*, 60–63.

had room, and she maintained contact with Amelot from then on. Amelot later moved in with Marguerite, and Marguerite was with her in the church of St.-Denis when she was cured of a crippling disease. This continuous contact between Amelot and Marguerite suggests that Amelot knew Marguerite, or knew of her, before she arrived in St.-Denis.[76]

The Bretons of Paris were especially inclined to stick together.[77] But we find other apparent migrant clusters as well. The tax assessment of 1292 contains only seven households or individuals who were identified as "from St.-Yon" (a town in the diocese of Paris). All seven resided on two streets in the parish of St.-Jacques.[78] One has the sense, however, that many people arrived in Paris with no contacts at all. Why else would there have been the profession of "commanderesses," women who provided references for those seeking positions as domestic servants? Those women apparently congregated on the rue des Commanderesses (now the rue de la Coutellerie) in the parish of St.-Jean-en-Grève.

In addition to structural factors in the economy and to obstacles shaped by patterns of migration, poor women in Paris had to worry about their vulnerability to rape and seduction as well. Criminal records from the later Middle Ages suggest that young men often considered single women, and especially poor single women, fair game for gang rape, largely because such women had neither fathers nor husbands to protect them.[79] Testaments indicate, moreover, that masters sometimes got their servants pregnant.[80] Thirteenth-century moralists described the habits of young men who chose to have sex with female servants because they were too embarrassed to frequent prostitutes, but when it came to imposing blame for these encounters

76. Ibid., 7–12.

77. Terroine, "Recherches," 1:89–100.

78. Géraud, *Paris sous Philippe-le-Bel*, 100–101.

79. Jacques Rossiaud, *Medieval Prostitution*, trans. Lydia G. Cochrane (Oxford, 1988), 1–30; Walter Prevenier, "Violence against Women in a Medieval Metropolis: Paris around 1400," in *Law, Custom and the Social Fabric in Medieval Europe: Essays in Honor of Bryce Lyon*, ed. Bernard S. Bachrach and David Nicholas, Studies in Medieval Culture, 28 (Kalamazoo, Mich., 1990), 263–84; Esther Cohen, " 'To Die a Criminal for the Public Good': The Execution Ritual in Late Medieval Paris," ibid., 285–86; Guido Ruggiero, *Violence in Renaissance Venice* (New Brunswick, N.J., 1980), 156–70.

80. Nicholas, *Domestic Life*, 104–6; Barbara Hanawalt, *Growing Up in Medieval London: The Experience of Childhood in History* (New York, 1993), 186–88. See also: Claude Gauvard, *"De Grace Especial": Crime, état et société en France à la fin du moyen âge* (Paris, 1991), 391; Karras, *Common Women*, 55, 87.

they chose to stigmatize the female victims.[81] Along similar lines, city governments often gave light sentences to—or pardoned or ignored—the perpetrators of sexual violence against women.[82]

The facts that men committed acts of sexual violence and seduction against poor women more often than they did against elite women, and that moralists and courts were especially inclined to overlook the misdeeds of male perpetrators when the victims were poor, point to the importance of cultural attitudes in shaping the experiences of poor women—a theme to which we will return later on. For the moment, however, we will turn to elite attitudes toward poor men.

81. Humbert of Romans, *De eruditione religiosorum praedicatorum*, bk. 2, tractatus 1, chap. 98, "Ad famulas divitum," ed. Marguerin de la Bigne, *Maxima bibliotheca veterum patrum et antiquorum scriptorum ecclesiasticorum*, vol. 25 (Lyon, 1677), 505; reprinted in *Prediche alle donne del secolo* XIII, ed. Carla Casagrande (Milan, 1978), 50. On Humbert, see Alexander Murray, "Religion among the Poor in Thirteenth-Century France: The Testimony of Humbert de Romans," *Traditio: Studies in Ancient and Medieval History, Thought and Religion* 30 (1974): 289–90.

82. Rossiaud, *Medieval Prostitution*, 1–30; Prevenier, "Violence against Women," 263–84; Esther Cohen, " 'To Die a Criminal for the Public Good,' " 285–86 (in 1389–92, 28 men were pardoned in Paris for participating in nineteen gang rapes and fifty-five confederates in those crimes were never prosecuted); Ruggiero, *Violence in Renaissance Venice*, 156–70.

CHAPTER TWO
ADAM'S CURSE

One of the paradigms that influenced the ways in which thirteenth-century clerical authors constructed genders was the description in Genesis 3:16–19 of the punishments that God imposed on Adam and Eve:

> To the woman He said, "I will greatly increase your hardship and your pregnancies: in pain you shall bring forth children, and you shall be under the control of your husband, and he shall rule over you." And to Adam he said, "Because you have listened to the voice of your wife and have eaten of the tree from which I commanded you not to eat, cursed is the ground that you work: in toil you shall eat of it all the days of your life. Thorns and thistles it shall bring forth for you, and you shall eat the crops of the earth. By the sweat of your face you shall eat bread until you return to the ground from which you were taken. . . ."
> (Translated from the Vulgate)

This text associates both man and woman with physicality and bodily pain. The curses on Adam and Eve focus on the physical matter from which each has been created—Adam from earth and Eve from the human body. Moreover, manual labor and reproductive labor are both bodily engagements with the physical realm; as a result of the Fall neither form of labor can bring forth fruit without bodily toil and pain. Interpreted in this way, the Genesis passage undermines simplistic assertions that in Western culture, woman is identified with body and physicality while man is associated with soul and immateriality. In the Genesis passage both Adam and Eve are deeply identified with body and physicality. The operating distinction points more to a division of labor—productive and reproductive—and thus, by implication, to a division of realms—public and domestic.

In the Middle Ages, the men who controlled the production of the written word in Latin Christian society seem to have taken this kind of gender distinction very seriously. Indeed, the identification of men with productive labor and women with reproductive labor was so deep and widespread that it even affected public record keeping: in tax and court records alike, men were more likely than women to be identified by profession, and women were identified by relationship to husband, father, or other family members much more often than were men. Thus, for example, in the Parisian tax assessment of 1292, 40 percent of the women were identified in relational terms while only 10 percent of the men were so identified. Conversely, in 1300 over 90 percent of the men were identified by the craft or trade that they practiced while less than 80 percent of the women were so identified.[1] Similarly, in discussions about parental responsibilities toward children, moralists assumed that parents should provide for the education of sons and for the marriage of daughters.[2]

While adhering to the differences between men and women laid out in Genesis 3, clerical authors of the thirteenth and fourteenth centuries nevertheless represented lower-status men and women (as well as Jewish men and women) as more closely tied to, and defined by, the body than elite men and women.[3] In making this assertion, I wish to challenge a predominant consensus that took hold in the 1980s and 1990s among medievalists, including myself, who were interested in questions of gender: that all women were more closely associated with the body and its appetites than were all men. This consensus distorted our understanding of medieval gendered constructs be-

---

1. Caroline Bourlet, "L'anthroponymie à Paris à la fin du XIIIe siècle d'après les rôles de la taille du règne de Philippe le Bel," *Genèse médiévale de l'anthroponymie moderne*, ed. Monique Bourin and Pascal Chareille, vol. 2–2 (Tours, 1992), 16, 23. For discussions of similar patterns, see: Heath Dillard, *Daughters of the Reconquest: Women in Castilian Town Society, 1100–1300* (Cambridge, 1984), 16–21; Isabelle Chabot, "La reconnaissance du travail des femmes dans la Florence du bas Moyen Age: contexte idéologique et réalité," *La donna nell'economia secc. XIII–XVIII*, ed. Simonetta Cavaciocchi (Florence, c. 1990), 565. For an interesting discussion of the ways in which systems for classifying women competed and interacted in official documents see Cordelia Beattie, "The Problem of Women's Work Identities in Post Black Death England," in *The Problem of Labour in Fourteenth-Century England*, ed. James Bothwell, P. J. P. Goldberg, and W. M. Ormrod (York, Eng., 2000), 1–19.

2. Thomas of Chobham, *Thomae de Chobham Summa confessorum*, art. 5, dist. 5, quest. 3, ed. F. Broomfield (Louvain, 1968), 312–13.

3. On the gendering of Jewish men and the association of all Jews with the body, see: Steven Kruger, "Becoming Christian, Becoming Male?" in *Becoming Male in the Middle Ages*, ed. Jeffrey Jerome Cohen and Bonnie Wheeler (New York, 1997), 21–41; and Kruger, "Medieval Christian (Dis)identifications: Muslims and Jews in Guibert of Nogent," *New Literary History* 28 (1997): 185–203.

cause it separated those constructs from other categories of difference. What we need to do instead is to follow the examples of feminists of color and post-colonial feminists, analyzing medieval gender categories within the hierarchical "grids" of difference that medieval people constructed.[4]

My examination of medieval elite constructions of poor men builds upon three strands of recent scholarship concerning medieval gender categories, while also suggesting ways in which these categories were more complex than any of these strands allows.

According to the first strand of scholarship, medieval thinkers created a mind/body binary, associating men with the first component of the binary—rationality and matters of the spirit—while associating women with the second component—irrationality, the body, and lust. This position has been laid out succinctly by Caroline Bynum: "Male and female were contrasted and asymmetrically valued as intellect/body, active/passive, rational/irrational, reason/emotion, self-control/lust, judgment/mercy and order/disorder."[5] As we shall see, however, medieval clerical authors in fact constructed various hierarchies of masculinity, and associated lower-status

---

4. bell hooks, *Feminist Theory: From Margin to Center* (Boston, 1984); Norma Alarcón, "The Theoretical Subject(s) of This Bridge Called My Back," in *Making Face, Making Soul/Haciendo Caras: Creative and Critical Perspectives by Feminists of Color*, ed. Gloria Anzaldúa (San Francisco, 1990), 356–69; Nalini Persram, "Politicizing the *Féminine*, Globalizing the Feminist," *Alternatives* 19 (1994): 275–313; Elizabeth Spelman, *Inessential Woman: Problems of Exclusion in Feminist Thought* (Boston, 1988), esp. chap 7; Patricia Hill Collins, *Black Feminist Thought: Knowledge, Consciousness, and the Politics of Empowerment* (Boston, 1990); Maxine Baca Zinn and Bonnie Thornton Dill, "Theorizing Difference from Multiracial Feminism," *Feminist Studies* 22 (1996): 321–31; Chela Sandoval, "U.S. Third World Feminism: The Theory and Method of Oppositional Consciousness in the Postmodern World," *Genders* 10 (spring 1991): 1–24; Sharon Farmer and Carol Braun Pasternack, eds., *Genders and Other Identities in the Middle Ages: The Interplay of Differences* (Minneapolis, 2002).

Several medievalists have already analyzed the unique ways in which Jews, Muslims, and peasants were gendered, but they have not suggested that we need to rethink medieval gender categories in general. In addition to the references in note 3, see: Louise Mirrer, *Women, Jews, and Muslims in the Texts of Reconquest Castile* (Ann Arbor, 1996); Paul Freedman, *The Image of the Medieval Peasant as Alien and Exemplary* (Stanford, Calif., 1999), chaps. 5 and 7.

5. Caroline Bynum, " 'And Woman His Humanity': Female Imagery in the Religious Writings of the Later Middle Ages," in *Fragmentation and Redemption: Essays on Gender and the Human Body in Medieval Religion* (New York, 1991), 151.

men both with necessary bodily labor and with moral weaknesses arising from the body. According to the authors of sermon literature, propertied individuals—both male and female—were stronger in virtue than these men, and hence these authors called upon both men and women of property to control the sexual appetites of lower status men and women.

The second strand in the predominant scholarly view that medieval women were asymmetrically associated with the body involves the reduction of a woman's character—most especially if she was a saint—to bodily signs. Brigitte Cazelles, for instance, has argued that in high medieval French translations of the lives of late antique saints, female saints were repeatedly disrobed for a voyeuristic audience, and their saintliness was largely reduced to a passive but willing suffering of bodily torments.[6] Similarly, Amy Hollywood has argued that in the saints' lives that were written by western European men in the high Middle Ages, "the identification of women with the body demands that their sanctification occur in and through that body. . . . the medieval hagiographer wants externally sensible *signs* of visionary and mystical experience in order to verify the claims to sanctity of the woman saint."[7] An extreme example of this stress on visible signs is the thirteenth-century mystic, Douceline of Digne, whose ecstatic raptures put her into a virtually catatonic state: she was totally unaware of what was going on around her, and lost all bodily sensation. Daniel Bornstein has argued that Douceline's audience was often more interested in the insensibility of her body than in the content of her visions, and thus, again and again, people tested her body in order to prove to themselves that it really did lose sensation during her raptures. Some of those tests—such as forcing needles under her fingernails, or pouring hot lead over her feet—were so cruel that she remained unable to use her hands or to walk for long periods of time.[8]

---

6. Brigitte Cazelles, "Introduction," in *The Lady as Saint: A Collection of French Hagiographic Romances of the Thirteenth Century* (Philadelphia, 1991), 43–61.

7. Amy Hollywood, *The Soul as Virgin Wife: Mechthild of Magdeburg, Marguerite Porete, and Meister Eckhart* (Notre Dame, Ind., 1995), 35; emphasis in original.

8. *La vie de Sainte Douceline: Texte Provençal du XIVe siècle*, ed. and trans. R. Gout (Paris, 1927), 108–9, 115, 126; Claude Carozzi, "Douceline et les autres," *La religion populaire en Languedoc du XIIIe siècle à la moitié du XIVe siècle*, Cahiers de Fanjeaux, vol. 11 (Toulouse, 1976), 256–61; Daniel Bornstein, "Violenza al corpo di una santa: Fra agiografia e pornografia," *Quaderni medievali* 39 (1995): 31–46. See also Walter Simons, "Reading a Saint's Body: Rapture and Bodily Movement in the *Vitae* of Thirteenth-Century Beguines," in *Framing Medieval Bodies*, ed. Sarah Kay and Miri Rubin (Manchester, 1994), 16–20.

In fact, however, as we shall also see, poor men—as well as women—were also subjected to bodily tests. Whether they labored with their hands or begged in order to survive, poor people who did not choose their poverty were stigmatized by that very lack of choice—the involuntary nature of their poverty. In the minds of people of property and those who controlled the written word the poor could not be trusted. As a result, in certain judicial settings, in which the bodily health or lack of health of individual poor people was a central issue, men of power subjected poor men and women to bodily tests because they were more willing to believe the signs that marked the bodies of the poor than they were to believe the words that poor people uttered.

The third strand of medieval gender scholarship with which we are concerned argues that in the Middle Ages there was an asymmetrical association of women with the use of cosmetic adornments, which distorted the true appearance of the individual. According to Marcia Colish, early Christian and patristic authors simultaneously borrowed and transformed Stoic invective against those who altered their natural appearance with depilatories, razors, and other devices. For pagan Stoics, Colish argues, this had been a gender-neutral theme, but Christians turned it into an asymmetrical invective against women's adornment and use of makeup.[9] Dyan Elliott has carried that analysis forward into the high Middle Ages, arguing that while western European Christian authors continued to associate women with the use of unnatural adornment, they sometimes encouraged married matrons to use makeup and other enhancements to their beauty in order to prevent their husbands from falling away into the sin of adultery.[10] Yet clerical authors in western Europe also associated poor men—especially those who begged—with the use of makeup. As our later discussion will show, men who begged were, in many ways, perceived as not masculine. Moreover, those who were suspected of faking their ailments in order to avoid manual labor were frequently accused of behaving like certain women—especially old women and deceptive prostitutes—who employed bodily deception and cosmetics in order to deceive the consumers of their appearance.

9. Marcia Colish, "Cosmetic Theology: The Transformation of a Stoic Theme," in *Assays: Critical Approaches to Medieval and Renaissance Texts*, ed. Peggy A. Knapp and Michael A. Stugrin (Pittsburgh, 1981), 3–14.

10. Dyan Elliott, "Dress as Mediator between Inner and Outer Self: The Pious Matron of the High Middle Ages," *Mediaeval Studies* 53 (1991): 279–308.

Clerical discussions of hierarchies of masculine labors reached a peak in the third quarter of the thirteenth century, after the secular clergy of Paris attacked the new religious orders—especially the Franciscans and the Dominicans—because they practiced mendicancy, or holy begging, as an aspect of their voluntary poverty.[11] Members of the secular clergy claimed that able-bodied beggars who lived on the alms of the faithful violated Saint Paul's injunction, "if anyone does not wish to work, neither should he eat" (2 Thess. 3:10).

Bonaventure, who was master general of the Franciscan order from 1257 to 1274 and one of the leading defenders of the mendicant religious orders, responded to these criticisms by building on Saint Augustine's work. Augustine had exempted monks engaged in spiritual endeavors such as preaching, administering the sacraments, and performing administrative tasks for the church from the monastic obligation of doing manual labor.[12] Similarly, Bonaventure pointed out that Christians (by which he meant, primarily, Christian men) were not all called upon to practice manual labor. Rather, the work of men could be divided into three categories: inferior or corporeal work (that which was necessary for such tasks as preparing clothing and food); exterior or civil work (such as that of governors, knights, and merchants); and finally, spiritual work (that of preachers and priests, for instance).[13] It was valid for the members of the mendicant orders to accept the alms of the faithful because they engaged in this third type of work, "the labor of wisdom," which was superior to corporeal work.[14] Indeed,

---

11. On the seculars' criticisms of the mendicant orders see: Penn R. Szittya, *The Antifraternal Tradition in Medieval Literature* (Princeton, N.J., 1986), chap. 1; D. L. Douie, *The Conflict between the Seculars and the Mendicants at the University of Paris in the Thirteenth Century*, The Aquinas Society of London, Aquinas Paper 23 (London, 1954); Michel-Marie Dufeil, *Guillaume de St.-Amour et la polémique universitaire parisienne, 1250–1259* (Paris, 1972). For a general discussion of the social meanings of voluntary poverty, see Lester K. Little, *Religious Poverty and the Profit Economy in Medieval Europe* (Ithaca, 1978).

12. Augustine also exempted monks from upper-class backgrounds from this obligation because they could not endure the strain: Birgit van den Hoven, *Work in Ancient and Medieval Thought* (Amsterdam, 1996), 144.

13. Bonaventure, *Quaestiones disputatae de perfectione evangelica*, quaest. II, art. III, conclusion, in *Doctoris Seraphici S. Bonaventurae Opera Omnia*, ed. College of Saint Bonaventure, 10 vols. (Quaracchi, 1882–1902), 5:161.

14. Bonaventure (attributed), *Expositio super regulam Fratrum Minorum*, chap. 5, in *Doctoris Seraphici S. Bonaventurae Opera Omnia*, 8:420. See also Bonaventure,

Bonaventure argued, there was only one category of men for whom manual labor was a precept—those "poor strong ones who are most fit for corporeal work, and least fit for spiritual work." Without the precept of manual labor, he went on, these men "would not know how to avoid idleness suitably."[15]

Thomas of Cantimpré, a member of the Dominican order who died in 1270, concurred with Bonaventure's position. In response to the critics of the mendicant orders, Thomas argued that spiritual labor was "more fruitful" and "more dignified" than manual labor, and that manual, or corporeal labor, was imposed upon those who were appropriately subordinated to others because it protected them from the dangers of idleness.[16]

In a different context, Humbert of Romans, who was master general of the Dominican order from 1254 to 1277 and the author of one of the great preaching treatises of the thirteenth century, made a similar mind/body distinction between lower-status and lettered men.[17] In a chapter concerning sermon material for boys who were studying Latin grammar, Humbert wrote that every occupation involved the acquisition of either mechanical

---

Apologia pauperum contra calumniatorem, chap. 12, par. 12–40, in *Doctoris Seraphici S. Bonaventurae Opera Omnia*, 8:320–29.

15. Bonaventure, *Quaestiones disputatae de perfectione evangelica*, quaest. II, art. III, conclusion, in *Doctoris Seraphici S. Bonaventurae Opera Omnia*, 5:161.

16. Thomas of Cantimpré, *Bonum universale de apibus*, bk. 2, chap. 10, no. 7; bk. 1, chap. 15 (Douai, 1627), 161, 55. Thomas Aquinas, another Dominican, also pointed to a hierarchy of labors in his response to the seculars, but that hierarchy was less central to his overall argument: *Contra impugnantes dei cultum et religionem*, chap. 7, in *Sancti Thomae Aquinatis Doctoris Angelici Ordinis Praedicatorum Opera Omnia*, 25 vols. (Parma, 1852–1873; reprint ed., New York, 1950), 15:41. In the sections of the *Summa theologiae* that dealt with whether or not members of religious orders should beg and whether or not they were required to do manual labor, Aquinas avoided constructing a hierarchy of labors, suggesting instead that "manual labor" referred to all forms of useful work for society, including preaching and serving at the altar: *Summa theologiae*, 2a2ae, quaest. 187, art. 3 and 4, ed. and trans. Blackfriars, 61 vols. (New York, 1964–81), 47:156–57, 160–61, 168–69.

The early thirteenth-century churchman Jacques de Vitry had also created a hierarchy of labors with preaching at the top: Jacques de Vitry, "Sermo XXXV ad Fratres Minores," in *Sermones vulgares*, in *Analecta novissima spicilegii Solesmensis Altera continuatio*, ed. Joannes Baptista Cardinalis Pitra, vol. 2 (reprint ed., Farnborough, 1967), 400–402.

17. For a discussion of the new preaching, and Humbert's role in promoting it, see Little, *Religious Poverty*, chap. 11.

knowledge—which pertained to the body—or the knowledge of letters, which pertained to the soul, and since the soul was more noble than the body, the acquisition of knowledge of letters was more noble than the acquisition of mechanical knowledge. Similarly, in a chapter concerning sermon material for the learned, Humbert compared those with wisdom to the angels and those who lacked intellect to beasts.[18]

Bonaventure, Thomas of Cantimpré, and Humbert of Romans left no room for doubt concerning the superiority of spiritual and intellectual over manual labor. But what about the labors of propertied laymen, especially those who engaged in the physically demanding activities of warfare? Did the physicality of the use of arms draw these men down to the level of ordinary laborers? Not at all. In the ideology of the three orders, which had been elaborated by members of the church hierarchy, "those who fought" were clearly superior to "those who worked" because they took up arms in order to defend the weak and the poor. The vernacular literature of the twelfth and thirteenth centuries went even further in bolstering the prestige of the knightly aristocracy, emphasizing that these men possessed the spiritual qualities of courage, chivalry, largesse, and romantic love—characteristics that nobles claimed to be altogether lacking in men of the lower orders of society.[19] Bonaventure, moreover, classified the labor of a knight with the labor of governors and merchants. According to Bonaventure, the labor of these men, which was "exterior" or "civil," stood in an intermediary position between the "interior" or "spiritual" labor of prelates and preachers and the "inferior" or "manual" labor of peasants and other laborers. Governors,

18. Humbert of Romans, *De eruditione religiosorum praedicatorum*, bk. 2, tract. 1, chap. 63, "Ad scholares in grammatica," in *Maxima bibliotheca veterum patrum et antiquorum scriptorum ecclesiasticorum*, ed. Marguerin de la Bigne, vol. 25 (Lyon, 1677), 487; ibid., bk. 2, tract. 1, chap. 56, "Ad omnes litteratos," p. 484. See also bk. 2, tract. 1, chap. 71, "Ad omnes laicos," p. 491, where he argues that like she-asses, who feed next to the oxen who do the plowing, "simplices"—that is to say, laypeople—should be content with the doctrines of their betters, that is to say, the clergy. Humbert was building on the twelfth-century *glossa ordinaria* to the book of Genesis, which interpreted both the binary male/female and the binary man/beast to stand for the relationship between clerics, who should lead, and simple laypeople, who should obey: see Philippe Buc, *L'ambiguïté du livre: Prince, pouvoir, et peuple dans les commentaires de la Bible au moyen âge* (Paris, 1994), 71–112.

19. On the ideology of the three orders, see Georges Duby, *The Three Orders: Feudal Society Imagined*, trans. Arthur Goldhammer (Chicago, 1980). See also Paul Freedman, *The Image of the Medieval Peasant as Alien and Exemplary* (Stanford, Calif., 1999), chap. 7.

merchants, and knights drew on their intelligence in order to do their work, but they directed their intelligence toward the external, rather than the internal, needs of humanity.[20]

Along with other writers, these three assumed that male members of the working poor had a stronger association with the body, and a weaker association with things pertaining to the soul, than did elite men. This does not imply, however, that they considered lower-status workingmen to be effeminate. Rather, they constructed a hierarchy of "masculinities," which were distinguished from "femininities" not by the difference between mind and body, but by the difference between men's productive labor (that is to say, work in the public sphere) and women's reproductive, or domestic, labor (that is, work in the domestic sphere). Men who worked with their hands were "masculine" because they engaged in productive labor, but their masculinity was inferior to that of prelates, preachers, and governors, who engaged in productive labor with their minds rather than with their bodies; or of knights, whose bodily labor was driven and perfected by intellectual traits.

Of course, it followed naturally that men who labored with their bodies rather than their minds were less informed about matters of the spirit, and more likely to give in to the rule of their appetites, than were men who labored with their minds. Thus, according to Humbert of Romans, hired laborers were "exceedingly" ignorant of things pertaining to their own salvation, and they were prone to drunkenness. He said nothing about these faults in his sermon material for either propertied laymen or propertied laywomen.[21] In their sermon material for male and female servants, moreover, thirteenth-century clerics associated both male and female members of the working poor with the rule of the sexual appetites. Humbert of Romans explicitly mentioned that some male and female servants engaged in sexual sins; he made no such statement in his sermon material for propertied lay-

---

20. See above, note 13.

21. Humbert, *De eruditione*, bk. 2, tract. 1, chap. 88, "Ad operarios conductivos," p. 500. Humbert's sermon material for elite laymen (urban officials and "maiores"— nobles, magnates and courtiers) is ibid., bk. 2, tract. 1, chaps. 73, 74, 80–84, pp. 492–93, 495–98; his sermon material for elite laywomen (noblewomen and rich urban woman) is ibid., bk. 2, tract. 1, chaps. 95–96, p. 504; reprinted in Carla Casagrande, *Prediche alle donne del secolo XIII* (Milan, 1978), 45–48. In his sermon material for peasant women, Humbert included credulity and simplicity among their faults, but not drunkenness: *De eruditione*, bk. 2, tract. 1, chap. 99, p. 505; reprinted in Casagrande, *Prediche*, 52–53.

men.[22] The early thirteenth-century churchman Jacques de Vitry and the mid-century Franciscan Gilbert of Tournai also mentioned sexual sins in their sermons about servants, and they went so far as to suggest that women who governed large households, as well as men of similar means, should assume responsibility for guarding the chastity of both their male and female servants.[23] Gilbert counseled "prudent" wives to "cast down lascivious and youthful manservants," and to "beware lest her male and female servants pollute her house with their incontinence."[24] Moreover, he placed the matron's responsibility for the behavior of her servants within a context that associated all of her household duties with aspects of "governance": she was to educate her children, humble male servants, and correct female servants.[25]

Discussions of the hierarchy of labors in the writings of Bonaventure, Humbert of Romans, Thomas of Cantimpré, and others represent only one of the possible discourses that distinguished laboring men from propertied men. In other contexts, clerical authors distinguished any member of the involuntary poor—including those who had to labor in order to survive—from those who did not need to labor, or to beg, for a living. Thus, we learn in the *Miracles of Saint Louis* of a woman named Jehanne, from the parish of St.-Merry in Paris, who after she was cured "earned her own living because she was poor."[26] Similarly, Jacques de Vitry opened a preaching story intended for regular canons with these words: "I heard of a certain poor lay-

22. Humbert, *De eruditione*, bk. 2, tract. 1, chap. 76, "Ad familiam divitum in civitatibus," p. 494. In his discussion of sermon material for devout nobles, Humbert did mention those who "kneel before prostitutes," but only to highlight that such nobles would nevertheless remain chaste (ibid., bk. 2, tract. 1, chap. 82, p. 496). Humbert said nothing about prostitutes in his chapters concerning nobles in general and bad nobles: ibid., bk. 2, tract. 1, chap. 80–81, pp. 495–96. For his sermon material for other elite laymen see the previous note.

23. Jacques de Vitry, "LXIV, Sermo ad servos et ancillas," in "Deux sermons de Jacques de Vitry (+1240) *Ad servos et ancillas*," ed. Jean Longère, in *La femme au moyen âge*, ed. Michel Rouche and Jean Heuclin (Mauberge, 1990), 278–80. Gilbert of Tournai, "Ad ancillas et servos sermo primus," Paris, Bibliothèque Nationale de France, ms. lat. 15943, fols. 175r–177r.

24. Gilbert of Tournai, "Ad coniugatas, sermo tercius," in Casagrande, *Prediche*, 94–95.

25. Ibid., 93–97. Although nonelite people also had servants, they did not usually have many servants in their households. Thus, it is reasonable to assume that Gilbert addressed his sermon to propertied women.

26. Guillaume de St.-Pathus, Confesseur de la Reine Marguerite, *Les miracles de Saint Louis*, ed. Percival B. Fay (Paris, 1931), 135; similarly, about a poor man who earned his living, 158.

man, who, laboring with his own hands, acquired each day a meager meal for himself. . . ."[27]

In this story, intended to inspire the voluntary poor to embrace their poverty, Jacques emphasized the carefree joy with which this poor working-man praised God each evening, contrasting his devout joy to the anxiety-ridden life of a rich man. In other contexts, however, moralists made it clear that the virtue of the involuntary poor was always suspect, precisely because their poverty was not voluntary: the simple poor desired not to be poor, and hence, they wished to gain more wealth. As Thomas Aquinas put it, "spiritual danger comes from poverty when it is not voluntary, because a man falls into many sins through the desire to get rich, which torments those who are involuntarily poor."[28] Similarly, the twelfth-century decretist Huguccio characterized the involuntary poor as filled "with the voracity of cupidity."[29]

According to the moralists, poor people were supposed to be satisfied with their lot in life. In his sermons, Jacques de Vitry counseled that if the poor were "patient and constant in the path of poverty and the test of affliction" they would "deserve to arrive from poverty to true wealth, and from tribulation to eternal delight."[30] The assumption, however, was that many poor people were not satisfied with such promises. Jacques described evil poor people who detested and blasphemed God for their afflictions.[31] Humbert of Romans wrote of poor people who "curse and hate their poverty, and bear it impatiently," and he described laborers who cursed both Adam—for afflicting mankind with the punishment of manual labor—and the day of their birth.[32] Guillaume le Clerc, a vernac-

27. Jacques de Vitry, "Sermo XXX ad Canonicos Regulares," in *Sermones vulgares*, 389. See also "Sermo XXXV ad Fratres Minores," ibid., 404.

28. *Summa theologiae*, 2a2ae, quaest. 186, art. 3, resp. ad 2, 47:108–11.

29. Brian Tierney, *Medieval Poor Law: A Sketch of Canonical Theory and Its Application in England* (Berkeley, Calif., 1959), 11. See also the thirteenth-century moralist John of Wales who characterized the involuntary poor as desirous of wealth: Jenny Swanson, *John of Wales: A Study of the Works and Ideas of a Thirteenth-Century Friar* (Cambridge, 1989), 133.

30. Jacques de Vitry, "Sermo secundus ad pauperes et afflictos," Bibliothèque Nationale de France, ms. lat 3284, fol. 117r. As is the case with a number of Jacques de Vitry's "Sermones Vulgares," this one was not included in Pitra's printed edition. See also Honorius of Autun, *Sermo generalis*, PL 172:864; Gilbert of Tournai, "Ad pauperes et afflictos sermo primus," Bibliothèque Nationale de France, ms. lat. 15943, fol. 100r; Swanson, *John of Wales*, 133.

31. Jacques de Vitry, "Sermo secundus ad pauperes et afflictos," fol. 117r.

32. Humbert of Romans, *De eruditione*, bk. 2, tract. 1, chap. 86, "Ad pauperes," p. 499; ibid., chap. 78, "Ad laicos in villis," 494.

ular poet who wrote in the 1220s, asserted that thousands of poor people were "felons, greedy, slanderous, proud, envious, and—as long as they can hold onto a penny—full of debauchery."[33] He went on to say that rather than praising God for giving them the gift of poverty, they challenged Him for creating them "in such a way that we never have earthly goods."[34]

BODILY TESTS OF POOR MEN

Desire—an insatiable appetite for that which one lacked—was, according to clerical authors, the essence of ordinary poverty, both of the working and of the nonworking poor. By contrast, in some contexts the mere fact of having wealth—especially wealth generated by landed property—seemed to speak to the possessor's superior virtue. In secular and church courts alike poor people's testimony was considered less trustworthy than that of people who possessed wealth.[35] In an effort to prevent fraud, church courts conducting inquests into saintly miracles almost always interviewed multiple witnesses to a miracle, especially if the principle witness to the miracle was poor. The inquisitors were especially cautious with poor witnesses because it was believed that they were susceptible to bribes, that they might fake illnesses in order to get more alms, or that they might fake miraculous cures in order to gain notoriety and perhaps increase their incomes as a result.[36] We

33. Guillaume le Clerc de Normandie, *Le Besant de Dieu*, ed. Pierre Ruelle (Brussels, 1973), lines 1113–14, 1117–20, p. 99.

34. Ibid., lines 1147–50, p. 100.

35. R. H. Helmholz, *Marriage Litigation in Medieval England* (London, 1974), 156; Cordelia Beattie, "The Problem of Women's Work Identities in Post Black Death England," 1–19; P. J. P. Goldberg, ed. and trans., *Women in England c. 1275–1525* (Manchester, 1995), 159–61 (this last is a translation of depositions concerning the trustworthiness of two poor witnesses in a marriage case that came before the church court of York in 1355).

36. On the susceptibility of poor witnesses to bribes, see Gratian, *Decretum*, Secunda pars, causa 4, quaest. 2 et 3, c. 3, in *Decretum Gratiani emendatum* (Rome, 1588), col. 910. The *glossa ordinaria* to the *Decretum* argued that poor people could be accepted as witnesses if they were not suspected of anything; ibid., gloss on the word *locuples*. This point was repeated by Johannes de Erfordia, *Die Summa confessorum des Johannes von Erfurt*, 2.7.1, ed. Norbert Brieskorn, 3 vols. (Frankfurt-am-Main, 1980–81), 3:1509. Aquinas acknowledged the position taken in the gloss, but favored that of Gratian: *Summa theologiae*, 2a2ae, quaest. 70, art. 3, 38: 138–39.

know, in fact, that the churchmen looking into saintly miracles occasionally caught people who pretended to have been cured.[37]

Given the suspicions surrounding the testimony of the poor, it is not at all surprising that William of Canterbury, who was one of the authors of the *Miracles of Thomas Becket*, defended the testimony of elite witnesses, even when there were no corroborating witnesses, on the basis of their social status alone. Concerning the testimony of one noblewoman, for instance, he asserted:

> we have heard . . . the woman, and examined her, in the manner proper for her noble birth, and we can presume the truth of her account from her pilgrimage and devotion. For although faith is rare, because many people say many things, nevertheless, just as we conclude that beggars are liars, so we do not at all assume the same of nobles who win divine favor by making a pilgrimage.[38]

Apparently influenced by the same way of thinking, the clerics who conducted the inquest concerning the miracles of Saint Louis asked each witness how much he or she was worth. Those with wealth answered that they had property worth so many livres; those without wealth tended to answer that they had nothing, and that they lived by their own labor.[39] In so answering, those without property placed themselves in the inferior of two groups—the haves and the have-nots—thereby indicating that their sworn testimony was worth less than that of the individuals with property.

These examples of clerics' tendency to give greater weight to the testimonies of witnesses with wealth and status provide a context for the evidence in *The Miracles of Saint Louis*, which suggests that men of power were more inclined to subject the poor, rather than persons of property, to bodily examinations and tests in order to establish their actual state, or status. My analysis of "bodily inspections" focuses on the fifty-two miracles for which it is possible to establish the social status of the beneficiary, and which were not reported as "secondary" miracles (miracles that were mentioned inci-

37. Ronald C. Finucane, *Miracles and Pilgrims: Popular Beliefs in Medieval England* (New York, 1977), 70–71.

38. William of Canterbury, *Miraculorum Gloriosi Martyris Thomae, Cantuariensis Archiepiscopi*, bk. 6, no. 140, ed. James Craigie Robertson, *Materials for the History of Thomas Becket*, Rerum Britannicarum Medii Aevi Scriptores 67, vol. 1 (London, 1875), 524.

39. H.-François Delaborde, ed., "Fragments de l'enquête faite à Saint-Denis en 1282 en vue de la canonisation de Saint Louis," *Mémoires de la Société de l'Histoire de Paris et de l'Ile-de-France* 23 (1896): 21, 26, 31, 33, 41–42, 44, 46, 50, 52, 54, 56, 59, 61, 62, 64, 71.

dentally by witnesses who had been summoned to testify to another miracle).[40] Sixteen of these fifty-two miracles benefited propertied individuals (nobles, beneficed clergy, monks, and propertied townspeople), six of whom were women and ten were men. The other thirty-six miracles benefited poor people—the indigent and those without property who worked with their hands for a living. Twenty-one of the poor beneficiaries were women, and fifteen were men.[41]

The first noteworthy difference between miracles benefiting propertied individuals and those benefiting poor people concerns the locations where the miracles took place. Thirty-four of the thirty-six poor people received their miraculous assistance from Saint Louis at his tomb in the Basilica of St.-Denis, while ten of the sixteen propertied beneficiaries were in their homes, in the homes of close relatives, at work, or in their own neighborhoods. Of the remaining six, only four had to travel to Louis's tomb in St.-Denis, and two of those four were of relatively modest means: the daughter and wife of bourgeois butchers in St.-Denis, and a tailor or tailor's assistant who inherited property in his home village. The other two propertied beneficiaries had access to Louis's relics without traveling to his tomb: they

40. Many of the secondary miracles involved the same beneficiaries as the primary miracles, so that their inclusion would distort the statistics.

41. Guillaume de St.-Pathus, *Les miracles*. Propertied men and boys: miracles 12, 13, 24, 29, 38, 40, 50, 60, 61, 65. Propertied women and girls: miracles 1, 3, 46, 53, 55, 64. Poor men and boys: miracles 7–9, 14, 15, 17, 18, 20, 25, 28, 33, 45, 47–49. Poor women and girls: miracles 2, 4, 5, 21, 30–32, 34–37, 39, 41–44, 51, 52, 57–59. Included among the poor are a Cistercian *conversa*, two sisters at the Filles Dieu (a house for reformed prostitutes), and a woman associated with the Beguinage of Paris, since all of these women would have come from modest backgrounds. The boy in miracle 19 has not been included. He was identified as the son of Agnes la Buschiere, who lived in the parish of St.-Merry; Agnes's husband was identified as Jehan de Clamart. This may be the "Anès, la buchière" who lived on the rue de la Barre in the parish of St.-Merry and was assessed, together with her two daughters, for a middle-level tax of twelve sous in 1292 and 1296 and for sixteen sous in 1297. The husband may be the same as the Jean de Clamart who owned a vineyard in 1272–76. See Hercule Géraud, *Paris sous Philippe-le-Bel, d'après des documents originaux et notamment d'après un manuscrit contenant "Le Rôle de la Taille" imposée sur les habitants de Paris en 1292*, reprint with introduction and index by Lucie Fossier and Caroline Bourlet (Tübingen, 1991), 75; Karl Michaëlsson, *Le livre de la taille de Paris, l'an 1296* (Göteborg, 1958), 113; Michaëlsson, *Le livre de taille de Paris, l'an 1297* (Göteborg, 1962), 99; Anne Terroine, *Un bourgeois Parisien du XIIIe siècle: Geoffroy de Saint-Laurent, 1245?-1290*, ed. Lucie Fossier (Paris, 1992), 220, 235.

were cured when the royal entourage bearing Louis's body stopped in their towns in Italy, on the way back to France from Tunisia, where Louis had died.[42] Although many of the propertied beneficiaries made pilgrimages to Louis's tomb after they received his aid in order to fulfill their vows to him, the ten who received help within their homes, work spaces, or neighborhoods were not subjected to the same degree of public scrutiny and physical examination during their illnesses that the sick and disabled pilgrims who traveled to Louis's tomb had to endure.[43]

There are several reasons for the differences in the locations of the miracles benefiting propertied individuals and those benefiting the poor. In a few cases, propertied beneficiaries had access to items of clothing that had belonged to Louis, so that they did not need to travel in order to make physical contact with the saint's power. When Lorenz, the prior of the Cistercian abbey of Chaalis, fell ill the sacristan of the abbey brought him a cloak that had belonged to Louis, which the abbey kept as a relic. The prior kissed the cloak, wrapped himself in it, then slept through the night using it as a blanket. His recovery began during that night (figure 1).[44] Aelis l'Aveniere, the wife of Louis's former squire, possessed several feathered hats that had belonged to the king. When the Seine rose and flooded her cellars, she ordered one of her servants to make the sign of the cross over the water with one of the hats, and the water began to recede.[45] Poor people did not have privileged access to items that had once belonged to the king, and hence they needed to travel to his tomb in order to make physical contact with his holy powers.

In most cases, the different locations of elite and lower-status miracles (those, that is, that came to be inscribed in the official record) resulted, in part, from the authorities' demands for reliable evidence. In the case of

---

42. Guillaume de St.-Pathus, *Les miracles*. For a complete list of miracles involving propertied and poor beneficiaries, see the previous note. Poor beneficiary not at the tomb: miracles 30, 47. Modestly propertied beneficiaries at the tomb: miracles 3, 24. Other propertied beneficiaries at the tomb: miracles 13, 53. Propertied beneficiaries in Italy when Louis's relics passed through their towns: miracles 64, 65.

43. These "at home" miracles are indicative of the growing pattern observed by André Vauchez, of conditional vows—vows that were kept only if a saint came to the individual's assistance; *La sainteté en occident aux derniers siècles du moyen âge: D'après les procès de canonisation et les documents hagiographiques* (Rome, 1981), 521–29. However, Vauchez did not attempt a status analysis of those who were most likely to make, and be helped by, conditional vows.

44. Guillaume de St.-Pathus, *Les miracles*, miracle 12.

45. Ibid., miracle 46.

FIGURE 1. Lorenz, Prior of the Abbey of Chaalis, Cured by Saint Louis's Cloak Guillaume de Saint-Pathus, *Les miracles de Saint Louis*, miracle 12. Bibliothèque Nationale de France, ms. fr. 5716 (illuminated c. 1330), p. 355. Photograph courtesy Bibliothèque Nationale de France, Paris.

propertied individuals who had been cured by Saint Louis, the authorities were apparently willing to trust the testimony of witnesses rather than relying on the physical evidence of the beneficiaries' bodies. When propertied individuals fell ill, even for short periods of time, their houses often filled with people, such as physicians, who would later serve as distinguished and highly credible witnesses. Guillaume de St.-Pathus mentioned that six of the sixteen propertied beneficiaries consulted physicians (figure 2). By contrast, he stated that only two of the thirty-six poor beneficiaries saw physicians. Another two consulted surgeons, but surgeons were of a much lower social status than that of physicians.[46] Even under normal circumstances, moreover, propertied individuals lived in large households with many servants. By contrast, poor people who suffered short illnesses—as opposed to

46. Ibid., passim. Propertied beneficiaries consulting physicians: miracles 38, 40, 50, 60, 64, 65. Poor beneficiaries consulting physicians: miracles 7, 58. Poor beneficiaries consulting surgeons: miracles 21, 33.

FIGURE 2. Dudes, A Canon of Paris, Consults Physicians

On the right, physicians examine Dudes's urine. On the left, Dudes later dreams that he is at Saint Louis's tomb and that Louis comes to him and cures him. Guillaume de Saint-Pathus, *Les miracles de Saint Louis*, miracle 38. Bibliothèque Nationale de France, ms. fr. 5716, p. 508. Photo courtesy Bibliothèque Nationale de France, Paris.

prolonged disabilities—suffered more privately, in households that were much more limited in numbers. Because their witnesses were less prestigious and less numerous, poor people were probably less confident about coming forward with stories about diseases that were relatively short-lived and not visible to so many people; and, in any case, the men who controlled the written word were apparently less willing to record poor people's accounts of such illnesses. Thus, while half of the propertied beneficiaries in the *Miracles of Saint Louis* had endured the ailments that Louis cured for one month or less, only three of the poor people (about 8 percent) had been ill for a month or less.[47]

47. Ibid. Propertied beneficiaries cured after being ill one month or less: miracles 1, 12, 29, 38, 40, 50, 53, 55; poor beneficiaries cured after being ill one month or less: miracles 18, 25, 28. The length of time that the poor person in miracle 37 was ill cannot be determined. It might have been one month or less.

Men of power were much more likely to believe the stories of poor people who had suffered disabilities for a long time, because their sufferings had been observed by the community at large, including, often, the beneficiary's parish priest. Moreover, once they traveled to the tomb of the saint, poor people submitted to the scrutiny of church authorities at the shrine, and thus the evidence of their appearance, both before and immediately after their cures, became a part of official memory.

The surviving fragment of the inquest into Saint Louis's miracles gives us a striking example of the careful observations of officials at his tomb. Thomas of Hauxton, who had been appointed by the prior of St.-Denis to watch over the infirm people at the tomb, provided an eyewitness account of the dramatic cure of Amelot of Chambly, a woman who had probably been the victim of spinal tuberculosis. For three years, between 1268 and 1271, Amelot had begged in the streets of St.-Denis, crawling about the town with the aid of a short walking stick, while she held her chin about eighteen inches from the ground (figure 3). Like many other people in St.-Denis, Thomas of Hauxton had seen Amelot begging in her pitiful condition. Unlike most others, however, he was standing right next to her when she was cured at Louis's tomb. Thomas told the inquisitors that in 1271, not long after Louis's relics had been placed in their sepulchre at St.-Denis, Amelot visited the tomb for six consecutive days. On the sixth or seventh day, while she was lying right at his feet, Thomas heard the bones in Amelot's back make a sound "as if they were being broken and violently shaken," and then he heard her call out "Lord, Saint Louis!" Next he saw her cast away her walking stick and straighten herself out without any assistance. Thomas ran to get the prior, who asked Amelot to walk, which she did—from the tomb to the main altar and back again—without any assistance. Finally, Thomas saw Amelot sit down and weep, calling out her thanks to Saint Louis.[48]

We find a similar pattern of differing treatment of propertied and poor beneficiaries when they appeared before the panel of clerics who conducted the inquest concerning the miracles in 1282–83. In his narratives concerning twelve of the thirty-six poor people, Guillaume of St.-Pathus goes to some trouble to tell us not only about the diseases that these people had suffered, and how they were cured, but also about what the clerics conducting the inquest did during their meetings with the beneficiaries. In eleven out of the twelve cases—seven women and four men—Guillaume described the inquisitors' visual examinations of the beneficiaries' bodies. In the twelfth

48. Delaborde, ed., "Fragments de l'enquête," 19–20. See also Guillaume de St.-Pathus, *Les miracles*, miracles 9 and 59, for accounts of the monks' encounters with people who were healed at the tomb.

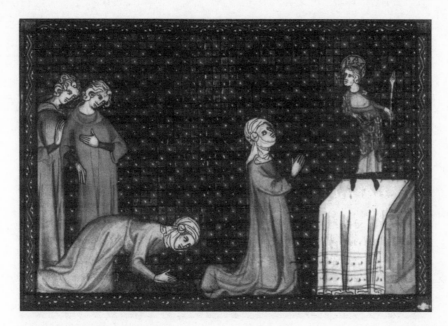

FIGURE 3. Amelot of Chambly
On the left we see Amelot bent over with her debilitating disease; on the right, she kneels erect and cured before a statue of Saint Louis. The artist, working c. 1330, made no effort to be consistent in his depictions of Saint Louis's tomb. In this case, as with figures 4 and 5, the statue of Louis stands on what appears to be an altar covered with a white linen cloth. Guillaume de Saint-Pathus, *Les miracles de Saint Louis*, miracle 5. Bibliothèque Nationale de France, ms. fr. 5716, p. 318. Photo courtesy Bibliothèque Nationale de France, Paris.

case, involving the cure of a deaf-mute boy, he described the questions that the inquisitors asked.[49]

One of the eleven was Moriset, a youth who had had a huge oozing tumor on his leg, which forced him to use crutches and smelled so bad that his fellow residents in the public hospital of the town of Saumur did not want him to come near them (figure 4). Guillaume tells us that after Moriset was cured: "[He] came before the inquisitors and their notaries, and the inquisitors and their notaries saw the place where the tumor had been, where now he had no malady or rupture. And also the traces of the scars were evident, still large and red, as is normal for newly healed and closed wounds."[50]

49. Guillaume de St.-Pathus, *Les miracles*. Visual inspections of poor men and boys: miracles 7, 14, 20, 47. Visual inspections of poor women and girls: miracles 34, 35, 36, 39, 42, 51, 52. Examination of poor deaf-mute boy: miracle 15.

50. Ibid., miracle 14, p. 49.

FIGURE 4. Moriset of Ranton

On the left Moriset exposes his oozing tumor. On the right, he kneels before Saint Louis's tomb. Guillaume de Saint-Pathus, *Les miracles de Saint Louis*, miracle 5. Bibliothèque Nationale de France, ms. fr. 5716, p. 370. Photo courtesy Bibliothèque Nationale de France, Paris.

Likewise, in the case of Raou the Cobbler, who was crippled for over a year with an oozing infection that had begun with a wound in his foot, but then spread to his knee and up his thigh, Guillaume tells us: "The inquisitors of the said miracle and their notaries saw the said Raou healed and healthy . . . going about without crutches or any other aid . . . and they saw his right foot and the thigh and the knee and the underside of the knee, and they saw about ten traces of closed wounds of the above-mentioned openings, small and large, which were now all closed up and flat."[51]

Guillaume's accounts of the inquisitors' interest in the bodies of poor beneficiaries differ strikingly from his descriptions of the inquisitors' meetings with people with property. Although his narrative suggests that several of the propertied beneficiaries appeared before the inquisitors, he gives us only one direct report of an examination that the inquisitors made of a person of property, the daughter of a bourgeois of St.-Denis. That examination

51. Ibid., miracle 20, p. 70.

was verbal: the inquisitors asked the girl, who had miraculously recovered from drowning, if she had fallen into the water and why she had approached the water in the first place.[52] In Guillaume's accounts, none of the propertied beneficiaries were physically examined by the inquisitors, and none had to lift their garments in order to reveal scars on their knees, thighs, or anywhere else on their bodies.

Differences in the kinds of diseases that afflicted those with and without property, and that each group bothered to report, may go some way in explaining the inquisitors', or Guillaume's, greater interest in inspections of the poor. After all, unlike Raou's and Moriset's oozing tumors, the short-lived fevers, pains, and unconsciousness that five of the propertied beneficiaries had endured would have left no visible marks upon their bodies.[53] Nevertheless, these differences do not explain Guillaume's silence about bodily inspections of eight other propertied beneficiaries, all of whom had suffered from lasting disabilities, or ones that would have left marks even when cured. One of those eight had had an oozing tumor, much like that of Moriset. Another six had been paralyzed or were otherwise unable to use a limb or limbs—like five of the poor people who were inspected by the inquisitors. Yet another had suffered from an unsightly facial swelling.[54]

A better explanation for this asymmetrical approach to the bodies of the poor lies, as I have already suggested, in the lack of trust that men of power had in the verbal testimony of the poor. Another explanation probably lies in the greater sense of decorum that lettered men observed in discussing the intimate details of the illnesses of propertied individuals, and in approaching their bodies. The overall effect, however, was to subject

52. Ibid., miracle 1, p. 7. In miracles 3, 13, 40, and 50, which all involve propertied beneficiaries who were cured, we are told that they remained healthy up until the time of the inquest, which suggests that they came before the canonization panel. In miracle 19, a miracle involving a boy whose parents may have been bourgeois property owners (see note 41), Guillaume reports on what the inquisitors and their notaries saw, but he does not describe the encounter as a bodily inspection: "[They] saw the said Giefrein healthy and sound. Nevertheless, he was very pale and squint-eyed" (ibid., 67).

53. Ibid., miracles 12, 38, 40, 50, 53.

54. Ibid., passim. Propertied beneficiary with oozing tumor: miracle 64. Propertied beneficiaries who had been paralyzed or were unable to use arms or legs: miracles 3, 24, 55, 60, 63, 65. Poor who had been paralyzed or were unable to use arms or legs, who were inspected by the inquisitors: miracles 34, 35, 36, 42, 52. Propertied beneficiary with facial swelling: miracle 29.

the poor to a type of voyeurism not unlike the voyeurism in the lives of women saints, and to reinforce the idea that embodiment was more central to the identities of the poor than it was to the identities of people of property.

MALE BEGGARS AND FEMALE ARTIFICES OF DECEPTION

In the writings of Jacques de Vitry, Bonaventure, Humbert of Romans, and Gilbert of Tournai, laboring men represented a lower form of masculinity, resting upon the "robust" body, which made a valuable, if inferior, contribution to society. But what about nonlaboring poor men who could not work because of bodily disability? Because they lacked robust bodies and passed their time without engaging in bodily labor, male members of the nonlaboring poor relinquished, as far as clerical authors were concerned, the most essential element of their masculinity. The mere fact that they did not labor, moreover, rendered them even more morally suspect than the working poor. Without labor, they had no protection against the dangers of idleness, as a popular story about two cripples (or a blind man and a cripple) proclaimed. According to the story, which was first told in the twelfth century, and repeated again and again in the thirteenth through fifteenth centuries, two disabled beggars did not wish to be cured of their disabilities because they would have to give up their soft life and go to work. According to the twelfth-century version of the story, when the prospect arose of being cured by Saint Martin, one of the beggars said to the other: "Behold, brother, we live a life of soft leisure . . . and it is this infirmity by which we are cast down that lays claim to all of this for us. But if—God forbid!—we were to be cured, manual labor, to which we are unaccustomed, would inevitably weigh us down."[55]

A variety of thirteenth-century texts elaborated the theme that disabled poor people were not only addicted to idleness but also despicable in their

55. André Salmon, ed., *De reversione beati Martini a burgundia tractatus*, in *Supplément aux chroniques de Touraine* (Tours, 1856), 31–32. On the date of this text, see Sharon Farmer, *Communities of Saint Martin: Legend and Ritual in Medieval Tours* (Ithaca, 1991), 305–6. The story was probably first written between 1137 and 1156. Jacques de Vitry included a version of the story in his collection of *ad status* sermons, and Jacob of Voragine included a version in *The Golden Legend* (see below, note 65); Gustave Cohen, "Le thème de l'aveugle et du paralytique dans la littérature française," in *Mélanges offerts à Émile Picot par ses amis et ses élèves*, vol. 2 (Paris, 1913; reprint ed., Geneva, 1969), 393–404.

wretchedness. Some of their sufferings were punishments for sins.[56] The poor were overindulgent, lustful, drunkards, envious, petty, deceitful, and avaricious.[57] Moreover, some of them failed to pray for the souls of those from whom they received alms.[58]

On an official level most of the sins that beggars committed did not stand in the way of giving alms to the involuntary poor. Drawing on Saint Augustine's distinction between the hatred that one should have for the sin, and the love one should have for the person of the sinner, high medieval moralists maintained that it was lawful to give alms to poor sinners as long as one did so to help them in their poverty rather than to support their sins.[59] The argument was incorporated into the *glossa ordinaria* to Gratian's *Decretum*, which was compiled around 1247, and it was reiterated by the Dominicans Thomas Aquinas and John of Freiburg.[60]

Still, stories about the sinful behavior of poor disabled beggars worked to reinforce the ambivalence and disgust that almsgivers, or would-be almsgivers, already felt in responding to the appeals of the needy. Moreover, such stories bolstered the ideas that poverty and disease were punishments for sin, and that it was preferable to support the voluntary, rather than the involuntary, poor. As Saint Jerome had argued, in a passage that was frequently quoted by Franciscans and Dominicans in the thirteenth century, it was better to seek spiritual advocates by giving alms to the poor in spirit

56. John Boswell, *The Kindness of Strangers: The Abandonment of Children from Late Antiquity to the Renaissance* (New York, 1988), 338–39.

57. On drunkenness, lechery, and gluttony, see, for example: Jehan le Marchant, *Le livre des miracles de Notre-Dame de Chartres*, ed. M. G. Duplessis (Chartres, 1855), miracle 20, pp. 113–15; *Le garçon et l'aveugle: jeu du XIIIᵉ siècle*, ed. Mario Roques, trans. into modern French by Jean Dufournet (Paris, 1989), lines 113–42, 207–8, 224–28, pp. 100–101, 106–9.

58. Thomas of Chobham implies that beggars fail to pray for their benefactors when he warns that to do so is a mortal sin: *Summa confessorum*, art. 6, dist. 4, quest. 6, p. 297.

59. Augustine, *Enarrationes in Psalmos*, Ps. C, c. 5, in *Sancti Aurelii Augustini Enarrationes in Psalmos LI–C*, Corpus christianorum series latina 39 (Turnhout, 1956), 1410.

60. *Decretum Gratiani emendatum*, Prima pars, dist. 86, chap. 7, 482, glosses on the words *donare* and *talibus;* Thomas Aquinas, *Summa theologiae*, 2a2ae, quaest. 31, art. 2, resp. ad 2, 34:226–27; Thomas Aquinas, *In quattuor libros sententiarum*, bk. 4, dist. 15, quaest. 2., art. 6, resp. ad 2, in *S. Thomae Aquinatis Opera omnia*, ed. Robertus Busa, vol. 1 (Stuttgart, 1980), 510; John of Freiburg, *Summa confessorum reverendi patris Joannis de Friburgo* (Lyon, 1518), bk. 3, tit. 8, quaest. 8, fol. 102r.

rather than to the simple poor, "among whose rags [pannos] and bodily filth [illuviem corporis] burning desire [flagrans libido] has domain."[61] Jerome's language about the begging involuntary poor evokes the rags of menstruating women and the susceptibility of female flesh to the rule of the passions.[62] Here, we are taken beyond the boundaries of the hierarchy of masculinities, into the realm of the feminine.

Unlike other sinful beggars, the hoarding, avaricious beggar—the one who was not truly needy at all—elicited serious fears that the entire charitable enterprise was corrupted by those whose broken bodies were only seeming evidence of need.[63] Thirteenth-century authors evoked the presence of hoarding beggars over and over again. Story after story worked to deconstruct the very certainty that seemed to lie in the broken bodies of beggars, suggesting that the beggar who was both wealthy and disabled was ubiquitous, and that he (for the stories were almost always about men) had become rich by begging. In the satirical play *Le garçon et l'aveugle* the blind man promises the boy, whom he wishes to recruit as a guide, "if you're good at my trade you'll get rich quick"; and he later proves the truth of his claim by showing the boy the well-filled purse that he has hidden away at home.[64] In Jacob of Voragine's version of the story about the two disabled beggars who did not wish to be cured by Saint Martin, the two "gained much money" by begging together; thus, "they had no wish to regain their health at the price of their profit."[65] According to the early thirteenth-century

61. Jerome, *Liber contra Vigilantium*, 14, *PL* 23:350; "Against Vigilantius," trans. W. H. Freemantle, *The Principal Works of St. Jerome*, The Nicene and Post-Nicene Fathers, vol. 6 (Grand Rapids, Mich., 1954), 422; Thomas Aquinas, *Contra impugnantes dei cultum et religionem*, chap. 7, *Sancti Thomae Aquinatis Doctoris Angelici Ordinis Praedicatorum Opera Omnia*, 15:43; Bonaventure, *Apologia pauperum*, chap. 12, p. 329.

62. See Isaiah 64:6 and Jerome's own *De perpetua Virginitate Beatae Mariae*, *PL* 23:202–3, for the use of "panni" to refer to menstrual rags.

63. According to Thomas Aquinas, there were two spiritual fruits to corporal charity: that of the cause of the act of charity—being endowed with love of God and neighbor—and that of the effect of the act of charity—the prayers of the recipients; *Summa theologiae*, 2a2ae, quaest. 32, art. 4, 34:248–51. No one went so far as to say that there was no spiritual fruit in giving alms to the wrong persons, but the recipients were supposed to be worthy; ibid., quaest. 32, art. 9, 34:266–69.

64. Roques, ed., Dufournet, trans., *Le garçon et l'aveugle*, lines 43–44, 203–6, pp. 94–95, 106–7.

65. Jacobus de Voragine, *Legenda aurea*, chap. 166, ed. Th. Graesse (Dresden, 1846), 750; trans. Granger Ryan and Helmut Ripperger (New York, 1941), 673.

moralist Thomas of Chobham, beggars "frequently collect alms in great quantity, and they do not use the money collected, but reserve it until their deaths, with great avarice."[66] The Dominican author Stephen of Bourbon, told a story about a blind beggar who accumulated so much wealth that he took up the profession of moneylending, and crossed over into a more prosperous social stratum.[67]

These stories tell us much more about the anxieties and prejudices of lettered men than they do about the actual possibilities of getting rich by begging. The acquisitiveness of these hoarding beggars highlighted the "burning desire" (to use Jerome's words) that was at the heart of ordinary poverty. The alleged success of these hoarding beggars suggests that for poor people, begging may have been more lucrative than working. Thirteenth-century working wages were quite inadequate and hardly lent themselves to accumulation: working women rarely made enough to support themselves, and working men rarely made enough to support a family of four.[68] Indeed, some wives of working men supplemented their husbands' wages by begging.[69] Vaguely aware of inadequate wages, lettered men may well have imagined that the poor felt a pull to beg rather than to work, and that begging might indeed provide a source of hidden wealth, even for the disabled.

The imagined success of these hoarding beggars also points to elite anxieties about status boundaries. In their imaginings about beggars who rose in the social hierarchy, lettered men expressed their fears that people such as these would not stay in their place. In their claims that poor individuals rose by means of usury, lettered men reinforced the idea that the upward mobility of the poor could only result from the most sinful of activities.

This elite disapproval of hoarding also reveals a great deal of insensitivity toward the plight of the disabled. Implicit to the theme of avaricious hoarding was the idea that beggars should use up all of the alms that they collected before they went out begging again. But the marketplace of charity had cycles of plenty and shortfall, just like the marketplace of labor, and

66. Thomas of Chobham, *Summa de arte praedicandi*, chap. 3, ed. Franco Morenzoni (Turnhout, 1988), 88.

67. Stephen of Bourbon, *Tractatus de diversis materiis praedicabilibus*, ed. A. Lecoy de la Marche, *Anecdotes historiques, légendes et apologues tirés du recueil inédit d'Etienne de Bourbon Dominicain du XIIIe siècle* (Paris, 1877), no. 414, p. 361.

68. See above, pp. 5, 23–24.

69. See below, chapter 5, and Farmer, "Down and Out and Female in Thirteenth-Century Paris," *American Historical Review* 103 (1998): 356–57.

some people—like Amelot of Chambly—were so crippled and bent that it was nearly impossible for them to go out begging in inclement weather.[70] For these reasons, the disabled needed to store away a bit of extra income to prepare for hard times. According to the moralists, however, beggars had no right to make such plans for the future.

The fact that most disabled beggars who hoarded were male, in the elite imagination, points to discomfort with the "softness" and lack of productiveness of the disabled poor. Men from this social stratum were supposed to have robust bodies and to use those bodies in productive ways; the disabled, by contrast, were weak and dependent, much like the women of the elite imagination. Descriptions of disabled men who preferred the "soft" and profitable life of begging to the harsh demands of work expressed elite anxieties about the bodies of lower-status males which no longer functioned in a manner that was appropriate to lower-status masculinity.

In addition to the sins and deceptions of beggars who really were disabled, moralists warned—again and again—about the deceptions of beggars who were not disabled at all, promulgating the suspicion that many "robust" men of the lower strata of society pretended not to be robust, because they preferred the "soft" life of the beggar to the harsh demands of paid labor. While this stereotype of the lazy beggar had been available since the late antique period, suspicions about the ubiquity of such beggars reached a new intensity in the thirteenth century.[71] Sometime before the middle of the century, the written collection of laws known as the *Customs of Touraine-Anjou* came to include a chapter encouraging justices in towns to banish unemployed, propertyless men who lingered in taverns and led an "evil life".[72] By the early fourteenth century, rulers in Spain and the Low Countries fol-

70. Delaborde, "Fragments de l'enquête," 32.

71. Jean Batany argued that the years around 1200 marked a turning point, at which increasingly negative attitudes toward the poor made their appearance: "Les pauvres et la pauvreté dans les revues des 'Estats du monde,' " in *Etudes sur l'histoire de la pauvreté*, ed. Michel Mollat, 2 vols. (Paris, 1974), 2:469–86. See also, on negative and ambivalent attitudes toward the poor: Michel Mollat, *The Poor in the Middle Ages: An Essay in Social History*, trans. Arthur Goldhammer (New Haven, Conn., 1986), 71, 109, 111–13, 128, 134; Bronislaw Geremek, *La potence ou la pitié: L'Europe et les pauvres du Moyen Age à nos jours* (Paris, 1987), 30–46; Jean-Louis Roch, "Le jeu de l'aumône au moyen âge," *Annales: Economies, sociétés, civilisations* 44 (1989): 505–27; Gerald B. Guest, "A Discourse on the Poor: The Hours of Jeanne d'Evreux," *Viator: Medieval and Renaissance Studies* 26 (1995): 153–80.

72. *Les établissements de Saint Louis*, bk. 1. chap. 38, ed. Paul Viollet, 4 vols. (Paris, 1881–1886), 2:54; trans. F. R. P. Akehurst, *The Etablissements de Saint Louis: Thirteenth-Century Law Texts from Tours, Orléans and Paris* (Philadelphia, 1996), 27.

lowed suit. Starting around 1268, edicts in Castile and León encouraged royal and municipal officials to arrest able-bodied persons who had no employment.[73] Around 1319 the municipal magistrates of St.-Omer ruled that "lazy servants" who had no means of livelihood and knew no craft should be banished from the town.[74] In 1321 King James II of Aragon and Valencia ruled that municipal magistrates in Valencia should punish individuals who defrauded the "poor of Christ" by seeking alms "under the false garment of poverty."[75]

Demographic growth probably provided one of the main stimuli for this increased suspicion on the part of the ruling elite. By the end of the thirteenth century the population of Europe had reached a peak to which it did not return until the sixteenth century or later. The underemployment and cycles of famine described in chapter 1 were among the results of this demographic saturation. Medieval intellectuals and rulers did not often analyze poverty in structural terms, and thus, as greater numbers of the unemployed and underemployed began to seek alms in the streets, men of power and lettered men tended to blame the beggars themselves for their plight.

In the rhetoric about beggars who fake their disabilities we also find lower-status men associated with a cosmetic transformation of their appearance similar to that of deceitful prostitutes and old women. The late twelfth-century Parisian moralist, Peter the Chanter, for instance, wrote about beggars who "make themselves tremulous, and putting on the various forms of the sick, change their faces just like Proteus."[76] Similarly, Peter's student, Thomas of Chobham, described beggars who went to church, not

73. See Teofilo Ruiz, "The Business of Salvation: Castilian Wills in the Late Middle Ages," in *On the Social Origins of Medieval Institutions: Essays in Honor of Joseph F. O'Callaghan*, ed. Donald J. Kagay and Theresa M. Vann (Leiden, 1998), 70.

74. Pagart d'Hermensart, ed., "Documents inédits contenus dans les archives de Saint Omer," *Bulletin historique et philologique du Comité des travaux historiques et scientifiques* (1900), no. 47, p. 77.

75. Luis Revest Corzo, *Hospitales y pobres en el Castellón de otros tiempos* (Castellón de la Plana, 1947), documents, p. 89 (document from Valencia dated 1321). Both Jacques de Vitry and Bonaventure made vague references to towns that passed statutes ordering the expulsion of able-bodied beggars: Jacques de Vitry, "Sermo LXI Ad agricolas et alios operarios," in *Sermones vulgares*, 436; Bonaventure, *Apologia pauperum*, chap. 12, p. 325. For an overview of late medieval vagrancy laws see Bronislaw Geremek, "La lutte contre le vagabondage à Paris aux XIVᵉ et XVᵉ siècles," in *Ricerche storiche ed economiche in memoria di Corrado Barbagallo*, ed. Luigi di Rosa (Naples, 1970), 213–36.

76. Peter the Chanter, *Verbum abbreviatum*, chap. 48, PL 205:152.

to hear sermons, but to "extort money through false tears and deceptions and many simulations."[77] Elsewhere, in his influential manual for confessors, Thomas wrote that beggars "frequently transfigure themselves into the appearance of the wretched, so that they seem more destitute than they really are, and thus they deceive others so that they will receive more."[78] The preeminent jurist at the University of Bologna, Azo, who wrote his *Summa* on the *Corpus juris civilis* between 1208 and 1210, also described the cosmetic deceits of able-bodied beggars, "who simulate bodily infirmity by applying herbs or ointments to their bodies in order to make swollen wounds." Azo went on to describe false beggars who made their bodies and limbs appear bent and shriveled, although there was nothing actually the matter with them.[79] An abbreviated version of Azo's description of false beggars was incorporated into the *glossa ordinaria* to the *Corpus juris civilis* towards the middle of the thirteenth century.[80]

Elite discussions of the deceits of false beggars can be placed within two interrelated discursive contexts. First, men of power and lettered men ex-

---

77. Thomas of Chobham, *Summa de arte praedicandi*, chap. 3, p. 88.

78. Thomas of Chobham, *Summa confessorum*, art. 5, dist. 4, quaest. 6, p. 297.

79. Azo, *Summa Azonis: Summa perutilis excellentissimi iuris monarche domini Azonis superrime maxima diligentia castigata* (Lyon, 1530), Liber undecimus codicis, 25, "De mendicantis validis," fol. 333v.

80. *Volumen legum parvum, quod vocant, in quo haec insunt: tres posteriores libri Codicis D. Iustiniani* (Venice, 1583), Codex, bk. 11, tit. 25, gloss on the word *lenitudinem*, col. 146. Other theologians and moralists of the mid–thirteenth and early fourteenth centuries were less specific in their descriptions of the deceits of false beggars. Bonaventure equated the poverty of "false beggars" with cupidity, and that of able-bodied beggars with indolence; Humbert of Romans wrote of the gullibility of village women who gave their goods to "vagabonds and false alms collectors"; Gilbert of Tournai advised hospital workers not to receive "ribalds or vagabonds or minstrels," and the Dominican John of Freiburg (d. 1314) argued that it was better to reprove able-bodied beggars than to give them alms, but he made no mention of their uses of deceit. At least one fifteenth-century Parisian anti-vagrancy law, by contrast, gave lurid descriptions of the deceptive artifices of false beggars: Bonaventure, *Apologia pauperum*, chap. 12, p. 325; Humbert of Romans, *De eruditione*, bk. 2, tract. 1., chap. 99, "Ad mulieres pauperes in villulis," p. 505, reprinted in Casagrande, *Prediche* 53; Gilbert of Tournai, "Ad servientes et hospitalinos sermo tertius" (actually this is his second sermon to hospital workers—the first sermon given that rubric in the manuscript, at fol. 94v, was for judges and lawyers), Bibliothèque Nationale de France, ms. lat. 15943, fol. 99v; John of Freiburg, *Summa confessorum*, bk. 3, tit. 8, quaest. 6, n. 61, fol. 102r; Geremek, "La lutte contre le vagabondage," 236.

pressed a desire to establish "distinguishing signs"[81] that would make known the true nature and status of individuals when they entered the public sphere. Such concern was neither gender- nor status-specific. Moralists, chroniclers, and legislators expressed the belief that kings and their subjects, clergy and laypeople, prostitutes and matrons, Jews and Christians, old women and young should be clearly and hierarchically marked off from one another so that people would know how to conduct themselves in their encounters with each other.[82] The conviction that able-bodied beggars should be clearly distinguishable from disabled beggars fit into this broader set of expressions.

In most cases, clothing of differing materials and colors provided the required signs to mark off status. In the case of old women and beggars, however, the body itself was the sign, and the cosmetic transformations of those bodies shared affinities with the shape shifting of the devil.[83] In their discussions of made-up beggars Peter the Chanter and Thomas of Chobham evoked images of "transfiguration" and of Proteus. Similarly, in his invective against old women who used makeup to look younger, the Dominican preacher Stephen of Bourbon compared them to masked jongleurs and to two-faced images of Janus, who appeared as an old man on one side and as a youth on the other.[84]

The disguises of false beggars were also considered one aspect of the larger problem of deceit in the marketplace. According to moralists and chroniclers of the thirteenth century, deceit was endemic to urban commerce: craftsmen substituted cheaper materials for costly ones; bakers falsi-

81. I have borrowed this expression from Diane Owen Hughes, "Distinguishing Signs: Ear-Rings, Jews and Franciscan Rhetoric in the Italian Renaissance City," *Past and Present*, no. 112 (1986): 3–59.

82. On kings and their subjects, see Jean, sire de Joinville, *Histoire de Saint Louis*, ed. Natalis de Wailly (Paris, 1868), chap. 6, pp.12–13; trans. René Hague, *The Life of Saint Louis* (New York, 1955), 30–32; on prostitutes and matrons, Ruth Karras, *Common Women: Prostitution and Sexuality in Medieval England* (New York, 1996), 21; on clergy and laity, Jews and Christians, canons 16 and 68 of the Fourth Lateran Council, in J. D. Mansi, ed., *Sacrorum conciliorum nova et amplissima collectio*, 53 vols. (Florence, 1759–98; reprint ed., Graz, 1960–1961), 22:1006, 1055; on old women and young, Stephen of Bourbon, *Tractatus de diversis materiis*, nos. 273, 274, 279, pp. 228–29, 231–32.

83. On the devil as the master of deception and transfiguration see Thomas of Chobham, *Summa de arte praedicandi*, chap. 8, pp. 203–13. On p. 205 Chobham compares the devil's deceptions to those of an ornamented prostitute.

84. Stephen of Bourbon, *Tractatus de diversis materiis*, nos. 274, 279, pp. 228–29, 231–32.

fied bread; prostitutes used makeup to transform undesirable bodies and faces into desirable ones.[85] In their attempts to gain alms under false pretenses, false beggars resembled all men and women who falsified goods in the marketplace. However, because beggars offered up their own bodies as products of charitable consumption, they shared a special affinity with prostitutes, who also placed their bodies on the market. It followed, therefore, that false beggars shared an affinity with those prostitutes who cosmetically transformed their bodies and faces into more desirable objects of consumption.

According to Thomas of Chobham and Peter the Chanter, prostitutes transformed licit wages into illicit wages when they falsified their appearances with cosmetics. Thomas argued that while a prostitute's profession was sinful, she licitly earned her living with the labor of her own body, and hence she should be allowed to keep her earnings. However, concerning those prostitutes who distorted their appearance with makeup, Thomas thoroughly agreed with Peter the Chanter that such women collected their payments under false pretenses, and should not be allowed to keep their earnings—"because," Thomas asserted, "then the one who hires [such a woman] believes that he has bought an appearance that is not there."[86]

Those who gave alms to false beggars were also, in a sense, buying an appearance that was not really there. Just like the man who gave money to a

85. On craftsmen, see van den Hoven, *Work in Ancient and Medieval Thought*, 240; on bakers, Jean of St.-Victor, *Excerpta e Memoriali Historiarum, auctore Johanne Parisiensi, RHGF* 21:663; trans. William C. Jordan, *The Great Famine: Northern Europe in the Early Fourteenth Century* (Princeton, N.J., 1996), 162.

86. Thomas of Chobham, *Summa confessorum*, art. 5, dist. 4, quaest. 5, p. 296. See art. 7, dist. 2, quaest. 6, chap. 3, and art. 7, dist. 2, quaest. 20, pp. 352, 403–4, for similar arguments. Chobham's argument about prostitutes being able to keep their earnings was partially based, as was that of Ivo of Chartres (d. 1115), on Justinian's *Digest: Digestum vetus seu Pandectarum Iuris civilis tomus primus* (Venice, 1584), bk. 12, tit. 5, chap. 4, col. 1323; Ivo of Chartres, *Decretum*, 8:307, *PL* 161:651. Chobham was original, however, in stressing the labor of the prostitute's own body.

For Peter the Chanter's discussions of prostitutes' wages see *Verbum abbreviatum*, *PL* 205:144; and *Summa de sacramentis et animae consiliis*, ed. Jean-Albert Dugauquier, 5 vols. (Louvain, 1954–1967), 3:170–75. Peter argued (ibid.) that a prostitute should not restore her earnings to her customer, but neither could she licitly keep them, and hence she should give them to the church; the church, however, needed to avoid scandal in accepting gifts from such persons. For Peter's discussion of prostitutes who used makeup, see ibid., 172. For a similar argument, that prostitutes who used fraud or deceit had to make restitution, see Thomas Aquinas, *Summa theologiae*, 2a2ae, quaest. 62, art. 5, resp. ad 2, 37:116–17.

prostitute, the almsgiver expected an intimate favor in return: the beggar, whom the almsgiver believed to be both needy and unable to work, was supposed to say prayers for the soul of the one from whom he or she, accepted alms.[87] If the beggar was not truly disabled, then the one giving alms was "buying" prayers, in a sense, from the wrong person.

The deceptive use of cosmetics was not necessarily gender-specific. Nevertheless, bodily beauty was more intrinsic to female identity than to male. Not surprisingly, therefore, most of the medieval invective against the deceptive use of beautifying cosmetics was directed against women. There was, moreover, a special anxiety about two categories of women who used cosmetics: old women, because their efforts to look young created status confusion; and prostitutes, because their efforts to make themselves more beautiful created deception in the marketplace.

Most of the invective against the use of cosmetic distortions by beggars was directed against men rather than women. In the rhetoric of members of the clerical elite, male beggars with robust bodies who feigned weakness through deception assimilated themselves to old women and prostitutes, creating, with falsified bodies, both status confusion and deception in the marketplace. False beggars also rendered themselves effeminate because they did not fulfill their roles as lower-status males, who were expected to work with their bodies. Rather, they went to great lengths to assure that, much like women (as elite male authors constructed them), they could remain "soft" and inactive. They placed themselves in great moral danger, and they defrauded their "customers" by deceiving them into believing that they were doing charitable deeds for the truly disabled—and hence, at least in theory, for the deserving poor.

The evidence thus suggests that members of the elite closely associated poor men, as well as poor women, with the body. Indeed, men of power and lettered men sometimes paid greater attention to the bodily nature and shortcomings of poor men than they did to the bodily nature and shortcomings of elite women. This is not to imply, however, that persons of property made no distinctions between lower-status men and women, or that they never placed women in a closer relationship to the body or the physical realm than men. If we stop at various points along the hierarchy of social status we find that medieval clerical authors did make statements that drew stronger associations between women and the body than between men and the body. Humbert of Romans said more about the lust of peasant women than about the lust of peasant men; Humbert and Jacques de Vitry said

87. Thomas of Chobham, *Summa confessorum*, art. 5., dist. 4, quaest. 6, ed. Broomfield, p. 297.

more about the lascivious behavior of servant women than about the lascivious behavior of servant men.[88]

Nevertheless, if we ignore the differences between, on the one hand, discussions of servants and laborers, and, on the other hand, discussions of people of property, or if we fail to notice that Gilbert of Tournai and Jacques de Vitry exhorted wealthy matrons to control the sexuality of both their male and their female servants, our analysis becomes distorted. Indeed, when we fail to incorporate other categories of difference into our analysis of gender constructions, then it is we, and not the authors whom we study, who end up constructing simplistic gender categories that reduce all men, or all women, to a single set of essentialized stereotypes.

ALTERNATIVE PERSPECTIVES ON THE POOR

The poor paid a heavy price for elite discourses that aligned them with the body and its burning appetites. In the minds of lettered men and men of power, the embodied identity and bodily hunger of the poor rendered them all—men and women, working and nonworking—morally suspect, and suspicion led to the belief that many of them were not hungry at all. But what about the poor themselves? Did they create, or appropriate, counter-discourses concerning their hierarchical subordination, their moral inferiority, or the idle and unmanly nature of beggars? Unfortunately, the sources for this period have not preserved poor people's fully articulated constructions of social reality, as is occasionally the case with sources from the late Middle Ages. Nevertheless, it is worth exploring the possible meanings of some of the words and actions of people without property, and the discourses that they might have appropriated to their own uses.

The most obvious counter-discourse to those that identified a hierarchy of labors or of wealth and poverty with a moral hierarchy was that which stressed humanity's common ancestry in Adam and Eve.[89] Various authors of the thirteenth and early fourteenth centuries articulated this sentiment.

88. Jacques de Vitry, "Ad servos et ancillas"; Humbert of Romans, *De eruditione*, bk. 2, tract. 1, chap. 76, "Ad familiam diuitum in ciuitatibus"; bk. 2, tract. 1, chap. 78, "Ad laicos in villis"; bk. 2, tract. 1, chap. 98, "Ad famulas divitum"; bk. 2, tract. 1, chap. 99, "Ad mulieres pauperes in villulis"; pp. 493–95, 505–6; chaps. 98 and 99 reprinted in Casagrande, *Prediche*, 50, 52.

89. For general discussions of this theme see Freedman, *The Image of the Medieval Peasant*, chap. 3; and Albert Friedman, " 'When Adam Delved . . . ': Contexts of an Historic Proverb," in *The Learned and the Lewed: Studies in Chaucer and Medieval Literature*, ed. Larry D. Benson (Cambridge, Mass., 1974), 213–30.

We find it, for instance, in the *Roman de Fauvel*, a political satire that was written by persons close to the Parisian royal court in the early fourteenth century:

> We have all sprouted from one seed
> Thus there is no difference
> Between the peasant and the gentleman;
> We are all born from Adam and Eve. . . . [90]

The thirteenth- and early fourteenth-century lettered men who articulated this idea had no desire to dismantle the social hierarchy. Rather, in stressing the common ancestry of the human race they highlighted the message that nobility was a matter of virtue, not of blood.[91] Many thirteenth-century moralists, including Bonaventure and Humbert of Romans, shared this idea. Of course, everyone knew that people lacking virtue could rise to high places. This possibility was expressed in the *Roman de Fauvel*, in which an evil horse came to be crowned as king.

In 1307, when the poor and middling renters of Paris rose up against the property holders who had taken advantage of the revaluing of the currency, they expressed—in their actions if not in their words—a similar, although more constricted sentiment: that justice did not always lie in the actions of people of higher status, and that the subordinates of those people had the right to rise up in the defense of justice.[92] Like other rebellions of its kind, this one expressed the "moral economy of the crowd": a reaction against a perceived violation of accepted economic practices rather than a desire to undo social and political hierarchies per se.[93]

The corollary of the idea that powerful people could lack virtue was the idea that virtue could reside among the poor and powerless. Most of the thirteenth-century moralists expressed this idea on occasion. We see it, for example, in Jacques de Vitry's description of the poor laborer who joyfully

90. Arthur Langfors, ed., *Roman de Fauvel* (Paris, 1919), 44; cited by Friedman, " 'When Adam Delved,' " 219. For a discussion of the authorship and milieu of the *Roman de Fauvel* see Margaret Bent and Andrew Wathey, "Introduction," in *Fauvel Studies: Allegory, Chronicle, Music, and Image in Paris, Bibliothèque Nationale de France, ms. français 146*, ed. Bent and Wathey (Oxford, 1998), 1–25.

91. See, on this point, Friedman, " 'When Adam Delved' "; on the radical turn that this sentiment sometimes took in the later Middle Ages, see Freedman, *The Image of the Medieval Peasant*, chap. 3.

92. On this rebellion, see above, p. 35.

93. E. P. Thompson, "The Moral Economy of the English Crowd in the Eighteenth Century," *Past and Present*, no. 50 (1971): 76–136.

praised God each day. We see it as well in Guillaume de St.-Pathus's descriptions of some of the beneficiaries of the miracles of Saint Louis, which he synthesized from the testimonies of the witnesses, many of whom were members of the laboring poor. We learn, for instance, that Richard the Saddler and his wife Emmeline were "good people, and were considered good by the people living on their street."[94] Similarly, we learn that Avice of Berneville, a sixty-year-old woman living in Paris who had to beg for three years while she suffered from a crippling malady in her foot, "was a good woman" who wore a hair shirt, disciplined her flesh, and fasted after she regained her health.[95]

It seems likely that some poor people took to heart elite messages about the moral and spiritual dangers of begging, and about the deceits of false beggars. Evidence pointing to this possibility will be discussed later on. Nevertheless, as the testimony about Avice suggests, however negatively the working poor may have viewed begging and false beggars, they did not necessarily hold negative opinions about individual beggars. Indeed, testimony concerning another beggar, Guillot of Caux, indicates that the working poor were well aware that the daily existence of disabled beggars was a strenuous struggle for survival rather than a life of ease. A young man who had migrated to Paris from the diocese of Rouen, Guillot suffered for a number of years from a crippling disease that was so severe that his back seemed to be broken and his emaciated legs seemed to be detached from his torso. For two years, Guillot lodged in the home of Nicol the Champanois, who said of Guillot's malady that "he would not want to have it for all the kingdom of France."[96] Another witness declared that a mound of gold filling the entire church of St.-Denis would not suffice to convince him to suffer Guillot's malady.[97]

The recognition on the part of modest artisans and the working poor of the extent of the suffering of the nonworking poor went hand in hand with their recognition that for the disabled, begging itself was a form of physical labor. Concerning Amelot of Chambly, who had begged for her food during the years that her spine was bent, a smith named Robert of Cantarage, who lived in St.-Denis, declared that it was absurd to think that she could have feigned her malady, "given the great labor and difficulty" that was required of her in order to move about.[98] The dependency of disabled begging men

94. Guillaume de St.-Pathus, *Les miracles*, 112.
95. Ibid., 107.
96. Ibid., 59.
97. Ibid.
98. Delaborde, "Fragments de l'enquête," 25.

may have worked to unman them; nevertheless, Robert's words suggest that the working poor recognized that disabled beggars—both male and female—had to "labor" in order to survive.

Elite discourses about the poor played a role in shaping the forms of charity that people of property made available to the poor. Indeed, as we shall begin to see in the next chapter, the disabled and nonworking poor paid a concrete price for the ways in which the elite stereotyped and stigmatized them. Moreover, elite messages about masculine and feminine roles and realms, and about poverty and begging, also affected the ways in which people of lower status perceived the poor. For disabled poor men this meant that even people of this social level were uncomfortable with their dependency. For poor women, this sometimes resulted in their own submission to clerical expectations that they should do penance for real or imagined sexual sins, and in a tendency for married women's work to count for less than married men's work. Nevertheless, modest artisans and the working poor responded to the suffering of the nonworking poor in ways that differed from the responses of the elite. Among the reasons for those differences were their different ways of viewing and judging the nonworking poor.

CHAPTER THREE
MEN IN NEED

FIGURE 5. Louis the Deaf-Mute
On the left Louis twists his head and gestures with his hands. On the right, he kneels before Saint Louis's tomb. Guillaume de Saint-Pathus, *Les miracles de Saint Louis*, miracle 15. Bibliothèque Nationale de France, ms. fr. 5716, p. 379. Photo courtesy Bibliothèque Nationale de France, Paris.

The fifteenth miracle of Saint Louis concerns a deaf-mute whom the saint cured of deafness and endowed with the capacity to learn to talk (figure 5). The story of the deaf-mute—Louis, as he was later named in honor of the saint—points to a number of significant patterns in poor men's strategies of survival and networks of support. It suggests that the male gender paradigm described in the third chapter of Genesis, which stressed men's role in the productive sphere, exercised a compelling influence on lower-status men, sometimes even driving disabled boys to leave their natal homes and learn to earn their keep at an early age. It also suggests that there were important differences in the forms of charity that propertied individuals and those lower in the social hierarchy extended toward disabled poor men. We learn from this and other sources, moreover, that a young person's work environment sometimes came to replace an absent, or inadequate, home environment.

Much of this story takes place outside of Paris and St.-Denis. Nevertheless, Louis probably would have become a permanent charitable dependent of the abbey of St.-Denis had he not been cured of his deafness. Of necessity, a good deal of our evidence about poor men involves men who did not live in Paris or St.-Denis because the *Miracles of Saint Louis* contains only half as many stories about poor men and boys as it does about poor women and girls from those towns: eight as opposed to sixteen stories.[1]

Sometime around 1257, when he was about eight years old, the boy who eventually came to be called Louis was either found or left at Orgelet, a château belonging to a nobleman, Count John of Chalon, that was located near the Jura mountains, about thirty-five miles east/southeast of Chalon-sur-Saône (map 3).[2] Soon thereafter the deaf-mute boy was taken in by the smith at Orgelet, a man named Gauchier, who nourished the boy and taught him, over the next twelve years, to light the forge, use the hammer, and assist with various tasks. Gauchier also took the boy to church, where he learned to kneel and to raise his joined hands in prayer, despite the fact that he understood nothing of Christian belief. The people at the château tested his deafness by yelling through a horn into his ear, and found that he could hear nothing. To test his muteness, Gauchier's sons put hot coals on the boy's stomach; he cast them off, never uttering a sound.

Around 1269, when the youth was about twenty years old, he went to live in Lyon, which was about twenty-five miles southwest of Orgelet. There, he took up residence, and probably work as well, on another estate of the count and countess of Chalon/Auxerre. According to Guillaume de St.-Pathus, the countess's chamberlain did not wish to provide the youth with shoes, so in 1271, when King Philip passed through town with the remains of King Louis IX, the young man attached himself to the royal entourage, whose members provided him with sufficient alms for his support.

1. Guillaume de St.-Pathus, Confesseur de la reine Marguerite, *Les miracles de Saint Louis*, ed. Percival B. Fay (Paris, 1931). Poor men and boys residing in Paris and St.-Denis: miracles 7, 9, 17, 18, 20, 25, 48, 49. Poor women and girls living in Paris and St.-Denis: miracles 2, 4, 5, 30, 34–37, 39, 41–44, 51, 52, 58.
2. Ibid., miracle 15.

Map 3: The Journeys of
Louis the Deaf-Mute and Moriset of Ranton

Without knowing where he was or who he was with, the young man
ended up in the town of St.-Denis, where he learned to stay close to the
abbey in order to live off of its alms. Eventually, after three or four days, he
found himself in front of the tomb of King Louis IX, mimicking—as he had
long done in church—the gestures of the people around him. Suddenly, he
was aware of sounds—voices, footsteps, bells. The noise made no sense to
him—indeed it terrified him—so he immediately left St.-Denis and began
to retrace the journey he had taken to get there. First, he went to Paris,
where he lived off alms and slept in public squares or under market stalls
along the streets. Begging and sleeping in similar places the young man
eventually made his way back to Lyon, a traveling distance of about two
hundred miles, and from Lyon back to Orgelet, the place he apparently considered home (map 3).

At Orgelet, the young man deliberately communicated to Gauchier and others that he could now hear and make sounds. Gauchier took him in again, and the people at the château began to teach him the meanings of words, "just as children are taught from their infancy, or as one teaches birds."[3] When the countess of Auxerre heard that the young man could now hear, and that he was learning to speak, she placed him in her kitchen—because it was always full of people—and ordered the people there to teach him to talk. Each day they taught him new words, and when he did not remember them the next, they beat him "just as children are beaten in school when they do not know their lessons."[4] He was also taught the Paternoster and the Ave Maria.

The young man returned several times to the home of Gauchier, where the members of the household told him his own history and he recounted to them how he had first begun to hear and to utter sounds at the place that he now understood to be the tomb of King Louis IX. In honor of that fact, Gauchier told him, he should take the name of the king. Louis eventually recounted his story—and recited his Paternoster and Ave Maria—to the panel investigating the miracles of Saint Louis. He reassured the panelists, moreover, that although he had no religious faith at the time of his cure, he now believed that it was through the power of the saint that he had gained the ability to hear and to speak.[5] The man with this remarkable story became a carriage driver of the widow of the very king who was believed to have cured him.

Louis's story offers a remarkably rich window onto the world of the medieval disabled. The account of a deaf-mute's experience of medieval religion as a conceptually empty, purely gestural, phenomenon; his lack of any name (at least as far as he was aware) until after he gained the ability to speak; and his ability, despite his total lack of language, to find his way back from St.-Denis to Orgelet, enable us to enter the interior life of a medieval deaf person. The inquisitors' dilemma in attempting to construct this miracle according to the conventions of acceptable miracles, which stressed the necessity of the recipient's own faith in the saint, reminds us that not all disabilities are the same: deafness, before the invention of modern sign language, placed the individual on the margins of human

3. Ibid., 54.
4. Ibid.
5. Disability experts tend to concur that adults who have been deaf since birth and then gain the ability to hear cannot learn to speak competently. The evidence thus suggests that Louis' deafness must not have been congenital. See Steven Pinker, *The Language Instinct* (New York, 1994), 37–38, 293.

communication and hence of human dignity. This probably helps to explain why we detect no implicit or explicit objections to the cruel test that the sons of Gauchier conducted on the body of the future Louis in their attempt to establish his muteness. The role of beatings in Louis's linguistic education highlights the fact that in the Middle Ages corporal punishment was taken for granted not only as an ordinary, and accepted, form of punishment for children and young adults but also as a means of reinforcing the learning process.[6]

In addition to providing some fascinating details concerning the experiences of the medieval disabled, Louis's story suggests that the expectations of lower-class masculinity could place a heavy burden on boys, especially those who were disabled, at a very young age. By the age of eight Louis's natal family ceased to care for him and he was placed in a situation where he was expected to learn enough skills to earn his keep. We are reminded, here, of the large numbers of boys and youths in their early teens or even younger who left their natal homes, in the high and late Middle Ages, in order to migrate to towns. The expectation of self-sufficiency or of training for self-sufficiency affected boys in these age groups in a way that it did not affect girls of the same age.[7] We find the same gendered expectations at the Parisian hospital of St.-Esprit-en-Grève, a home for orphans that was founded in 1369: while both boys and girls received practical training for work from the age of ten or twelve, only girls continued thereafter to be dependents of the orphanage, until they crossed the threshold of adulthood when they married.[8]

We need to unpack the details concerning Louis's family origins, for the narrative about his life leaves a number of points open to interpretation. Just

6. Walter Ong, "Latin Language Study as a Renaissance Puberty Rite," in Ong, *Rhetoric, Romance, and Technology: Studies in the Interaction of Expression and Culture* (Ithaca, 1971), 124–25; Guibert of Nogent, *De vita sua sive monodiarum suarum libri tres*, bk. 1, chap. 5, trans. C. C. Swinton Bland, intro. and notes by John F. Benton, *Self and Society in Medieval France* (New York, 1970), 48; see below, p. 96.

7. See above, pp. 30–32.

8. Paule Bavoux, "Enfants trouvés et orphelins du XIVᵉ au XVIᵉ siècles à Paris," *Assistance et assistés jusqu'à 1610*, Actes du 97ᵉ Congrès National des Sociétés Savantes, Nantes, 1972 (Paris, 1979), 370; Joseph Berthelé, "La vie interieure d'un hospice du XIVᵉ au XVIᵉ siècle: l'Hôpital du Saint-Esprit-en-Grève à Paris," *L'Hôpital et l'aide sociale à Paris*, no. 7 (January–February 1961): 81–91; no. 8 (March–April 1961): 225–35; no. 9 (May–June 1961): 375–83; no. 10 (July–August 1961): 537–41; no. 11 (September–October 1961): 687–703; no. 12 (November–December 1961): 847–52.

what are we to make, for instance, of the contradictory claim that the boy was both "found" and "left" at the château of Orgelet? Here is the way that Guillaume de St.-Pathus puts it, in the opening lines of the story:

> Louis, carriage driver of queen Marguerite, widow of the blessed Saint Louis, when he was eight years old, was found, by chance, at the château of Orgelet fifteen years [*sic*—the text should read "twenty-five years"] before the time of this inquisition. And Gauchier the smith of Orgelet received him and nourished him and raised him in his house for twelve years. And a youth a little older than the said Louis led him to Orgelet and left him there.[9]

The inconsistencies in Guillaume's text probably reflect the differing perspectives of two of the witnesses to the miracle, perhaps Louis and Gauchier. Both versions of the story are quite plausible. If Louis was "found, by chance" at Orgelet, we can probably assume that he was a victim of abandonment. Handicapped children were overrepresented among the abandoned in the Middle Ages, and child abandonment began to rise in the thirteenth century.[10] A number of testaments from early fourteenth-century Paris mention abandoned children who were under the care of the cathedral of Nôtre-Dame.[11]

If, however, Louis was "left" by a "youth" who "led him to Orgelet," we may be dealing with a more benevolent effort on the part of Louis's biological family to prepare Louis for adulthood by arranging for him to receive practical training as a servant in a workshop. Details of the story fit this second scenario. At the time that he arrived at Orgelet Louis was eight years old, an age when some boys and a few girls entered formal apprenticeships in towns, and when rural boys had already begun their work training, often

9. Guillaume de St.-Pathus, *Les miracles*, 50. For the correction from fifteen to twenty-five years, see editor's note on p. 280: according to Guillaume, Louis spent twelve years living with Gauchier and he was cured in 1271, eleven years before the inquest—a total of at least twenty-three years. If we add in two years for the time Louis lived in Lyon, we get twenty-five years, and thus it appears that a scribal error, perhaps in the record that Guillaume used, changed "xxv" to "xv."

10. John Boswell, *The Kindness of Strangers: The Abandonment of Children in Western Europe from Late Antiquity to the Renaissance* (New York, 1988), 322–63.

11. For example: Jehanne du Faut, 1330; Jehan de Troyes, 1332; Jehanne Haudry, wife of Etienne Haudry, 1309: see appendix. For general discussion of care of abandoned children at Nôtre-Dame in the late fourteenth and fifteenth centuries see Bavoux, "Enfants trouvés." Bavoux was apparently not aware of this early fourteenth-century testamentary evidence.

under the supervision of their fathers, but sometimes with other men.[12] Moreover, the smith trained the future Louis to perform basic tasks in his workshop, he took him under his own roof, and he functioned, as many masters did with their apprentices, as a substitute parent. The boy stayed with the smith for twelve years, which was at the high end for most practical educations, but not for those of children who began their training at the young age of eight, or who, because of disability, would have required more extensive training than most children their age.[13] Still, it is unclear why we know nothing about Louis's background before the time of his arrival at Orgelet. If he was indeed left there intentionally by a member of his own family why did Orgelet remain his final destination when he regained his ability to hear and to make utterances? No original home ever emerges from behind the home in Orgelet. One assumes that if Gauchier had known where Louis came from that Louis would have returned to that place to tell, and to learn, his own story. Louis's biological family remains absent in this story, only to be replaced by the family of the workplace. And that family took quite seriously its responsibility to provide for him emotionally and physically and to educate him not only in a trade (or at least to be a useful servant in the workshop) but also spiritually.

Gauchier's intimate and sustained charitable generosity is exemplary of the kind of generosity that modest artisans and members of the working poor extended to the disabled poor. The offering of alms on the part of the noble entourage bearing Saint Louis's body back to St.-Denis is exemplary of elite charity towards the disabled poor, which tended to be more impersonal and less sustained. Admittedly, Louis's noble employer, the countess of Auxerre, also took an interest in his spiritual and practical education, and the account books of other members of the high nobility indicate that they too sometimes cared for dependent workers in their households when they became old or ill.[14] Nevertheless, the fact that the countess left the daily responsibility of educating Louis to her kitchen staff is consistent with the

12. On age of apprenticeship, see Françoise Michaud-Frejaville, "Bons et loyaux services: Les contrats d'apprentissage en Orléanais (1380–1480)," in *Les entrées dans la vie: initiations et apprentissages*, Congrès de la Société des Historiens Médiévistes de l'Enseignement Superieur Public (Nancy, 1982), 191–92. On rural boys, see Barbara Hanawalt, *The Ties That Bound: Peasant Families in Medieval England* (New York, 1986), 158–59.

13. On young apprentices, see Michaud-Frejaville, "Bons et loyaux," 203–4.

14. Jules-Marie Richard, *Une petite-nièce de Saint Louis: Mahaut Comtesse d'Artois et de Bourgogne* (Paris, 1887), 52–54.

evidence suggesting that daily support for the old and disabled usually came from modestly prosperous artisans and members of the working poor.[15]

PROPERTIED PARISIANS AND DISABLED POOR MEN

The urban geography of thirteenth- and fourteenth-century Paris suggests that propertied Parisians had a clear sense that two highly gendered age categories—that of youths, like Louis, who needed assistance in preparing for adulthood, and that of elderly women—were especially in need of charitable assistance. By 1342 Paris had ten shelters for poor widows, or "good women," and at least five hospices, or colleges, for poor schoolboys.[16] After 1363, moreover, the city included the Hospital of St.-Esprit-en-Grève, a bourgeois foundation that provided lodging, nourishment, and practical educations for both boy and girl orphans of legitimate birth, as well as dowries for the girls.[17]

In addition to these institutions, through which members of the Parisian elite inscribed the urban landscape with their charitable priorities, bourgeois Parisians repeatedly testified to their concern for the poverty of male and female youths and of elderly or mature women through municipal policies and charitable bequests. The city itself provided for its orphans by having the provost make arrangements for their care and for their practical training for adult work,[18] and individuals provided for widows, poor schoolboys and poor marriageable girls in their testaments. The frequency of testamentary donations, moreover, reflects the same hierarchy of concern that Parisian elites expressed through their institutions. Among the thirty-two bourgeois Parisian testaments that I have located, the greatest number of testators (eighteen) gave gifts to hospices for widows or older women; a

15. We find similar delegation of responsibility in aristocratic account books: Richard, ibid., 52–54.

16. To the four (or five, if we count St.-Thomas and St.-Nicolas of the Louvre as two different institutions) houses favored by the Parisian bourgeoisie, I have added Ave Maria College because it housed boys between the ages of eight and sixteen (for these institutions see below). However, I have not found any bourgeois testators giving gifts to Ave Maria College. On the hospices for poor women, see below, pp. 147–150.

17. Bavoux, "Enfants trouvés."

18. Ibid.; Gustave Fagniez, *Etudes sur l'industrie et la classe industrielle à Paris au XIIIe et au XIVe siècle* (Paris, 1877; reprint ed., New York, 1970), chap. 4.

slightly smaller group (fifteen) gave gifts to colleges for poor schoolboys; a still smaller group (twelve) set aside money for dowries for poor girls; and none expressed concern for elderly men.[19]

Upon first consideration, the gendered asymmetries in elite expressions of charitable concern for the life cycle crises of poor youths and mature women in Paris—the slightly greater concern for boys over girls at the point of entry into adulthood, and a far greater concern for older women than for older men—seem to reflect actual patterns of need. Demographic data from the late Middle Ages indicate that while a large number of widowed and older women headed their own households, older male heads of household living alone were extremely rare.[20] Moreover, the sources for the *Miracles of Saint Louis* point to a gendered imbalance among both youths and the elderly: among the laypersons of the working and nonworking poor who benefited from Louis's miracles, four of the eighteen women and girls (about 22 percent) were described as old or in their sixties, but only one of the fifteen men and boys (about 7 percent) was so described.[21] Among those beneficiaries who had to beg for a living before they were cured, six of the eight men (75 percent) were youths between the ages of fourteen and twenty-five, while four of the six women (about 67 percent) were over thirty.[22] Three of the four mature women, moreover, were single or widowed.

These statistics suggest that elite responses to the needy poor, which emphasized the poverty of young men entering the workforce and of older women without men, actually matched the needs of the poor. However,

19. See appendix.

20. Roger Mols, *Introduction à la démographie historique des villes d'Europe du XIVe au XVIIIe siècle*, 3 vols. (Gembloux, 1954–1956), 2:222; Charles Phythian-Adams, *Desolation of a City: Coventry and the Urban Crisis of the Late Middle Ages* (Cambridge, 1979), 92; Maryanne Kowaleski, "The History of Urban Families in Medieval England," *Journal of Medieval History* 14 (1988): 56.

21. Guillaume de St.-Pathus, *Les miracles*. Lower-status laywomen identified as old or in their sixties: miracles 4, 35, 43, 57; other lower-status laywomen/girls: miracles 2, 5, 31, 32, 36, 37, 39, 41, 42, 44, 51, 52, 58 (this women is identified as in her forties in the text, and as "old" in the rubric for the chapter), 59. Lower-status man identified as sixty years old: miracle 9; other lower-status men/boys: miracles 7, 8, 14, 15, 17, 18, 20, 25, 28, 33, 45, 47, 48, 49.

22. Ibid. Youths who begged: miracles 8, 14, 15, 17, 18, 20; other male beggars: miracles 9, 45. Women beggars over thirty: miracles 5, 35, 44, 52, and possibly 59 (this woman was over thirty either at the time of the inquest or at the time of her cure). Other woman beggar: miracle 42 (no age given, but she was married and had children).

there were important disjunctures between, on the one hand, the actual needs of women without men and boys on the threshold of adulthood, and, on the other hand, the charitable generosity of the elite. The most obvious disjuncture between elite expressions of charitable concern for young men and the needs of the begging youths of the *Miracles of Saint Louis* involved differences of status and opportunity. Bourgeois testators directed most of their money to promising boys and youths who were young enough, or already educated enough, to pursue lettered educations; but the young men in the *Miracles of Saint Louis* had already missed the opportunity to begin training for lettered professions, and instead they earned their bread, until misfortune befell them, by the sweat of their brows. Louis the deaf-mute trained from the age of eight in the workshop of a smith on a rural estate. Thomas of Voudai became blind when he was twelve years old and already watching pigs for the people of his village. Moriset, also a young swineherd, became lame at some point early in his working life. Guillot of Caux, a migrant to Paris, was presumably working when he began to suffer from a paralysis at the age of eighteen. Jehan of La Haye began to suffer from dizzy spells and muscular failure while he was migrating to Paris, also at the age of eighteen, in order to find work; Raou the Cobbler, also an immigrant to Paris, was living and working in Paris when he suffered a leg injury that developed into a debilitating infection.[23]

These were not the kind of boys or young men whom bourgeois donors preferred to help. Rather, in directing their generosity to colleges for students, bourgeois donors hoped to reproduce themselves by fostering a new generation of men who would contribute to the commercial and legal professions, thereby enhancing the wealth and prosperity of Paris. Of course, such intentions did not preclude helping boys from poor backgrounds.[24] But disabled boys were altogether a different matter, as we learn from educational treatises and from the statutes of Ave Maria College, a hospice for schoolboys between the ages of eight and sixteen that was founded in 1339 on the Left Bank by a cleric named Jean of Hubant. The statutes stipulated that the boys who held scholarships at the college were to be poor, of legiti-

23. Ibid., miracles 8, 14, 15, 17, 18, 20. Concerning Moriset, we can assume his youth by the fact that he is given a diminutive name, and that he is identified as "the son of the deceased Jehan Poilebout of Ranton" (ibid., p. 45).

24. Schoolboys of the College of St.-Honoré begged, which suggests that they came from modest backgrounds; J. M. Reitzel, "Medieval Houses of Bons-Enfants," *Viator: Medieval and Renaissance Studies* 11 (1980): 202–3. Moreover, some of the orphans at the Hospital of St.-Esprit-en-Grève gained entry into colleges at the University of Paris: Bavoux, "Enfants trouvés," 370.

mate birth, from good families living by their own labor, capable of being taught, and free of physical deformities.[25]

Neither did bourgeois donors favor men who were pursuing advanced university degrees, which usually led to careers in the church. Thus, they tended to avoid support for the forty or more colleges associated with the University of Paris—most notably the Sorbonne, Narbonne, Du Plessis, Harcourt, Cholet, Navarre, and Lemoine—which had been founded by 1348.[26] Instead, Parisian bourgeois testators directed their assistance to four colleges that provided support for younger students. The first of these, the Dix-huit, or St.-Christophe, which was affiliated with the Hôtel Dieu of Paris, was founded in 1180.[27] The second, the hospice of poor students of St.-Honoré, was located on the Right Bank, north of the Louvre and outside the walls of Philip Augustus. It was founded between 1204 and 1209 by two bourgeois couples.[28] The third, St.-Thomas (or St.-Nicolas) of the Louvre, was founded before 1210.[29] The fourth, the Bons Enfants of St.-Victor, was established before 1248 on the rue St.-Victor on the Left Bank. (For the locations of these institutions, see map 1.)[30] I have found only one exception to this pattern of bourgeois Parisian charity—a testator who gave sums of money not only to these four hospices but also to poor beneficiaries of the Sorbonne.[31] This pattern of bourgeois disinterest in students pursuing higher university degrees occurred in medieval England as well.[32]

In making donations in behalf of "poor students" some bourgeois donors

25. Astrik L. Gabriel, *Student Life in Ave Maria College, Medieval Paris: History and Chartulary of the College* (Notre Dame, Ind., 1955), 105, 323, 352.

26. Astrik Gabriel, "The College System in the Fourteenth-Century Universities," in *The Forward Movement of the Fourteenth Century*, ed. Francis Lee Utley (Columbus, Ohio, 1961), 82, 110 n. 26.

27. *Chartularium universitatis Parisiensis*, ed. Henricus Denifle, vol. 1 (Paris, 1889), no. 50.

28. Reitzel, "Medieval Houses of Bons-Enfants," 202.

29. Denifle, *Chartularium universitatis Parisiensis*, 1, no. 10. Most Parisian testaments refer to the schoolboys of St.-Nicolas of the Louvre rather than St.-Thomas of the Louvre: Gervais Ruffus, 1260; Pierre la Pie, 1302; Simon Piz d'Oue, 1307; Robert Evrout, 1306; Marie, wife of Robert Evrout, 1307; Etienne Haudry, 1312; Jehanne, wife of Etienne Haudry, 1309; Margaret, wife of Pierre Loisel, 1330; Jehan de Troyes, 1332; see appendix.

30. Reitzel, "Medieval Houses of Bons-Enfants," 183.

31. Testament of Jehanne la Fouacière, 1313; see appendix.

32. Gabriel, "The College System," 85. Corpus Christi College at Oxford is the one exception.

probably hoped to help members of their own families. The statutes of Ave Maria College stated that in the selection of the "poor students" who would hold residential scholarships there, preferential treatment was to go first to the founder's own relations, and then to inhabitants of his natal village. We know, in fact, that Hubant's own nephew held a scholarship at Ave Maria, as did the son of the mayor of Ste.-Geneviève.[33] In the Middle Ages and Renaissance, as Richard Trexler has so convincingly argued,[34] legitimate charity for the poor was extended to all people who met with difficulties in living up to the standards of their social group. Hence, propertied individuals gave preference to those forms of charity that helped their own kind, if not their own families.

This is not to say that Parisians of means totally disregarded charity for the working poor. We encounter this concern in the arrangements that both the provost of Paris and the Hospital of St.-Esprit-en-Grève made for the practical educations of orphans. We also encounter it in the foundation in 1344 by Jehan Roussel and his wife Aalis of a block of housing for respectable poor people; and in five Parisian testaments, in which the bourgeois testators designated that sums of money were to be given to "poor households."[35] Roussel's foundation and the five testaments may have served the disabled and elderly poor as well as the working poor. However, the statutes for the interlocking charities associated with Ave Maria College suggest that preference may have been given to the working poor.[36]

According to Jean of Hubant's statutes for Ave Maria College, it consisted of a central institution—the college itself—which was to provide food and clothing for six boys between the ages of eight and sixteen who held regular scholarships, and for two other resident students whose endowment supported them at a lower standard of living. Additionally, the property of the college included several out buildings, which provided housing for six

33. Gabriel, *Student Life*, 106–7.

34. Trexler, "Charity and the Defense of Urban Elites in the Italian Communes," in *The Rich, the Well-Born, and the Powerful: Elites and Upper Classes in History*, ed. Frederic Cople Jaher (Urbana, Ill., 1973), 64–109.

35. On the Maison Roussel, see Bronislaw Geremek, *The Margins of Society in Late Medieval Paris*, trans. from the French by Jean Birrell (Cambridge, 1987), 83; and AN, S 5073b, no. 40. The five testators were: Jehanne de Malaunay, 1310; Philippe de Cormeilles, 1329; Jehanne du Faut, 1330; Margaret, wife of Pierre Loisel, 1330; Jehanne la Fouacière, 1313; see appendix.

36. The following discussion is from Astrik Gabriel, *Student Life*. However, my reading of the statutes, which Gabriel publishes, is not always the same as that of Gabriel.

more students of this lower status, for ten aged poor women and for ten poor households.[37]

Hubant went to great lengths to assure that none of the dependents of the college would be young women, who, presumably, would have provided too much sexual temptation for the boys.[38] Perhaps for this reason he assumed that the poor households would all be headed by men. Concerning these male heads of household, Hubant warned against "false beggars or those living on false begging" stipulating that preference should be given instead "to those working the earth or earning their bread with other work, unless they are blind or have another disability or are old and for that reason have to beg."[39] This language may seem to suggest that Hubant's charitable housing was offered equally to laboring, disabled, and elderly poor men. However, the illuminations for the statutes indicate that he gave preference to functioning laborers: the illumination depicting the poor householders shows ten male heads of household. Eight of them—a baker, a wine seller, a cobbler, a smith, a tailor, a mason, a carpenter, and a butcher—hold the tools of their trade, while two hold walking sticks, probably to indicate that they went out begging each day. The illumination thus gives the impression that laboring heads of household were the preferred residents.[40] Along similar lines, the inscription on the facade of the hospice for the poor that Nicolas Flamel built in 1407 indicated that the house was intended for poor "laborers" rather than the feeble and disabled.[41] The sources for these two institutions thus suggest that because of their discomfort with the nonworking poor, bourgeois Parisians preferred to extend their charity to able-bodied workingmen rather than to disabled and elderly men.

We might expect that hospitals provided the best venue through which Parisians of property extended their assistance to the nonworking disabled poor. Like members of the bourgeois and aristocratic elites in other towns, propertied Parisians both founded and supported the various Parisian hospitals that housed poor sick persons. By the end of the thirteenth century Parisian aristocrats had founded at least three hospitals: the Maison-Dieu Philippe de Magny (or St.-Eustache), the Maison-Dieu Jean l'Ecueillir, and

37. Ibid., 98–116; "Statutes of Ave Maria College," ibid., 322, 345, 347–48.
38. The servant had to be a man, or, if a woman, old. The householders could not have young wives, and they had to move out when their daughters or other female household members reached the age of ten: "Statutes of Ave Maria College," in Gabriel, *Student Life*, 323–24, 375.
39. Ibid., 375.
40. Gabriel, *Student Life*, 173 and plate 22.
41. Nigel Wilkins, *Nicolas Flamel: Des livres et de l'or* (Paris, 1993), 36.

the Maison-Dieu St.-Gervais.[42] These were joined, in the first half of the fourteenth century, by at least two bourgeois foundations: a hospital founded by Ymbert of Lyon in 1316, and one founded by Arnoul Braques in 1348.[43] Bourgeois Parisian testators made frequent donations to these and other hospitals. In 1330, for instance, Margaret, the wife of Pierre Loisel, gave twenty sous tournois for distribution to the poor at the Hôtel Dieu of Paris, and five sous tournois each to the hospitals of St.-Mathurin, St.-Gervais, St.-Catherine, Philip de Magny, St.-Marcel and Nôtre-Dame of the Fields. Additionally, she left six deniers to each of the thirty-nine leprosaria and seventeen Hôtels Dieu that sought alms each Monday on the Grand Pont.[44] Some testators gave gifts in kind, especially beds, to the Hôtels Dieu. While these gifts helped the poor, they could also serve as concrete reminders of the social ties of the donors. Thus, in 1313, Jehanne la Fouacière gave to the Hôtel Dieu of Paris "her best furnished bed with a coverlet, which once belonged to Lady Margaret, Queen of France of illustrious memory, widow of the blessed Louis."[45]

The Hôtel Dieu of Paris, which had been founded by at least the ninth century, was the largest hospital in Paris.[46] Located near the cathedral of

42. Léon Le Grand, "Les maisons-Dieu et léproseries du diocèse de Paris au milieu du XIVe siècle," *Mémoires de la Société de l'histoire de Paris et de l'Ile-de-France* 25 (1898): 53, 67, 82–83.

43. Ibid., 54. According to one fifteenth-century document, the hospital founded by Ymbert of Lyon in 1316 originally provided temporary shelter for female beggars. However, neither the foundation documents nor the early fourteenth-century testaments that make reference to Ymbert of Lyon's hospital indicate that it was a women's hospice: AN, LL 7, fols. 57v–60r (copies of foundation documents of 1316); AN, L 1053, no. 12 (1348 *vidimus* of Ymbert of Lyon's testament of 1316); testament of Jehanne du Faut, 1330, gift to "hospitali defuncti Ymberti de Lugduno" (see appendix). In the 1360s Parisians responded to the dangers of the French war with England by digging a defensive moat on the north side of the city; as a result, the Convent of the Filles Dieu was compelled to move from its original location to Ymbert of Lyon's hospital: Paul and Marie Louise Biver, *Abbayes, monastères, couvents de femmes à Paris des origines à la fin du XVIIIe siècle* (Paris, 1975), 68; L'Abbé Lebeuf, *Histoire de la ville et de tout le diocèse de Paris, rectifications et additions, ville de Paris et ancienne banlieue, par Fernand Bournon* (Paris, 1890), 43. The 1483 document claiming that Ymbert's hospital had sheltered female beggars is printed in Jacques Du Breul, *Le théâtre des antiquitez de Paris* (Paris, 1639), 662–63.

44. Testament of Margaret, wife of Pierre Loisel, 1330; see appendix.

45. Testament of Jehanne la Fouacière, 1313; see appendix.

46. Le Grand, "Les maisons-Dieu," 54.

Nôtre-Dame, and under the jurisdiction of its chapter, it had 279 beds in the fifteenth century, which could hold two or three inmates each, although the hospital rarely held as many as four hundred inmates. Those 279 beds were intended to hold poor and feeble people, the seriously ill, abandoned children, and a number of pensioners. An additional 24 beds were reserved for poor pregnant women when they went into labor.[47] Bronislaw Geremek has estimated that in the fourteenth and fifteenth centuries the hospitals and hospices of Paris offered, on the average, between one thousand and twelve hundred places for sick and poor people, excluding lepers and pilgrims.[48] These numbers would not have gone far in meeting the needs of the twenty thousand or so beggars who resided in Paris in the period before the onset of the Black Death in 1348.

Indeed, the best evidence suggests that most hospitals—with the exception of those that housed the blind—were not intended to provide assistance for mobile individuals suffering from prolonged disabilities. A number of hospitals passed statutes indicating that disabled people who were capable of moving around were not to be given beds.[49] Similar rules seem to have been in effect in the hospitals of Paris as well. Seventeen of the miracles of Saint Louis involved poor adults residing in Paris or St.-Denis who experienced lasting disabilities.[50] In only one case, however—that of a married woman named Jehanne of Serris—are we told that the sufferer entered a hospital because of her paralysis.[51] Jehanne, moreover, was soon taught to use crutches and sent home, where she survived by begging each day. In one other story, involving a young man named Guillot of Caux, who was crippled for at least five years, we are told that he entered the Hôtel Dieu only when he had a fever and could not beg.[52]

The Parisian hospice for the blind, the Quinze-Vingts, provides the one notable exception to the general lack of interest of the Parisian elite in providing institutional assistance to the disabled poor. It is significant that the initiative for this exceptional institution came not only from a king, but from a king who was known for his unusual level of charitable generosity

47. E. Coyecque, *L'Hôtel-Dieu de Paris au moyen âge: Histoire et documents*, 2 vols. (Paris, 1891), 1:25, 60–75.

48. Geremek, *The Margins*, 176.

49. Annie Saunier, *"Le pauvre malade" dans le cadre hospitalier médiéval: France du nord, vers 1300–1500* (Paris, 1993), 13.

50. Guillaume de St.-Pathus, *Les miracles*, miracles 2, 4, 5, 7, 9, 17, 18, 20, 35, 37, 39, 42, 43, 44, 51, 52, 58.

51. Ibid., miracle 42.

52. Ibid., miracle 17.

and concern for the poor. It is also significant that while this institution provided shelter for poor blind men and women, its residents were expected to earn their keep by begging. Founded by Saint Louis around 1260, the Quinze-Vingts could house up to three hundred people—blind men and women and their guides, who were often the spouses, children, or siblings of the blind residents.[53] Begging was so important at the Quinze-Vingts that blind persons who married while residing there were allowed to marry only sighted individuals, who would be able to serve as their guides. Those who married other blind persons had to leave the Quinze-Vingts and forfeit half of their possessions.[54]

A number of bourgeois testators made donations to the Quinze-Vingts in the thirteenth and early fourteenth centuries, just as they did to other hospitals.[55] Still, stories like the satire *Le garçon et l'aveugle*, which portrayed a blind man as both avaricious and lascivious, suggest that people of property and letters continued to harbor distrust for blind beggars; and Rutebeuf's satirical poems, "Les ordres de Paris," and "Le chanson des ordres," suggest that some Parisians had reservations about King Louis IX's foundation:

> The king has united in one refuge
> (But I'm not sure why)
> Three hundred blind people, row by row.
> They go around Paris in groups of three
> All day long never ceasing to bray
> "For the three hundred who can't see a thing!
>
> The order of the blind,
> Such an order is less than nothing.[56]

53. Léon Le Grand, "Les Quinze-Vingts: Depuis leur fondation jusqu'à leur translation au faubourg Saint-Antoine, XIIIᵉ–XVIIIᵉ siècles," *Mémoires de la Société de l'Histoire de Paris et de l'Ile-de-France* 13 (1886): 113–25.

54. "Reglèment donné auz Quinze-Vingts par Michel de Brache, aumônier du roi Jean (1351–1355)," in Le Grand, "Les Quinze-Vingts," part 2, *Mémoires de la Société de l'Histoire de Paris et de l'Ile-de-France* 14 (1887): 158; reprinted by Mario Roques, ed. and Jean Dufournet, trans., *Le garçon et l'aveugle, jeu du XIIIᵉ siècle* (Paris, 1989), 141.

55. These include Guillaume au Long Nez, 1327; Jehan de Troyes, 1332; Robert le Vinetier, 1311; Jehan Langlais, 1316; Girart de Troyes, 1298; Emeline, wife of Nicolas, minister of the Quinze-Vingts, 1303; Thomas le Tailleur, 1307; Sédile of Laon, 1316; Pierre la Pie, 1302; see appendix.

56. Rutebeuf, *Oeuvres complètes*, 2 vols., ed. Michel Zink (Paris, 1989), 1:232, 394.

Whatever the level of bourgeois enthusiasm for the Quinze-Vingts, it did not meet the needs of all of the blind in and around Paris: the three blind individuals in the *Miracles of Saint Louis* all lived within twenty-five miles of Paris, but not one of them became a resident at the Quinze-Vingts. Two of the three begged in order to survive.[57]

The principal assistance that propertied Parisians offered to disabled members of the nonworking poor came in the form of alms—given, as we see in the story about Louis the former deaf-mute, informally in the streets and at the gates of monasteries; or, as we learn from testaments and confraternal statutes, during funeral processions and at confraternal banquets.

ARTISANS, THE WORKING POOR, AND DISABLED POOR MEN

More sustained care of the disabled poor tended to come from artisans of modest means and from the working poor. Nevertheless, even these groups seem to have felt greater discomfort, or less empathy, with dependent nonworking men than with dependent, nonworking women. Thus, while families, employers, and neighbors provided the most important and sustained care for the men and women in the *Miracles of Saint Louis*, they appear to have done so less frequently for men and boys than for women. Twelve of the sixteen needy lay women and girls aged ten or more (75 percent) in the *Miracles* received help from family, employers, neighbors, and companions, while we are told that only seven of the twelve men and boys aged ten and older (about 58 percent) received such assistance.[58] Similarly, we are told that only six of the sixteen women and girls ten and older (about 38 percent) had to resort to begging in order to survive, while the *Miracles* indicate that eight of the twelve men and youths (about 67 percent) had to do so.[59] It is possible that these statistical differences reflect differences in reporting as well as differences in practice: as we will see later on, clerics were not entirely comfortable with women beggars. Nevertheless, the evidence also

57. Guillaume de St.-Pathus, *Les miracles*. Blind persons who begged: miracles 8, 59. Blind person who did not beg: miracle 51.

58. Ibid. Women/girls aged ten and older receiving help: miracles 2, 4, 5, 31, 32, 37, 39, 44, 51, 57, 58, 59. Women/girls ten and older, no evidence of help: miracles 35, 42, 43, 52. Men/boys aged ten and older receiving help: miracles 7, 9, 15, 17, 25, 28, 33. Men/boys aged ten and older, no evidence of help: miracles 8, 14, 18, 20, 45. The boys and girls in miracles 36, 41, 48, and 49 were clearly younger than ten; the boy in miracle 47 was probably younger than ten.

59. Ibid. Women who begged: miracles 5, 35, 42, 44, 52, 59. Men/youths who begged: miracles 8, 9, 14, 15, 17, 18, 20, 45.

suggests that older girls and women received more support in times of need than did older boys and men.

We might expect that families would have provided the most important source of support for disabled workers. Medieval discussions of charitable giving usually stressed that charity began at home.[60] But to what degree did familial support work among propertyless laborers who, if male, frequently did not earn enough to support a nuclear family, and if female, frequently did not earn enough to support themselves? Indeed, how effective was family support among poor peasants, whose children—especially those who inherited nothing—fed the immigrant population of Paris?

The story of Moriset, a young swineherd from the diocese of Poitiers, has much to tell about nomadism in search of work among the noninheriting rural poor, and about the inability of poor families to support their disabled members.[61] It also points, once again, to the gender-specific pressures of self-sufficiency, which affected male youths in their teens even if they were disabled.

Although we are never told Moriset's age, the facts that he is identified by a diminutive first name, and as "the son of the deceased Jehan Poilebout" suggest that he was probably in his teens or even younger.[62] He came from the village of Ranton, half-way between Angers and Poitiers and a few miles west of Loudun. For reasons that the text never explains, however, he took up employment watching pigs for a cleric who lived in the town of St.-Jean d'Angely, about seventy-five miles south of Ranton (map 3). Because he felt ill—or perhaps because it was Holy Week—Moriset returned, in the spring of 1281, to the house of his brother Colin in Ranton. When he awoke on the morning after his arrival his legs had "contracted": his heels would not touch the ground and for that reason he was forced to walk on the balls of his feet using crutches for balance. Unable to work, Moriset remained in his brother's house for several months. However, "because his brother was a poor man and had five children and a wife, it was a difficult thing for him to nourish Moriset."[63] So Moriset decided to go to the town of Saumur, about twenty miles to the north, where his stepmother had taken up work as a servant in the Maison-Dieu after her husband's death. When Moriset arrived at the hospital, however, he learned that his stepmother had died a month ear-

60. Brian Tierney, *Medieval Poor Law: A Sketch of Canonical Theory and Its Application in England* (Berkeley, Calif., 1959), 57; Trexler, "Charity and the Defense of Urban Elites," 76.

61. Guillaume de St.-Pathus, *Les miracles*, miracle 14.

62. Ibid., 45.

63. Ibid., 46.

lier. But his half-brother was still there, and Moriset remained at the hospital for the next two months, from mid-August to late November.

By now an oozing ulcer, so malodorous that it annoyed the other residents at the hospital, had developed on Moriset's left thigh. People encouraged him to seek a cure at the shrine of Saint Sulpice in the diocese of Paris, so, in late November or early December of 1281, Moriset set out for that destination. His progress was painfully slow, however, so when he reached the town of Tours, which is about thirty miles west of Saumur, he decided to wait out the winter. Sometime in the spring Moriset progressed another thirty miles or so, to the town of Blois. Before mid-May he traveled another seventy-five miles, to reach his destination.

Moriset stayed at the shrine of Saint Sulpice for three days, but nothing happened. In the meantime, however, he learned of the miraculous cures that were taking place thirty miles away, at Saint Louis's tomb in St.-Denis. Finally, on the Wednesday after Pentecost—May 20, 1282, over five months after he left Saumur—Moriset arrived at St.-Denis, where, on the very same day, he cast off his crutches and walked around the interior of the church, although with some difficulty. By the next week, when he appeared before the panel of inquisitors, Moriset was no longer using crutches, his ulcer had drained, and the wounds had closed.

We do not know what happened to Moriset in the end. He may have retraced his journey of over 195 miles to Ranton or the even longer distance to St.-Jean d'Angely. It is also quite plausible, however, that he stayed, and found work, in St.-Denis or Paris. A journey that began with the purpose of a cure may have resulted, after so much travel, in Moriset's finding work in Paris or St.-Denis. After all, Moriset's ties to family and employment were relatively weak, and Paris and St.-Denis worked as powerful magnets on the labor market.

Moriset's story illustrates the inability of poor families to care for adults and youths who became disabled for long periods of time. In all likelihood, his plight was gender-specific: while the *Miracles of Saint Louis* includes stories of married women with lasting disabilities whose husbands could not provide full support for them, and about immigrant single women in their late twenties who received no support from their families, it contains no such stories about unmarried girls in their teens. One suspects that between the ages of twelve and twenty disabled girls were more likely to receive help from their natal families than were disabled boys. The data on women's older ages of migration that were discussed in chapter 1 support this hypothesis.

Moriset's story also illustrates the fate of widows, who frequently had to migrate to find work after their husbands' deaths, and the weak links of communication among family members once such migrations took place: Moriset did not know of his stepmother's death until he arrived in Saumur. In this case, the distance that served as an obstacle to family communication was only twenty miles. In the cases of three male beggars in the *Miracles of Saint Louis* who are mentioned as residing (or as being on their way to reside) in Paris, the distance was even greater: seventy, eighty, and over a hundred miles.[64] Two of them were only eighteen when disability struck them. No mention is made of support from their families for any of them; the distance that they had migrated constituted one of the factors contributing to that absence.

The story of Richard of Bricqueville, a village in the Calvados region of the diocese of Bayeux, also provides a view of sibling care, but within a family with more substantial resources than those of Moriset's family.[65] Sometime around 1268, Richard, who originated in Bricqueville but was then living with his sister and her husband in St.-Denis, fell victim to a paralysis that forced him to use crutches and drag his feet behind him. However, this disability did not compel Richard to depend upon his sister and brother-in-law for financial support: he continued to work, at least intermittently, as either a tailor or a sewer in a tailor's workshop, and he had an inheritance in his native village upon which he could draw.[66] Indeed, perhaps because he had become more dependent upon that inheritance, Richard returned, during his four-year illness, to his native Bricqueville. Sometime around 1272, however, at the time of the Lendit—the important commercial fair that took place during two weeks in June on the plain of Lendit, between Paris and St.-Denis—he went to visit his brother, who was a student in St.-Denis. The brother encouraged Richard to visit Saint Louis's tomb. He did so, and was cured. When he returned without crutches to his sister's house his sister cried for joy and neighbors gathered at her house to celebrate the event with a meal.

64. Ibid., miracles 17, 18, 20.

65. Ibid., miracle 24.

66. Guillaume de St.-Pathus calls Richard a "cousturier de dras." In the *Livre des métiers* the gild of tailors was identified as that of the "tailleurs de robes," while the term "couturier" occurred only in the phrase "valet couturier"—"journeyman/woman sewer." However, it is possible that the expressions "couturier de robes" (which occurs in the tax assessments) and/or "couturier de dras" (the term used for Richard of Briqueville) referred to persons of higher status. Janice Archer, "Working Women in Thirteenth-Century Paris" (Ph.D. diss., University of Arizona, 1995), 192–94; René de Lespinasse and François Bonnardot, eds., *Le livre des métiers d'Etienne Boileau* (Paris, 1879), 116.

Two aspects of Richard's story may be gender-specific. First, the rural inheritance that devolved on him may have been more substantial than that which devolved on his sister or younger brother. And second, if Richard was actually a tailor (and thus a master artisan) his was a profession that consisted almost entirely of men: the Parisian tax assessments of 1297–1300 included an annual average of thirty-five men and no women who were listed as "tailleur de robes" and an annual average of four men and no women who were listed as "couturier de robes."[67] If, however, Richard was only a sewer, he practiced a skill that was exercised by many women, for unusually equal pay: the tax lists of 1297–1300 included an annual average of ninety-nine men and fifty-three women who were listed as "couturier/es"; in 1292 the average assessment of the male sewers was 2.14 sous, while that of the female sewers was 2.13 sous.[68]

The *Miracles of Saint Louis* does not include any stories about poor married townsmen who suffered lasting disabilities. Such stories would provide important insights into the survival strategies, or the failure of such strategies, among poor urban families that suffered the worst possible type of long-term financial crisis: the loss of the principal breadwinner's ability to work.[69] In such a case, we might well imagine, neither the wife's work nor her begging could have made up for the man's loss of income, and it is entirely unclear what kind of income the man would have brought in by begging.

As we have already learned from the story of Louis the deaf-mute, employers sometimes assumed parental roles vis-à-vis their employees, even providing support for disabled dependent workers when natal families failed to do so. Because training and apprenticeship were often tied to migration,

67. Archer, "Working Women in Thirteenth-Century Paris," 258.

68. Ibid.; Hercule Géraud, *Paris sous Philipp-le-Bel, d'après des documents originaux et notamment d'après un manuscrit contenant "Le Rôle de la Taille" imposée sur les habitants de Paris en 1292*, reproduction of the 1837 edition with introduction and index by Caroline Bourlet and Lucie Fossier (Tübingen, 1991). Calculations of average tax assessments are my own.

69. Three married poor men were beneficiaries of Louis's miracles. One, a leatherworker residing in St.-Denis, lost the use of his leg for two days because he had spoken ill of Saint Louis. The other two lived in the countryside. The first, a royal forester, had to use a cane for three or four years but was apparently able to continue working. The second, a peasant who may have owned his own land, was unable to walk for an unknown length of time, apparently less than a year. His wife, father, and sister helped him arrange his trip to St.-Denis, but only his sister accompanied him, because his wife was pregnant and his father was too old: Guillaume de St.-Pathus, *Les miracles*, 25, 28, 33.

many young employees must have found themselves in need of such support. Boys and young men often left their families and even their native regions in order to seek work or to begin training as servants or apprentices. Girls and young women also left home to become servants and apprentices. However, girls and women tended to migrate at later ages than did boys— something that was closely related to the fact that far more young men entered into apprenticeship contracts than did young women. In the surviving notarial records of the late fourteenth- and early fifteenth-century Orléanais, for instance, Françoise Michaud-Frejaville found 337 apprenticeship contracts for boys and young men and 40 for girls and young women.[70] Kathryn Reyerson found 208 contracts for boys and young men and 30 for girls and young women from Montpellier, for the period 1293–1348.[71] The proportion of girls entering formal apprenticeships in thirteenth-century Paris was probably higher than this, since Paris had five female gilds—four listed in the *Livres des métiers*, which was compiled between 1261 and 1271, and one other established toward the end of the thirteenth century.[72] Even so, it is likely that boy apprentices far outnumbered girls. We need to remember, however, that even for boys, apprenticeship—which was the beginning of the road to becoming a master artisan—was not the norm. Many, if not most, Parisian laborers worked outside of the gild structure. During the summer construction season, for instance, 54 to 59 percent of the workers at construction sites in Paris were not enrolled in the gilds.[73]

In most cases, young servants and apprentices resided with their masters, who thus assumed responsibilities as their adult guardians.[74] It is not entirely clear, however, to what extent these young people could depend upon the

70. These numbers are for the period 1380–1440. The proportion of girls was even lower for the period between 1440 and 1490, for which Michaud-Frejaville found 428 contracts for boys and 16 for girls: "Bons et loyaux," 186.

71. Kathryn L. Reyerson, "The Adolescent Apprentice/Worker in Medieval Montpellier," *Journal of Family History* 17 (1992): 354.

72. See below, chap. 5, and Farmer, "It Is Not Good That [Wo]man Should Be Alone: Elite Responses to Singlewomen in High Medieval Paris," in *Singlewomen in the European Past, 1250–1800*, ed. Judith Bennett and Amy Froide (Philadelphia, 1999), 83.

73. Bronislaw Geremek, *Le salariat dans l'artisanat parisien aux XIIIᵉ–XVIᵉ siècles*, trans. from the Polish by Anna Posner and Christiane Klapisch-Zuber (Paris, 1982), 70–71.

74. Steven A. Epstein, *Wage Labor and Guilds in Medieval Europe* (Chapel Hill, N.C., 1991), 110–11; Philippe Didier, "Le contrat d'apprentissage en Bourgogne aux XIVᵉ et XVᵉ siècles," *Revue historique de droit français et étranger* 54 (1976): 43.

emotional and material support of their guardians in times of sickness as well as health. During the initial period of their training even healthy servants and apprentices generally cost their masters more than they returned in labor. Masters of servants could recover some of their early losses by withholding wages until the end of a period of service. Masters of apprentices recovered these expenses in one of two ways: they either retained the apprentices a number of years after their training had been completed, thus profiting from several years of underpaid or unpaid labor, or they had the apprentices and their families pay in advance for the expense of their training. Apprentices whose training was paid for in this way generally owed fewer years to their masters than did those in the same craft who did not pay.[75]

The records concerning the responsibilities of masters when their dependent workers became ill offer contradictory evidence. Contracts of apprenticeship sometimes implied that apprentices could depend upon the material support of their masters during times of illness, but only a few of these contracts spelled out the length of time that such support might last. One contract from thirteenth-century Montpellier, for instance, indicated that the master would provide food, clothing, and shoes for up to a month of illness; similarly, a contract from fifteenth-century Orléans indicated that a master weaver would support his apprentice for up to a month of illness without demanding additional time from the apprentice at the end of his term of service.[76] It is usually impossible to determine what happened to apprentices and servants who became ill for longer periods of time, or to those whose work agreements or contracts, as was usually the case, included no such specific arrangements. However, one court case from late fourteenth-century Paris involving an apprentice who needed medical attention indicates that the parents were sometimes held responsible for bearing the financial burden of consultations with physicians and other medical practitioners.[77]

In addition to providing material support and professional training, masters were also expected to assume parental roles in other ways as well: it was taken for granted, for instance, that they would employ corporal punishment and that they would provide appropriate moral and intellectual train-

75. Fagniez, *Etudes sur l'industrie*, 60; Epstein, *Wage Labor*, 143–47. Not all of the Parisian gilds offered both options.

76. Reyerson, "Adolescent Apprentice," 363; Michaud-Frejaville, "Bons et loyaux," 205.

77. Fagniez, *Etudes sur l'industrie*, 65.

ing for their young charges.[78] In twelfth- and thirteenth-century Genoa, moreover, many apprenticeship contracts stipulated that apprentices were required to attain their masters' permission before marrying.[79] Sermon literature also stipulated that masters and mistresses were supposed to watch over the moral behavior and provide for the spiritual education of their servants. Jacques de Vitry told an exemplary story about a mistress who sometimes stayed at home on Sundays so that her maidservant could go to church to hear the sermons;[80] both Jacques and Gilbert of Tournai cautioned masters and mistresses to watch over the chastity of their male and female servants; and Gilbert praised a mistress who severely beat a servant and then cast her into a river because she had gossiped to the mistress about a man who lusted after the mistress.[81]

Unfortunately, sermon literature and initial contracts do not enable us to evaluate the spiritual, emotional, and charitable relations that actually evolved between masters and their dependent workers. Occasionally, however, we detect strong apprentice-master bonds in testaments, especially those of masters who had no children. In 1310, for instance, a Parisian currier named Jehan le Grand included a former apprentice among his primary heirs: he bequeathed twenty livres each to his former apprentice, John of Ulmeyus, to his nephew, to his niece Emmeline, and to Emmeline's daughter. Emmeline also inherited the incomes on several properties, with the understanding that she and her heirs were to have masses performed for the soul of her uncle.[82] Similarly, in Genoa a childless master shoemaker left to his apprentice twenty lire, the tools of his shop, the shop itself, and the use of his house for life.[83] Several artisans in late medieval London also made their apprentices their principal heirs.[84]

Testaments give us occasional glimpses into quasi-familial bonds between apprentices and masters. Conversely, court and gild records offer glimpses of the occasional breakdown of the parental role that masters and

78. Epstein, *Wage Labor*, 105–11; Didier, "Le contrat," 43–47.

79. Epstein, *Wage Labor*, 111.

80. Paris, Bibliothèque Nationale de France, ms. lat. 3284, fol. 177a, "Sermo primus ad coniugatos."

81. See above, p. 48, and Gilbert of Tournai, "Ad coniugatas, Sermo Tercius," ed. Carla Casagrande, *Prediche alle donne del secolo XIII* (Milan, 1978), 95.

82. See appendix.

83. Steven A. Epstein, *Wills and Wealth in Medieval Genoa, 1150–1250* (Cambridge, Mass., 1984), 133–34.

84. Barbara Hanawalt, *Growing Up in Medieval London* (New York, 1993), 171.

mistresses were expected to fulfill. For instance, the mid-thirteenth-century gild statutes from Paris—the *Livre des métiers* of Etienne Boileau—referred to the problem of runaway apprentices, leaving to our imagination the various reasons why apprentices might feel the need to run away.[85] Late four-teenth-and early fifteenth-century court records from Paris point to one such reason: the right to exercise corporal punishment sometimes evolved into intolerable physical abuse. In two such court cases, the apprentices were relieved of the necessity of fulfilling their contractual obligations to their masters because their masters had injured them during beatings. A third case leads us to believe that a young girl died as a result of the beatings she received from her master.[86]

Court records and wills offer only rare glimpses into the qualitative relations between masters and their working dependents. In addition to the story of Louis the deaf-mute, the *Miracles of Saint Louis* includes two other stories—those of Orenge of Fontenay and Guillot the Cripple—that fill out this picture, providing evidence concerning the charitable lengths to which some artisans would go in their support for sick and disabled dependent workers.[87]

Guillot's story illustrates the care that a young worker-in-training could receive from an employer in an urban artisanal home/workshop. Sometime around 1259 Guillot, who was twelve at the time, migrated about 165 miles from his home in Varenguebec, a village in the diocese of Coutances in Normandy, to Paris. Guillot took up work with a bourgeois fuller named Robert Reboule, quite possibly the same individual living on the "Foulerie"—a street where most of the fullers resided, later called the rue de la Mortellerie, which ran along the right bank of the Seine, between the Place de Grève and the Porte Barbeel (see map 1)—who was assessed for a tax of ten sous in 1292.[88] If this was indeed the same Robert Reboule, we are dealing with a propertied artisan of modest but not insignificant means: Robert's tax assessment was slightly below the average assessment for non-Lombards and non-Jews, which was 14.6 sous in 1292.[89]

85. Fagniez, *Etudes sur l'industrie*, 73.
86. Ibid., 67–69.
87. Guillaume de St.-Pathus, *Les miracles*, miracle 7. Orenge of Fontenay is more fully discussed in chapter 5.
88. Géraud, *Paris sous Philippe-le-Bel*, 128, 286.
89. I have calculated this average myself, reworking the average given by David Herlihy for the entire tax assessment, including Lombards and Jews: Herlihy, *Opera Muliebra: Women and Work in Medieval Europe* (New York, 1990), 135.

About a year and a half after Guillot went to live and work with Robert a swelling developed in his foot. Guillot was forced to limp for the first year after the swelling appeared, and to use crutches for the following nine years. Eventually the swelling developed into an open wound, which gave off pus through nine openings and caused such a stench that the other members of Robert's household blamed him for allowing the young man to continue living there. Robert, however, remained firm in his support for the boy, providing both advice and material support even after Guillot ceased to be able to work.

During the ten years of his suffering, Guillot sought help from a number of sources: he had a surgeon pierce his foot, he received care from an unlicensed doctor, and he twice went on pilgrimage to the church of Saint Eloy in Noyons, a town about fifty-five miles northeast of Paris. Robert Reboule advised the youth to say confession before he made his second pilgrimage to Noyons, and he sent his own servant to accompany Guillot on the journey. Toward the end of Guillot's ordeal, Robert advised him that he should probably have his foot amputated by a carpenter so that he could rejoin "the people who earn their bread."[90] The carpenter, however, dissuaded Guillot from following this advice.

Finally, in 1271, after King Louis's bones had been deposited in St.-Denis, Guillot went on crutches to the tomb. He returned to Robert's house that day feeling much better but still using his crutches, and Robert advised him to say confession and return to the tomb. Guillot followed the advice, staying at the tomb for nine days, during which time he rubbed dust from the tomb into the putrescent openings on his foot. Within three or four days after he applied the dust, the wound on his foot dried up and the openings closed. Guillot returned to Robert's house, exchanging his crutches for a cane. After about four months, he was able to walk without any artificial aid, though he still limped slightly.

There are important differences and similarities between the story of Guillot the Cripple and that of Louis the deaf-mute. Unlike Robert Reboule, Gauchier extended most of his charitable generosity at the onset of his relationship with the future Louis. After a period of initial training, Gauchier received his "payment" from Louis in the form of labor. Robert Reboule, by contrast, supported Guillot during a period of disability that far exceeded the initial period of Guillot's healthy labor. Guillot may have been able to work, in some limited capacity, for part of the ten-year period when he was disabled, but the text makes it clear that by the end of that period he could not work at all.

90. Guillaume de St.-Pathus, *Les miracles*, 25.

Both employers understood their responsibility to include not only practical instruction, but also the kinds of personal and spiritual support and guidance that parents might be expected to provide. This responsibility helps to explain why Robert continued to provide for Guillot even when Guillot could no longer work for him. However, the provisions of the contracts from Montpellier and Orleans, and the Paris court decision that was mentioned earlier all suggest that Robert's generosity far exceeded most contractual expectations.

It may be significant that both Guillot and the future Louis were boys under the age of fifteen, and hence their masters were especially aware of their vulnerability. Amelot of Chaumont, a domestic servant in the home of a prominent bourgeois in St.-Denis named Jehan Augier, became ill at about the age of thirty; her master moved her to the Maison-Dieu of St.-Denis, where she died.[91] Similarly, when Agnes of Pontoise, also a domestic servant working in a bourgeois household, became blind, she had to resort to begging. Agnes was probably about thirty at the time.[92] But age alone does not explain the fate of these two servants. Orenge of Fontenay, a wool carder living in the home of Maurice the weaver in Paris, was in her thirties when she became too disabled to work. Maurice allowed her to continue to live in his home throughout the four years of her disability.[93] One significant difference between the care extended by Maurice the weaver and Robert Reboule and that extended by Jehan Augier and Agnes's employer may have been the status of the employer: Maurice and Robert were modest craftsman, while the other two were propertied bourgeois. Indeed, Jehan Augier was from a family that had served the king since the early thirteenth century.[94] Propertied individuals, as I have already argued, were less likely than modest artisans to provide sustained care for the disabled.

After completing their apprenticeships artisans generally entered the labor market as skilled *valet* or journeyman/journeywoman workers who might sell their labor by the day or the week. A few eventually set up their own workshops as master artisans within the gild, but they had to wait

91. Ibid., 12. If Jehan Augier acted at all like Mahaut, countesse of Artois, he paid something to the hospital for taking Amelot; Richard, *Une petite nièce*, 52.

92. Guillaume de St.-Pathus, *Les miracles*, 180. See chapter 1, note 43 on the difficulty of determining Agnes's age.

93. Ibid., 177.

94. Anne Terroine, *Un bourgeois Parisien du XIIIe siècle: Geoffroy de Saint-Laurent, 1245?-1290*, ed. Lucie Fossier (Paris, 1992), 35.

until they met the gild's requirements for master artisans. Many *valets*, as they were called, had the skills of master artisans but were never able to afford the cost of crossing the line separating skilled employees from independent master artisans.[95] Some gilds granted gild membership to *valet* workers, but the rights and obligations of the *valets* differed from those of the masters.

Gild membership had distinct advantages. For instance, a limited number of artisanal gilds expressed concern for older men or mature men who had to leave the labor force because of age or disability: the *Livre des métiers* shows that the tailors', glovemakers', roasters', and cobblers' gilds set aside the proceeds of fines for assistance to old or sick members.[96] Along similar lines, the goldsmiths built a hospice, in 1399, for sick and older members of the gild and for widows of gild members.[97] In 1319, moreover, the squirrel, or vair, curriers established a mutual aid society, which provided members with three sous per week during periods of illness. This was, however, a form of insurance rather than a form of charity: those who desired the benefits of the society paid ten sous as an entrance fee and one denier each week after that.[98] According to the *Livre des métiers*, the iron bucklemakers' and strapmakers' gilds also paid the entrance fees for orphaned or poor children of members.[99]

It is impossible to determine how often gilds were called upon to provide aid for sick and old members and for the poor and orphaned children of members, or indeed, how much revenue they had at their disposal to provide such aid. Drawing on account books from late fourteenth-century England, Ben McRee has argued that in practice gilds provided less aid than their statutes implied, and that the gilds promising such aid were the wealthier ones, whose members were the least likely to require such aid. Unlike McRee's gilds in late medieval England, however, the thirteenth-century Parisian gilds that provided charitable aid to members were not wealthy. Indeed, the average individual practicing these crafts was assessed for a tax that fell well below the average assessment. In 1292, when the overall average tax assessment was 14.6 sous, the average assessment for glove-

95. Geremek, *Salariat*, chap. 3; Epstein, *Wage Labor*, 115.

96. Lespinasse and Bonnardot, eds., *Le livre des métiers*, pp. 116, 146, 184, 195.

97. Jean Baptiste Michel Jaillot, *Recherches critiques, historiques et topographiques sur la ville de Paris depuis ses commencemens connus jusqu'a présent*, vol. 1, pt. 3 (Paris, 1775), p. 45.

98. Fagniez, *Etudes sur l'industrie*, 39, 290–91.

99. Lespinasse and Bonnardot, eds., *Le livre des métiers*, pp. 49, 189.

makers, strapmakers, cobblers, tailors, bucklemakers, and roasters was between 4.9 and 9.8 sous.[100]

Of course, the tax assessments of the wealthiest individuals in any tax list
distort the average. In 1292 less than 1 percent of the assessees were liable
for 18 percent of the total for that same population. Thus, it helps to look at
the percentage of individuals who were assessed to pay the lowest taxes.
When we look at the numbers in this way, we find that individuals in one of
these six crafts clustered at the very bottom rung of the tax assessments, and
that individuals in three of the crafts clustered in the bottom two rungs.

In the assessment of 1292, 16.5 percent of taxpaying units were assessed
at the lowest tax of twelve deniers or one sou. Among the six crafts providing charitable aid to members and children of members, that of the roasters
had a greater percentage of individuals paying the lowest tax: five of the
twenty roasters in the tax assessment, or 25 percent, were assessed for the
lowest tax.

When we move up to the next rung of the 1292 assessment, including all
of those who were assessed for either one or two sous, we find that three of
the six crafts had a higher than average percentage of individuals who were
assessed for the two lowest taxes. Thus, while 38.7 percent of the tax-paying
units were assessed for one or two sous in 1292, 55 percent of the roasters,
43 percent of the strapmakers, and 39 percent of the bucklemakers were assessed for one or two sous in the same year. The tailors came close to the
overall percentage, with 38.6 percent of those practicing the craft paying
one or two sous, and the glovemakers and cobblers clustered near the overall percentage, with 36.4 and 33 percent of those practicing the two crafts
being assessed for one or two sous. These six crafts, then, were far from
wealthy. Many of their members could have used the charitable assistance
that their gilds claimed to offer. However, it is impossible for us to determine how often such assistance was actually given. Moreover, migrants
would not have qualified for the assistance offered to the children of gild
members, and many of them, as I have already mentioned, never became
gild members at all.

Charity for disabled poor men and women came not only from family,
employers, and gild organizations, but also from neighbors and companions—modest individuals who realized that they, too, might someday find
themselves on the receiving end of charitable assistance. Gilbert of Sens, a
sixty-year-old suffering from a trembling ailment, frequently relied on his

100. Géraud, *Paris sous Philippe-le-Bel*. The averages were: glovemakers, 9.8 s.;
strapmakers, 7.3 s.; cobblers, 7.2 s.; tailors (tailleurs), 5.8 s; bucklemakers, 5.5 s;
roasters, 4.9 s. These are my own calculations.

neighbors and on the proprietors of his lodgings to help him hold his cup when he drank.[101] However, Gilbert had to provide for his own daily sustenance—both by begging at various churches, and by selling keys. Guillot of Caux, an eighteen-year-old whose legs were completely useless, also begged for his sustenance. However, he received lodgings from Herbert the Englishman, in the parish of St. Gervais, and Herbert's maidservant helped him dress, undress, and get in and out of bed each day.[102]

An important category of support for women, which will be discussed later on, was that of female companions. This does not seem to have been the case for men. None of the men in the *Miracles of Saint Louis* received such support. At first glance the tax assessments may appear to contradict this evidence, suggesting that men and women were almost equally inclined to be identified as companions. We find, for instance, that the Parisian tax assessment of 1292 lists thirty-eight pairs or clusters of men, and eight pairs or clusters of women, as companions. However, relative to their overall numbers in the tax assessment, women were slightly more likely than men to be identified as part of a pair or group of companions.[103] Moreover, the data suggest that many male companions were really business partners.[104] Female companions formed business alliances as well, but their relative

101. Guillaume de St.-Pathus, *Les miracles*, miracle 9.

102. Ibid., miracle 17.

103. The seventeen or eighteen women in the eight companionships of 1292 constituted between .78 percent or .83 percent of the total number of women (2,169) in that assessment; the eighty-five to ninety-one men in the thirty-eight clusters of male companions constituted between .70 and .75 percent of the total number of men (12,068) in that assessment; Géraud, *Paris sous Philippe-le-Bel*. Calculations are my own. For the total number of men and women I have employed the statistics of Caroline Bourlet for non-Lombard and non-Jewish assessees: "L'anthroponymie à Paris à la fin du XIIIe siècle d'après les rôles de la taille du règne de Philippe le Bel," in *Genèse médiévale de l'anthroponymie moderne*, ed. Monique Bourin and Pascal Chareille vol. 2-2 (Tours, 1992), 11.

104. Both the relatively high tax assessments of these men and their greater tendency to cluster into groups of more than two suggest that these "companions" were really business partners, and that their companionships were really "companies": nine of the thirty-eight male groups, or 23.7 percent, consisted of more than two individuals, and the average tax for individuals listed as male companions was between 22.5 and 24.1 sous, which was well above the average assessment of 14.6 sous in 1292. By contrast, only one of the eight groups of female companions (12.5 percent) consisted of more than two individuals, and the average tax assessment for each woman listed as a companion was between 5.1 and 5.4 sous, which was well below the average assessment.

poverty also suggests that they were far more likely to cling to each other for the sake of economic survival than for the sake of economic gain.

As we have seen, gendered expectations for lower-status men emphasized manual labor and self-sufficiency. Because of these expectations, disabled young men and boys were sometimes pushed out of their natal homes, much like able-bodied young men. Moreover, both propertied and nonelite individuals were more reluctant to help disabled boys and men than to help disabled girls and women from the same social strata. However, there were differences between elite and nonelite forms of support for disabled men. Propertied Parisians directed much of their charitable support toward institutions that helped able-bodied young men get a start in life. Their assistance for the disabled, by contrast, was limited primarily to almsgiving, and, occasionally, to financial assistance for dependent members, or former members, of their households. Nonelite individuals, by contrast, provided more sustained care—housing, daily assistance, and advice. Closer to the disabled poor, both in terms of daily contact and in terms of personal circumstances, modest artisans and the working poor, who realized that they too might someday find themselves in need of help, developed more empathy for the nonworking poor than did people of property.

CHAPTER FOUR
EVE'S CURSE

To the woman He said, "I will greatly increase your hardship and your pregnancies: in pain you shall bring forth children, and you shall be under the power of your husband, and he shall rule over you." And to Adam he said, "Because you have listened to the voice of your wife . . ."

—*Genesis 3:16–17 (translated from the Vulgate)*

E ve's punishments condemned her to pain in childbirth and to subordination to her husband, "who shall rule over you." Thus, medieval Christian biblical commentators assumed, women in general were defined by reproduction, by their relationship to men, and by their subordination to male authority.[1] The idea that the devil approached Eve rather than Adam supported clerical assumptions that women were less rational than men. On this account some clerics—such as the thirteenth-century Dominican Albertus Magnus—attributed them with a greater capacity for lust: "She seeks to be under what she does not have, because on account of the weakness of her reason she judges that what she does not have is better than what she does have. And therefore she seeks intercourse more frequently than does man."[2] Finally, the idea that Adam listened to Eve's voice lent support to clerical asser-

---

1. On wives' obedience to their husbands see Jacques de Vitry, "Sermo [primus] ad coniugatos," Paris, Bibliothèque Nationale de France, ms. lat. 3284, fol. 177v. Jacques told several *exempla* stories about disobedient and litigious wives. As a result of their quarrelsome and disobedient behavior, one wife had her tongue cut out, another drowned, and a third was pierced by a sharp nail: Thomas Frederick Crane, *The Exempla or Illustrative Stories for the Sermones Vulgares of Jacques de Vitry* (Reprint ed., New York, 1971), nos. CCXXI, CCXXII, CCXXVII, CCXXVIII, 92, 94–95. To a certain extent, Jacques tempered his stress on women's necessary obedience with a critical discussion of men who mistreated their wives: "Sermo [primus] ad coniugatos," fol. 177v.

2. Albertus Magnus, *Quaestiones super de animalibus* 5:4, ed. Ephrem Filthaut, *Alberti Magni Opera Omnia*, ed. Bernhard Geyer et al., vol. 12 (Cologne, 1955), 156;

tions that women exercised considerable influence—much of it negative—over men.

The story of Adam and Eve contributed to ancient and medieval gender paradigms. It is not surprising, therefore, that ancient and medieval male clerical authors had difficulty incorporating single women—those who were not "under the power" of a man—into their descriptions of the social world; in those places where they actually recognized the presence of single women, moreover, their perception that women were dangerous when not under male control often led them to treat such women harshly.[3] Along similar lines, because they associated women with the domestic realm—the only place where women could remain both safe and unthreatening—propertied and lettered men, both clerical and lay, had difficulty imagining women's work in the public sphere. These blind spots had important implications for women of lower status.

HIERARCHIES OF FEMININITIES

As the passage from Albertus Magnus indicates, clerical authors sometimes associated women with intellectual weakness and lust in such a way that their conceptualizations seemed to fall into a male/female binary that aligned men with mind and women with body. Nevertheless, female gendering, like male gendering, was complicated by other categories of difference. For our purposes, the most important of those differences was that of social status: in some contexts propertied women were associated with spiritual and intellectual aspects of the domestic and affective realms while lower status women were associated with bodily, sexual, and irrational aspects of those realms.

Hierarchical treatments of femininities were explicit in secular and ver-

---

trans. by Prudence Allen, *The Concept of Woman: The Aristotelian Revolution 750 B.C–A.D. 1250* (Montreal, 1985), 373.

3. On their tendency not to recognize the presence of single women see, for instance, the numerous discussions of Eve's creation from Adam's rib, which emphasized that women should thus neither dominate their husbands nor be their servants: Hugh of St. Victor, *Adnotationes Elucidatoriae in Pentateuchon*, chap. 7, PL 175:40; Humbert of Romans, *De eruditione religiosorum praedicatorum*, bk. 2, tract. 1, chap 94, "Ad omnes mulieres," ed. Marguerin de la Bigne, in *Maxima Bibliotheca veterum patrum et antiquorum scriptorum ecclesiasticorum*, vol. 25 (Lyon, 1677), 503–4; also in Carla Casagrande, ed., *Prediche alle donne del secolo XIII* (Milan, 1978), 43. See ibid., 6 n. 2, for other examples. See also R. Howard Bloch, *Medieval Misogyny and the Invention of Western Romantic Love* (Chicago, 1991), 24ff.

nacular literature about love. Andreas Capellanus and the poets who contributed to the genre of the French *pastourelle*, for instance, entertained
courtly audiences with the idea that the "game of love" differed as the social
status of the "players" changed, and they presented approving accounts of
aristocratic males who employed sexual force in their encounters with
lower-status women, whose "love" could be treated as a purely sexual, rather
than a spiritual and consensual matter.[4]

Less clear are the intersections of gender and social status in religious
discourse. The way in which women were gendered—the fact that they
were usually defined through a paradigm of reproductive rather than productive labor—inclined clerical authors to discuss propertied and lower-
status women together. In their *ad status* sermons, for instance, clerical authors usually categorized men according to their occupations or social
status, while categorizing women according to their sexual or married status: nuns and virgins (either consecrated virgins or young girls), widows,
and married women.[5] Thus, it is more difficult for us to determine the ways
in which social status complicated female gendering in pastoral and theo-

4. See especially Kathryn Gravdal, *Ravishing Maidens: Writing Rape in Medieval
French Literature and Law* (Philadelphia, 1991), chap. 3; and Paul Freedman, *Images of
the Medieval Peasant as Alien and Exemplary* (Stanford, Calif., 1999), chap. 7.
William D. Paden has recently argued that the figure of the shepherdess, as well
as her sexual encounters with aristocratic males, was the invention of the *pastourelle*
genre: "The Figure of the Shepherdess in the Medieval Pastourelle," *Medievalia et
humanistica* 25 (1998): 1–14. Clearly Paden is correct in pointing out that cross-cul-
turally the isolated task of watching sheep is usually assigned to men, largely, one assumes, because of the sexual and physical danger such isolation poses for women.
Nevertheless, there are examples of real-life medieval women who guarded sheep,
including one of the beneficiaries of Saint Louis's miracles, who, at the age of sixteen, "watched her sheep and those of her brothers in the fields"; Guillaume de St.-
Pathus, Confesseur de la reine Marguerite, *Les miracles de Saint Louis*, ed. Percival B.
Fay (Paris, 1931), 15. While the authors of the *pastourelles* probably stretched reality
by peopling the landscape with more shepherdesses than actually existed, the imagined sexual encounter between an aristocratic male and a lower-status woman, which
was facilitated by the woman's isolation, nevertheless worked to reinforce the idea
that whenever the circumstances provided an opportunity upper-status males could
take advantage of lower-status women.
5. Geneviève Hasenohr, "La vie quotidienne de la femme vue par l'église: L'enseignement des 'Journées chrétiennes' de la fin du moyen-âge," in *Frau und spätmittelalterlicher Alltag* (Vienna, 1986), 19–101; Carla Casagrande, "The Protected
Woman," trans. Clarissa Botsford, in *A History of Women in the West*, vol. 2, *Silences of
the Middle Ages*, ed. Christiane Klapisch-Zuber (Cambridge, Mass., 1992), 70–104.

logical literature than it is for us to determine such complications in male gendering.

Nevertheless, the sermon material of Humbert of Romans provides an important exception to this general rule, thereby revealing the intersections of social status with female gender stereotypes in clerical thought. In his manual of advice for preachers, Humbert classified women sometimes by social status, sometimes by profession, and sometimes by age. Thus, he offered preaching topics for those who might find themselves preaching to noblewomen, rich urban women, female servants, peasant women, prostitutes, girls, and a whole variety of professed religious women.[6]

If we divide Humbert's sermon literature for laywomen along lines of social status, what emerges is a clear pattern: he virtually ignored the issues of sexuality and sexual misbehavior in his discussions of propertied women, both noble and bourgeois, while in his discussions of lower-status women—servants, prostitutes, and peasants—he dwelt on these subjects, although not always exclusively. Moreover, his discussions of propertied women suggested that they were both capable of exercising and obliged to exercise their intellects within the domestic realm in order to enhance the spiritual and moral welfare of others. By contrast, he barely even hinted at the possibility that lower-status women might exercise a positive moral or spiritual influence on others.

Regarding rich urban women Humbert was most concerned with the ways in which many of them participated in the sins of their husbands by counseling them to practice usury, by failing to argue against the practice, or by employing the profits from it. He also discussed the ways in which many of these women neglected their charitable obligations and their own spiritual welfare, often abandoning themselves to the practical management of their households. He emphasized as well that many of them failed to care for the spiritual welfare of their children and husbands, when instead they should imitate Solomon's mother, who taught him many things that pertained to salvation, and Saint Cecilia, who converted her husband to Christianity. Regarding the children—but not the husbands—he indicated that rich urban women who failed to attend to their children's salvation did so because they loved them only carnally. Finally, he indicated that many such women did not care about what went on in their households, when, instead,

6. Humbert of Romans, *De eruditione*, bk. 2, tract. 1, chaps. 40–55, 96–100, in Bigne, *Maxima bibliotheca*, 25:475–84, 503–6, and Casagrande, *Prediche*, 43–56. Casagrande published all of Humbert's sermon material for laywomen, but she left out a number of his discussions of sermon materials for various categories of nuns.

they should follow the advice given to Sarah, the wife of Tobias (Tobit 10:13 in the Vulgate), who was told to honor her in-laws, love her husband, rule her family, and govern her household.[7]

The closest that Humbert came to discussing the sexuality of rich urban women was in his remarks on their love of display. Unlike Jacques de Vitry and Gilbert of Tournai, however, Humbert did not accuse them of inciting adultery through their use of excessive ornament.[8] In fact, in his entire chapter on women of this class, Humbert never even suggested that their sexuality was a major problem. Moreover, in emphasizing that many of these women failed to provide a positive spiritual and moral influence over the members of their households, he implied that they were indeed capable of exercising such influence, and that some of them actually succeeded at doing so.

Regarding noblewomen Humbert again avoided the question of illicit sexuality, although he did touch on their ability to lead their men astray.[9] As examples of evil women of the nobility, Humbert drew on the biblical stories of Jezebel, the wife of King Ahab, who introduced the Israelites to the worship of Baal, persecuted the prophet Elijah, and had Naboth unjustly stoned to death (1 Kings 16–21); Athalia, the mother of King Ahaziah, who avenged her son's death by destroying the royal house of Judah (2 Kings 11, 2 Chronicles 22:10); and Herodias, who hated John the Baptist because he had criticized Herod for marrying her, and used her daughter's allure to gain her husband's promise to kill the prophet (Mark 6:17—29).

Humbert's list of good noblewomen was considerably longer than his list of evil ones. Moreover, it included not only biblical women and postbiblical saints, but also the Virgin Mary herself. Humbert made it clear that noble-

7. Humbert of Romans, *De eruditione*, chap. 96, "Ad mulieres burgenses divites," in Bigne, *Maxima bibliotheca*, 25:504, and Casagrande, *Prediche*, 47–78. The Vulgate account of the advice of both parents to Sarah (Tobit 10:13) reads: "Monentes eam honorare soceros, diligere maritum, regere familiam, gubernare domum et se ipsum irreprehensibilem exibere." The New Revised Standard Version (Tobit 10:12) has only the father giving the following advice to Sarah: "My daughter, honor your father-in-law and your mother-in-law, since from now on they are as much your parents as those who gave your birth. Go in peace, daughter, and may I hear a good report about you as long as I live."

8. For a discussion of Jacques de Vitry's and Gilbert of Tournai's treatments of this theme, see D. D'Avray and M. Tausche, "Marriage Sermons in *ad status* Collections of the Central Middle Ages," *Archives d'histoire doctrinale et littéraire du moyen âge* 47 (1980): 71–119.

9. Humbert, *De eruditione*, chap. 95, "Ad mulieres nobiles," in Bigne, *Maxima bibliotheca*, 25:504, and Casagrande, *Prediche*, 44–45.

women of his own time could emulate such women, thus practicing personal virtue for themselves and providing a positive influence over others. Like Queen Esther, they could direct their hearts to hope in God rather than to external glory (Esther, Deuterocanonical Additions, 14: 16–19); like Saint Elizabeth, they could show their disdain for finery by secretly wearing a hair shirt under their sumptuous garments; like the wife of Pontius Pilate, they could attempt to prevent the evil deeds of their husbands (Matthew 27:19); and like Pharaoh's daughter, who rescued the baby Moses from the Nile, they could do pious works (Exodus 2:5–6).

In contrast to his discussions of propertied women, Humbert's discussions of lower-status women placed a heavy stress on sexual misconduct. Moreover, while virtually ignoring the possibility that such women might have a positive moral and spiritual influence, Humbert emphasized their negative influence in these areas.

Humbert divided his sermons to maidservants of the rich into three parts: sins of the flesh; sins with things (including theft and failure to carry out charitable deeds entrusted to them); and sins of the heart (such as anger, litigiousness, and pride).[10] The first and longest section was that on sins of the flesh. Humbert asserted that many maidservants committed such sins because of their close proximity to the men in the households in which they worked. Other maidservants, he claimed, provided the opportunity for sexual sins by procuring, while others participated in carnal sins by failing to put a halt to the illicit liaisons of others.

Regarding those maidservants who themselves engaged in illicit sex, Humbert made it clear that these women were responsible not only for their own misdeeds but also for the misdeeds and spiritual downfall of the men with whom they had sex: "Oh how many sons of families and youths who would have been ashamed to go to women in the streets lost their virginity with these [servant] women. And thus woe to such women, for they are guilty of all the subsequent sins that those young men later commit."[11] Along similar lines, Humbert argued that prostitutes threatened the spiritual well-being of men of every social, marital, and moral status. Through these "incendiaries of the world" the devil snared many men.[12]

Humbert began his chapter on peasant women with a long discussion of

10. Humbert, *De eruditione*, chap. 98, "Ad famulas divitum," in Bigne, *Maxima bibliotheca*, 25:505, and Casagrande, *Prediche*, 50–51.

11. Ibid.

12. Humbert, *De eruditione*, chap. 100, "Ad mulieres malas corpore, sive meretrices," in Bigne, *Maxima bibliotheca*, 25:506, and Casagrande, *Prediche*, 54–55.

their inclination to practice sorcery.[13] Although he conceded that these women turned to such practices because of their poverty and concern for the welfare of their families and flocks, his main explanation for their behavior was their weakness of mind: like Eve, who was so foolish that she believed the promises of the devil, they turned to sorcery because of their simplicity and credulity. From sorcery, Humbert turned to the theme of illicit sex, indicating that many peasant women received and consented to sexual propositions because there were no prostitutes in their villages. Finally, in a discussion of peasant women's failure to take care of the goods of their households, Humbert again stressed their simplicity and intellectual failings: they were so ignorant that they frequently gave their household goods to goliards and false beggars, thereby "taking away the things that are necessary to [their] husband[s] and children, while out of prudence [they] ought to provide those things which would sustain their households."[14] Humbert thus proclaimed prudent management of household goods as one of the highest goals for peasant women—a trait that he criticized as overly materialistic among rich urban women. As far as spiritual influence was concerned, all that he could imagine was the negative influence that peasant women might exert through their practice of sorcery.

Because the system of classification of women used by Jacques de Vitry and Gilbert of Tournai was largely that of the three sexually based orders of virgins, wives, and widows,[15] it is more difficult to find evidence of social distinction in their *ad status* sermons than in those of Humbert of Romans. Nevertheless, both of these authors composed several sermons for male and female servants, and Gilbert discussed the supervision of maidservants in one of his sermons for wives.[16]

---

13. Humbert, *De eruditione*, chap. 99, "Ad mulieres pauperes in villulis," in Bigne, *Maxima bibliotheca*, 25:505–506, and Casagrande, *Prediche*, 52–53.

14. Humbert, ibid., in Bigne, *Maxima bibliotheca*, 25:506, and Casagrande, *Prediche*, 53.

15. Actually, Jacques composed sermons to virgins, widows, and "married persons." See the list of his *ad status* sermons in Joannes Baptista Cardinalis Pitra, *Analecta novissima spicilegii Solesmensis, altera continuatio*, 2 vols. (Paris, 1885–1888; reprint ed., Farnborough, 1967), 2:346.

16. Jean Longère, ed. and introd., "Deux sermons de Jacques de Vitry (+1240) *Ad Servos et Ancillas*," in *La femme au moyen-âge*, ed. Michel Rouche and Jean Heuclin (Maubeuge, 1990), 261–96; Gilbert of Tournai, "Ad ancillas et servos [sermones] primus . . . secundus . . . tertius," Paris, Bibliothèque Nationale de France, ms. lat.

What emerges in Jacques's and Gilbert's discussions of servants and matrons is the clear sense that these two clerics held upper-status matrons accountable for the moral and spiritual welfare of both their children and the lower-status men and women who inhabited their domestic realms. Drawing, as Humbert did, on the passage of the Vulgate version of the book of Tobit concerning Tobias's wife Sarah, Gilbert wrote that the principal responsibility of a "wife" (by which he apparently meant a propertied wife, since he assumed that she had many servants) was to draw on her intellectual and moral capacities in order to govern her household: she should "educate" the children, "humble" male servants, "correct" female servants, and "guard" the house.[17] As we already noted in chapters 2 and 3, Gilbert and Jacques indicated that the matron's principal duties included guarding the chastity of both her male and her female servants, especially if men and women resided in the same house, ate together, and slept in proximity to one another.[18] Jacques, as we have noted, told a story praising a mistress who

15943, fols. 175r–180v; Gilbert of Tournai, "Ad coniugatas, Sermo tertius," in Casagrande, *Prediche*, 93–97.

Susan Mosher Stuard has argued, drawing primarily on Mediterranean sources, that the word *ancilla* refers to female slaves: "Ancillary Evidence for the Decline of Medieval Slavery," *Past and Present*, no. 149 (November 1995): 3–28. This was not exclusively the case for Jacques de Vitry and Gilbert of Tournai, whose word choice was determined by the language of the Vulgate (Ps. 122:2, Prov. 30:23), and who employed this word to distinguish female from male persons in serving/servile positions: see Jacques de Vitry, "Deux sermons," 271, 283; and Gilbert of Tournai, "Ad ancillas . . . sermo primus," fol. 175r–v. Jacques attempted to define various categories of "servus" in his second sermon "ad servos et ancillas." His definitions included slaves, serfs, and hired servants, suggesting that he considered all of these to be potential auditors for these sermons: "LXV, Sermo ad eosdem," in "Deux sermons," 285–86. I have found no evidence of domestic slaves in thirteenth- and early fourteenth-century Paris.

17. Gilbert of Tournai, "Ad coniugatas, Sermo tertius," 93–97. Like other moralists, Gilbert grounded his description of wifely duties in the biblical text concerning Sarah, the wife of Tobias: Tobit 10:12–13 in the Vulgate. He may have been influenced by Aristotelian writings as well; see Silvana Vecchio, "The Good Wife," trans. Clarissa Botsford, in *A History of Women in the West*, 2:105–35. On the influence of Aristotle on fourteenth-century discussions of wives, see Mireille Vincent-Cassy, "Quand les femmes deviennent paresseuses," in *Femmes, mariages, lignages, XIIᵉ–XIVᵉ siècles: Mélanges offerts à Georges Duby* (Brussels, 1992), 439.

18. Jacques de Vitry, "LXIV, Sermo ad servos et ancillas," in "Deux sermons," pp. 278, 279–80; Gilbert of Tournai, "Ad ancillas et servos sermo primus," fols. 175r–177r; Gilbert of Tournai, "Ad coniugatas sermo tercius," 94–95.

stayed home on Sunday and loaned her coat to a maidservant so that the servant could go to church and hear the sermon; and Gilbert praised a matron who whipped a maidservant and cast her into a river because she had spoken to her mistress about a man's sexual interest in the mistress.[19] Thus, while the organization of most of Jacques's and Gilbert's sermons obscures differences of social status, details within the sermons indicate that they held upper-status women responsible for the moral welfare and improvement of everyone—including the male and female servants—who fell under their governance within the domestic realm.

CLERICAL ATTITUDES TO SINGLE WOMEN

According to Genesis 2:18, in creating Eve, God declared and promised: "It is not good that man should be alone; let us make him a helper resembling him"(translated from the Vulgate). Unlike many of their Jewish counterparts, ancient and medieval male Christian commentators often interpreted this passage to mean that women were secondary, and thus hierarchically inferior, to men, that they were created for men, and that their principle raison d'être was procreation.[20] As Thomas Aquinas put it, in a passage borrowed neatly from Saint Augustine, "It was necessary for woman to be made, as the scripture says, as a helper to man not, indeed, as a helpmate in other works, as some say, since man can be more efficiently helped by another man in other works; but as a helper in the work of generation."[21] The account of the Fall in the third chapter of Genesis only served to underscore this reading: the normative clerical understanding of women

19. Jacques de Vitry, "Sermo [primus] ad coniugatos," fols. 177r–179v; Gilbert of Tournai, "Ad coniugatas sermo tercius," 95.

20. On Jewish readings of Genesis 1–3, which stressed marriage for both men and women and were less negative about women and sexuality, see Daniel Boyarin, *Carnal Israel: Reading Sex in Talmudic Culture* (Berkeley, Calif., 1993), 77–106. On alternative readings of Gen. 1–2, which sometimes stressed equality between Adam and Eve before the fall, see Philippe Buc, *L'ambiguïté du livre: Prince, pouvoir, et peuple dans les commentaires de la Bible au moyen âge* (Paris, 1994), chap. 1.

21. Thomas Aquinas, *Summa theologiae*, pt. 1, quest. 92, art. 1, response, ed. and trans. Blackfriars, vol. 13 (New York, 1963), 34; trans. Elizabeth Clark and Herbert Richardson, *Women and Religion: A Feminist Sourcebook of Christian Thought* (New York, 1977), 86. See Kari Elisabeth Børresen, *Subordination and Equivalence: The Nature and Role of Women in Augustine and Thomas Aquinas*, trans. Charles H. Talbot (Washington, D.C., 1981), 17–18, 157, for a discussion of Aquinas's reliance on Augustine.

was that they inhabited the social world through their relations with men, and they should always be under the authority of men. Women who never married did not fit this social vision.

It might have been otherwise. After all, in the ancient world Christianity had been unusual in providing women with a lasting alternative to marriage—the celibate life. A number of recent scholars have argued convincingly that many early Christian women celibates interpreted their sexual abstinence as a ticket to freedom from subordination to male authority. The male hierarchy, however, proclaimed that these women were wrong.[22] As Tertullian put it, "If the man is the head of the woman, of course [he is the head] of the virgin too, from whom comes the *woman* who has married."[23]

Ascetic women—both virgins and consecrated widows—were considered to be "married," for they were brides of Christ. Organized in the early church into orders of widows and virgins, and cloistered in the Middle Ages as nuns, these women were considered safe by male clerics both because they were subject to Christ's authority and because the church assumed the paternal role of protecting and controlling them.[24] However, uncloistered, semireligious women, like the Beguines who occupied two streets near the Franciscan convent on the Left Bank in Paris, were often viewed as a threat because they eluded clear lines of male authority.[25] Thus they ran into repeated opposition and condemnation from the church in the high Middle Ages. As the Moravian Bishop Bruno of Olomouc made clear in the report that he prepared for the Council of Lyon in 1274, clerics perceived uncloistered Beguines as "fleeing obedience both to priests and to husbands."[26]

22. Jo Ann Kay McNamara, *A New Song: Celibate Women in the First Three Christian Centuries*, Women and History, vol. 6/7 (New York, 1983), esp. 107ff.; Elizabeth Castelli, "Virginity and Its Meaning for Women's Sexuality in Early Christianity," *Journal of Feminist Studies in Religion* 2 (1986): 61–88; Dyan Elliott, *Spiritual Marriage: Sexual Abstinence in Medieval Wedlock* (Princeton, N.J., 1993), 25–50; Ross Shepard Kraemer, *Her Share of the Blessings: Women's Religions among Pagans, Jews, and Christians in the Greco-Roman World* (New York, 1992), 128–56, 191–98; Joyce Salisbury, *Church Fathers, Independent Virgins* (London, 1991).

23. Tertullian, "On the Veiling of Virgins," in *Fathers of the Third Century*, ed. A. Cleveland Coxe, Ante Nicene Fathers, vol. 4 (reprint ed., Grand Rapids, Mich., 1976), 31, cited by Bloch, *Medieval Misogyny*, 35.

24. On the paternal role of the church see Edith Pasztor, "I Papi del Duecento e Trecento di fronte alla vita religiosa femminile," in *Il movimento religioso femminile in Umbria nei secoli XIII–XIV*, ed. Roberto Rusconi (Citta di Castello, 1984), 29–67.

25. On the Beguines of the Left Bank, see below, pp. 144–45.

26. *Relatio de statu ecclesiae in regno Alemaniae (1273)*, ed. Jacob Schwalm, *Monumenta Germaniae Historica, Legum, Sectio IV*, vol. 3 (Hanover, 1904–6), 593; cited by

The perception that all women should be subordinated to male authority rendered single women both a threat to the social order and a logical contradiction. This perception also shaped Jacques de Vitry's and Gilbert of Tournai's classification of women by their sexual or marital status rather than their occupational or social status. Despite the fact that married women were considered inferior to virgins and widows because they did not practice chastity, marriage, in this system of classification, was the prism through which all women were viewed.

Humbert of Romans, Jacques de Vitry, and Gilbert of Tournai all moved outside of the marriage prism (but not the sexual prism) by composing sermons for servants. Humbert assumed that two of his three categories of poor women—servants and prostitutes—were single. In his discussion of these women, Humbert emphasized their sexuality even more than he did that of poor peasant women. Moreover, he emphasized not only the sexual transgressions of prostitutes and female servants but also the threat that those women posed to the social order: the married household and its progeny in the case of female servants, and the spiritual well-being of men of every social and moral status in the case of prostitutes.

Humbert considered only one category of single women—that of maid-servants—morally acceptable.[27] Like Jacques de Vitry and Gilbert of Tournai he found it possible to include single servant women within the acceptable gendered universe because they constituted a part of an extended household, and thus were subject, at least indirectly, to the authority of the household's male head. In other words, in his discussion of single women, Humbert did not stray very far from the Genesis paradigm, which emphasized women's sexual relations to men and the need to subordinate women to male authority.[28]

Since female servants stood outside of Jacques de Vitry's and Gilbert of Tournai's general system of classification for women, it would seem that these women constituted a special case that was almost an exception to the category "women" for these two authors. It also seems, in Gilbert's case, that only relatively prosperous wives—those with many servants—constituted his category "wives." In other words, the classification of women into

---

Jean-Claude Schmitt, *Mort d'une heresie: L'église et les clercs face aux béguines et béghards du Rhin supérieure du XIVe au XVe siècle* (Paris, 1978), 58.

27. The only other category of single women he discussed were prostitutes, about whom he said that those who persisted in their manner of living were "detestable"; *De eruditione*, bk. 2, tract. 1, chap. 100, in Bigne, *Maxima bibliotheca*, 25:506, and Casagrande, *Prediche*, 54.

28. See Casagrande, "The Protected Woman," for a similar argument.

three sexual categories begins to break down, for Jacques and Gilbert, when they discuss nonelite women.

Unlike Humbert of Romans, Jacques de Vitry and Gilbert of Tournai structured their sermons for servants in such a way that they appeared, at first, to give equal weight to the sexual dangers that both male and female servants posed to the households they served.[29] Nevertheless, observations in their sermons indicate that they did not consider male and female servants to be equal in the sexual dangers that they posed. All of the examples and *exempla* stories that Jacques drew on in order to illustrate his points about the sexual dangers of male and female servants involved women. Moreover, he associated such women with animals, and he did not hesitate to recommend the most brutal of punishments for them. For instance, in warning masters that they ought to give their male and female servants burdensome tasks so that they would not have the occasion for wandering and lusting, Jacques quoted Hosea 4:16: "Like a lusting cow she wandered."[30] He went on to explain that "cow" signified "a lascivious woman," who, "stimulated by diabolic frenzies follows bulls in order to satiate her desires."[31] Such women, he asserted, should be treated like a certain female cat who wandered through various houses looking for male cats until her master burned her beautiful tail and removed most of her beautiful hair. "In this way," Jacques concluded, "a ragged servant woman, vile and dejected, ought to be returned to the house."[32] Jacques also indicated that maidservants threatened the stability of the household in ways that menservants did not. Thus he wrote of the "intolerable evil" that occurred when maidservants supplanted their mistresses, stealing the affections of their masters and thus gaining control of the houses that they were supposed to serve. "Certain miserable men," he wrote, "are exceedingly infected with this crime," and

29. Humbert addressed sexuality extensively in his chapter on sermons for female servants, but he alluded only briefly, in his chapter on sermons for both male and female servants, to the "unclean sins" that could result from "evil familiarity" among comrades. Humbert seems to have been more concerned about thefts, quarrelsomeness, laziness, and fighting among male servants than he was about sexual sins—and in his reference to "unclean sins" he said nothing about the threat that such sins posed to the household in which the servants were working; *De eruditione*, bk. 2, tract. 1, chap. 76, "Ad familiam diuitum in ciuitatibus," in Bigne, *Maxima bibliotheca*, 25:493–94.

30. Jacques de Vitry, "LXIV, Sermo ad servos et ancillas," in "Deux sermons," 11a, p. 279.

31. Ibid.

32. Ibid., 11b, p. 279.

placed their maids before their wives even though their wives were more beautiful.[33]

Unlike Jacques de Vitry, Gilbert of Tournai did not draw on *exempla* stories to elaborate his discussions of the need to control male and female servants. Nevertheless, Gilbert did write about "vile" women servants who supplanted their mistresses by entering the beds of their masters.[34] Moreover, he claimed that maidservants posed a special threat to their households in another way, since, through their vain words about the attentions of certain men, they were capable of inciting lust in their mistresses or in their mistresses' daughters. Despite minor differences, then, Humbert of Romans, Jacques de Vitry, and Gilbert of Tournai shared the perspective that because of their sexuality female servants—the only single women whom they deigned to include in their constructions of the social universe—threatened the households that they served in ways that male servants did not.

LETTERED MEN AND WOMEN'S WORK

Because they tended to define women—and especially lower-status women—through their sexuality, and because they believed that all women should be subordinated to men, Parisian clerics tended to ignore the existence of a large number of working single women in the cities, who were neither household servants nor prostitutes. In addition to this blind spot, medieval clerical authors often failed to recognize the importance of women's productive labor for the marketplace, especially when the women in question were married. We see this, again, in the way in which Gilbert of Tournai and Jacques de Vitry classified women in their *ad status* sermons. Indeed, we even see it in Humbert of Roman's system of classification: as Carla Casagrande has pointed out, his "noble," "bourgeois," and "peasant" women were really wives of noble, bourgeois, and peasant men. Moreover the only legitimate working women whom he discussed were servants—single women whose work and residence were encompassed within patriarchal households.[35]

As we saw earlier, the narrowly focused association of men alone with

33. Jacques de Vitry, "LXV, Sermo ad eosdem," in "Deux sermons," 294.

34. Gilbert of Tournai, "Ad ancillas et servos sermo primus," fol. 175v.

35. Casagrande, "The Protected Woman." Women's "work" is mentioned in one of Gilbert of Tournai's sermons to married women, but he means by that the wife's role in the domestic sphere; "Ad coniugatas, Sermo tercius," in Casagrande, *Prediche*, 96. Casagrande mentions a number of moralists who advocated domestic work for women. However, with the exception of the secular author Philippe de Novarre, they postdated the thirteenth century. Mireille Vincent-Cassy has argued that in the

productive labor and of women with reproductive labor even shaped the way in which information about men and women was recorded in both secular and ecclesiastical records.[36] We see this pattern in the surviving record of the inquest into the miracles of Saint Louis. At the beginning of each interview, the panel of clerics who conducted the inquest apparently asked each witness a series of questions that established the witness's identity. All of the twenty-one witnesses whose testimonies survive were asked to state their names, where they were born, where they currently lived, how long they had lived there, and how old they were. Only when the witness was a woman, however, did the scribes record the identity of the witness's spouse: as an aspect of the reproductive sphere, marital status was essential to identifying a woman but not a man. Work, by contrast, was an aspect of the productive, or masculine sphere, and thus more central to men's identities: as part of the initial identifying information the scribes recorded the occupations of nine of the fourteen male witnesses whose testimonies survive.[37] By contrast, in the initial sections for the seven female witnesses whose testimonies survive, the scribes indicated neither whether the women worked nor in what capacity.[38] In a number of cases, involving both males and females, we learn later in the interview what the witness did for a living, but not because the interviewers asked for that information.

In his summaries of the material from the original inquest, Guillaume de St.-Pathus went even further than the inquisitors and scribes, filtering out information that the scribes at the inquest had recorded concerning women's work. Luce of Rémilly, a woman who was believed to have been cured of blindness at Louis's tomb, is a case in point. The surviving fragment of the original inquest includes the testimony of eight witnesses to Luce's cure. Four of those witnesses cited the facts that Luce now peddled

---

fourteenth and fifteenth centuries moralists became preoccupied with the idea that elite women were especially prone to the sin of idleness. Prescriptions for manual labor were intended to ward off idleness, and its consequence, adultery; "Quand les femmes deviennent paresseuses."

36. See above, p. 40.

37. The men whose work is named in the initial part of the redaction of the interview are 5–1, 5–3, 5–4, 5–5, 5–6, 5–7, 41–1, 41–2, 51–5. The others are 5–2, 41–3, 51–3, 51–6, 51–8: H.-François Delaborde, ed., "Fragments de l'enquête faite à Saint-Denis en 1282 en vue de la canonisation de Saint Louis," *Mémoires de la Société de l'Histoire de Paris et de l'Ile-de- France* 23 (1896): 19, 21, 24, 27, 29, 31, 33, 39, 42, 44, 59, 62, 64, 69. I am counting "literatus" (5–1) as a professional identification.

38. Ibid., 41–4, 41–5, 41–6, 51–1 (the initial part of the interview is missing), 51–2, 51–4, 51–7; pp. 46, 50, 52, 54, 56, 61, 67.

petty merchandise and victuals and that she could discern one coin from another as evidence that she had been completely cured of her blindness. Guillaume, by contrast, only mentioned that Luce could now identify coins.[39]

We do not know the degree to which Guillaume filtered out the evidence about women's work in most of his other sixty-four narratives. Nevertheless, the statistics are striking: at various places in Guillaume's narrative we learn what over one-half (thirteen out of twenty-four) of the married men did for a living. By contrast, we learn nothing about the work of twenty-three of the twenty-four married women—neither if they worked nor in what capacity. In the case of the twenty-fourth woman, we learn that she was a spinner because she made a vow that if her daughter was cured by Saint Louis she would stop spinning on Saturdays unless she was compelled to do so by extreme poverty.[40] We learn more about the occupations of single people, both male and female, but again the information is biased in favor of the men: Guillaume tells us what ten of the thirteen single laymen did for a living, and what seven of the thirteen single laywomen did.[41]

Guillaume's narratives are interesting not only for what they reveal concerning clerical authors' blindness to married women's necessary labor, but also for what they have to say about women's penitential labor—work that they performed in order to cancel the debt that they owed to God for sins that they had committed. This paradox underlies Guillaume's narrative concerning a lower-status Parisian woman named Jehanne of Serris. Jehanne's physical incapacity compelled her both to beg—apparently because she could not work—and to work, because she wanted to be cured. Because Guillaume's specific language about dependency, work, and begging is im-

39. Ibid., 58, 62, 67, 70; Guillaume de St.-Pathus, *Les miracles*, 158.

40. Guillaume de St.-Pathus, *Les miracles*. Married men whose work is identified: miracles 3, 6, 10, 25, 28, 31, 33, 36, 42, 46, 48, 49, 64. Married men whose work is not identified: miracles 1, 11, 16, 19, 22, 23, 41, 51, 52, 53, 65. Wife who spun: miracle 41. I am counting only the beneficiaries of the miracles, their parents, or their spouses. To determine Guillaume's gender bias, I have used all sixty-five miracle narratives for this statistic, and not just the stories that deal with Paris and St.-Denis.

41. Ibid. Single men whose work is identified: miracles 7, 8, 9, 13, 14, 15, 20, 24, 45, 63. Single men whose work is not identified: miracles 17, 18, 40. The marital status of the men in miracles 60 and 61 is not clear. The work of both is identified. Single women whose work is identified: miracles 2, 4 (this woman later married; we only know what she did before marriage), 39, 44, 55, 58, 59. Single women whose work is not identified: miracles 5, 32, 35, 37, 43, 57. It is unclear if the mother in miracle 54 is married, widowed, or single, so I have not counted her. Her work is not identified. I am counting only the beneficiaries of the miracles and their parents.

FIGURE 6. Jehanne of Serris

On the left nuns at the Hôtel Dieu of Paris help Jehanne walk to the altar of Saint Leonard in the Hôtel Dieu. In the center, she walks on crutches. On the right, she kneels before Saint Louis's tomb, which is represented, this time, as a bare altar or tomb with votive offerings hanging above. Those votive offerings include crutches; the artist may have intended to imply that they had belonged to Jehanne. Guillaume de Saint-Pathus, *Les miracles de Saint Louis*, miracle 42. Bibliothèque Nationale de France, ms. fr. 5716, p. 543. Photo courtesy Bibliothèque Nationale de France, Paris.

portant to our analysis, his account of this miracle follows almost in its entirety:

> In the year of Our Lord 1276, in the winter, a great malady took Jehanne of Serris [a village in the diocese of Paris from which Jehanne had emigrated to Paris], the wife of Jehan the Carpenter. . . . This malady seized her in such a way that, whereas before she had been healthy and robust in all her limbs, now she could not walk, stand, or use her feet and legs. It took her during the night, between the feast of the Purification [February 2] and the beginning of Lent. She went to bed healthy and robust on a Tuesday evening . . . and when she awoke she found herself so weak and ill in her thighs, legs, and feet that she could not use those members. . . . She was like that in her house for a month. . . .
>
> And since she was thus afflicted in her house, and she was poor and had no one to help her, and since her husband did not want to do that which was necessary for her, she was carried to the Hôtel Dieu of Paris, where she lay . . .

paralyzed and sick, until just after the feast of Saints Peter and Paul [June 29]. And afterwards the sisters of the Hôtel Dieu decided to make crutches for her. . . . and when she was taken out of her bed and the sisters assisted her, she went with great effort to the altar of Saint Leonard which is in that hospital [see figure 6]. . . . And when she went on crutches she placed her right foot firmly on the ground, but she could not control the left foot at all, and so she dragged it behind her.

And as soon as she was able to move about she wanted to go home to her husband and children . . . so she started to return to her house on crutches but she could not make it, and so her husband carried her all the way. . . . And after that it happened that her husband did not want to find that which was necessary for her, and so with great difficulty she went on crutches to the church of St.-Merry in Paris to seek alms.

And when Jehanne heard that many miracles were occurring at the tomb of Saint Louis and that sick people were cured there, she . . . had hope that she would be cured there by the merits of the blessed Saint Louis. And since she wanted to live by her own means when she went to the tomb, she spun some yarn until she gained three sous, which she carried with her. And on a Sunday morning she took the road to St.-Denis [a distance of about five miles] on her crutches and one of her daughters accompanied her, barefoot and in a woolen chemise. She went with great difficulty, and vespers were already ringing when she arrived. She was at the tomb each day for four days, then she was cured, and she offered a candle as long as she was tall.

. . . And afterwards she limped a little . . . but she was healthy and robust . . . and she took care of her needs just like any other healthy woman.[42]

Four passages in this narrative shed light on cultural attitudes towards women's work: Guillaume's apparent disapproval of Jehanne's husband for putting her in the public hospital; his blaming the husband for the fact that Jehanne has to beg; Jehanne's decision to pay for her pilgrimage not with the money that she gains by begging but with money that she earns with her own hands, by spinning; and Guillaume's statement that after her cure Jehanne "took care of her needs just like any other healthy woman."

These moments in Jehanne's story are illustrative of two largely unrelated discourses that thirteenth-century clerics developed about the role of manual labor in a woman's life. On the one hand clerics tended to associate men alone with productive labor and women alone with reproductive labor, and thus they tended to ignore the fact that many married women worked, assuming instead that labor and supporting the family were part of the masculine sphere. On the other hand, in discussing women's penitential behavior, clerics impressed upon women the idea that they should engage in

42. Ibid., miracle 42, pp. 131–34.

manual labor largely because begging was a tainted activity, especially if the person who begged was both involuntarily poor and a woman.

In the story about Jehanne of Serris, Guillaume's role in shaping the narrative and that of the panel of clerics upon whose inquest he relied are most evident in the silences about and language for necessary productive labor. While Guillaume identifies Jehanne's husband as a carpenter, he never tells us whether or not Jehanne worked before she became ill; and concerning the period after her recovery he reduces her activities, whatever they were, to "she took care of her needs [besoigne] just like any other healthy woman." Elsewhere in the miracles he uses a similar expression as a euphemism for necessary labor.[43] The fact that Jehanne begged once she returned to her household, despite the pain that she endured in order to reach her parish church, suggests that her household could not survive on the income-producing work of her husband alone. It seems that Jehanne's begging was a necessary "labor," one that contributed to the survival of the household, and it is thus reasonable to assume that before and after her illness Jehanne contributed to the survival of the household by generating income in some other way. In a household that constituted a single occupational unit of production, in which a husband and wife worked together at a single craft, Jehanne's economic contribution to her family's survival would have been valued but not easily measured. It is certainly possible that a husband and wife would have worked together in the carpentry craft; however, statistics from the Parisian tax assessments indicate that women were significantly underrepresented in this craft.[44] It seems more likely that Jehanne's begging compensated for the loss of income that she gained independently, perhaps by laboring in the home (spinning, carding, processing victuals), perhaps by hiring herself out, for instance, as a laundress.[45]

43. Ibid., miracle 23. Guillaume states that the mother and father of a three-year-old boy named Jehennet, who lived in the parish of St.-Jean-en-Grève in Paris, left the boy for several days in St.-Denis under the care of Ermengart of Senlis, and returned to their home "pour leur autres besoignes [for their other necessities/work]."

44. Janice Archer, "Working Women in Thirteenth-Century Paris" (Ph.D. diss., University of Arizona, 1995), 211–12, 108–10. Women made up 13.8 percent of the total number of taxpayers in the 1297–1300 tax rolls, but only 3.1 percent of the carpenters.

45. For an excellent discussion of historians' tendency to exaggerate the degree to which the members of medieval households were engaged in only one occupation, see Heather Swanson, "The Illusion of Economic Structure: Craft Guilds in Late Medieval English Towns," *Past and Present*, no. 121 (1988): 29–48. For an excellent discussion of women's makeshift economic activities as essential to household sur-

Guillaume also implied that Jehanne's difficulties, once she became ill, were in part the result of her husband's refusal to live up to his role as provider. Thus, Guillaume states that Jehanne was taken to the Hôtel Dieu of Paris "since . . . she was poor and had no one to help her, and her husband did not *want* to do that which was necessary for her"; and again, after she had returned from the hospital to her home, she started begging at her parish church because "her husband did not *want* to find that which was necessary for her."[46] But was Jehan the carpenter really as negligent as Guillaume suggested? Certainly, he was attentive enough to carry his wife home from the hospital, and it was probably he who carried her there in the first place. As a laborer whose salary may not have been sufficient to support a family, Jehan would have been doing the best he could by placing his wife in the hospital where she was at least assured of receiving daily meals. For similar reasons, concern for his family's welfare may have compelled Jehan to allow, or to encourage, his wife to beg, despite whatever he may have felt about the humiliation and pain that she went through in order to do this.

In these ways, Guillaume's representations—and possible misrepresentations—of the earning capacities and responsibilities of Jehanne and her husband, were clearly influenced by the association of men alone with necessary productive labor.

On first consideration, Guillaume's discussion of Jehanne's penitential labors seems implausible. Jehanne, who had been unable to walk a few blocks from the Hôtel Dieu of Paris to her home in the parish of St.-Merry, suddenly makes a pilgrimage on crutches to the town of St.-Denis, a trip of about five miles. Moreover, after begging for her livelihood she decides to earn some travel money by spinning yarn. However, Jehanne apparently viewed both her journey to the tomb of Saint Louis and the work with her own hands as penitential acts: acts of punishment or atonement for sins that she had committed.[47] While Guillaume creates confusion concerning who

vival, see Olwen Hufton, "Women and the Family Economy in Eighteenth-Century France," *French Historical Studies* 9 (1975): 1–22. The fragments of the Saint Louis inquest provide examples of wives living in Paris and St.-Denis who worked selling petty merchandise, spinning, and doing laundry; Delaborde, "Fragments de l'enquête," 49, 52, 58, 62, 66, 70.

46. "Et com ele . . . fust povre ne n'eust qui li aidast et son mari ne li vosist amenistrer ce qui li failloit," "son mari ne li voloit pas trouver ce que il li couvenoit," Guillaume de St.-Pathus, *Les miracles*, 131, 132.

47. On walking as "the fundamental and primordial form of penance," see Raymonde Foreville, "Les 'Miracula S. Thomae Cantuariensis,' " in *Assistance et assisté jusqu'a 1610, Actes du 97ᵉ Congrès National des Sociétés Savantes* (Paris, 1979), 452; cit-

actually walked barefooted—Jehanne, her daughter, or both—the end result would have been the same, since Jehanne's daughter would have suffered vicariously for Jehanne. By adding to her suffering with manual labor and by walking barefoot—whether in person or having her daughter do so—Jehanne apparently hoped to remove the stain of her sins and to pay off the debt that she owed to God, whether or not she had already gained God's forgiveness by confessing her sins.

It is likely that Jehanne was strongly motivated to perform these penitential acts (apparently, in the case of the pilgrimage, with much assistance from her daughter) because thirteenth-century churchmen sometimes argued that disabilities were signs of God's punishment for the sinful nature of humankind. Moreover, in addition to viewing her manual labor as an act of penance, Jehanne probably believed that God was more likely to deliver her from her suffering if she financed her trip to St.-Denis with the work of her own hands rather than by begging. At least one other pilgrim to Louis's tomb, the mother of a crippled girl, believed that "God would be more favorable to them" if they lived by their own labor while they waited at Louis IX's tomb for a cure, and thus she did not want alms to be given to her daughter.[48]

But why would Jehanne believe this? After all, she clearly fit the thirteenth-century category of the deserving poor: those who sought alms because they were incapable of supporting themselves by working.[49] Moreover, as the spirituality of the mendicant orders made clear, begging could also be considered penitential behavior. One problem that Jehanne faced was that there was a big difference between voluntary and involuntary begging: many involuntary beggars were held in suspicion, and that suspicion tended to rub off on honest beggars such as Jehanne. A second problem was that of gender: clerics did not want women to share in the activity of voluntary—or penitential—begging.

As we have already seen, the works of thirteenth-century moral theologians and hagiographers frequently reveal a harsh and judgmental attitude towards involuntary beggars, even going so far as to suggest that some disabled individuals faked their poverty in order to gain income by begging;

---

ing E.-R. Labande, "Eléments d'une enquête sur les conditions de déplacement du pèlerin aux Xᵉ et XIᵉ siècles," in *Pellegrinaggi e culto dei santi in Europa fino alla prima crociata*, Convegni del Centro di studi sulla spiritualità medievale 5 (Todi, 1963), 95–111.

48. Delaborde, "Fragments de l'enquête," 49.

49. See Brian Tierney, "The Decretists and the 'Deserving Poor,' " *Comparative Studies in Society and History* 1 (1958–59): 360–73.

other beggars, they indicated, faked their disabilities and illnesses in order to enhance their incomes.[50] The concern with faked disabilities and illnesses shows up in the sources for the Saint Louis miracles: the clerics who held the inquest asked the witnesses who had known a person thought to have been cured by Saint Louis if that person could have faked his or her condition. In the surviving fragment of the inquest, all of the witnesses who were asked that question answered no. Moreover, three of the witnesses who had known Luce of Rémilly, the blind woman, pointed to the fact that she had never begged while she was blind as proof that she had not faked her condition.[51] The underlying assumption, here, was that the only rationale for faking a disability was to gain more alms as a beggar. Even people who did not belong to the elite, then, perceived that some dishonest beggars did this.

But what of honest beggars such as Jehanne of Serris? We learn from the Saint Louis sources that a number of working poor people went out of their way to care for poor men and women who had to beg because of their disabilities. Ace the smith, for instance, gave shelter to Amelot of Chambly, whose body was bent in two with what seems to have been spinal tuberculosis. On days when the ground was too muddy for Amelot to go out begging, Ace provided food for Amelot as well.[52]

The Saint Louis sources suggest that artisans and the laboring poor were far more likely to sympathize with beggars than were their more elite clerical contemporaries, for whom even honest and truly disabled beggars were objects of suspicion. Passages in the works of Thomas of Chobham are illustrative of this greater distrust on the part of clerics. Chobham maintained that many of those who truly needed to beg were nevertheless guilty of the sin of envy, and that others may have started out needing to beg, but they then hoarded the alms that they collected, committing the sin of avarice.[53] It was the widespread belief, moreover, that poverty and illness were the consequences of sin. Thus, most hospitals—including the Hôtel Dieu of Paris—gave communion to entering inmates

50. Peter the Chanter, "Verbum abbreviatum," *PL* 205:152–53; Thomas of Chobham, *Summa confessorum*, art. 5, dist. 4, quest. 6, ed. F. Broomfield, Analecta Mediaevalia Namurcensia 25 (Louvain, 1968), 297; Thomas of Chobham, *Summa de arte praedicandi*, chap. 3, lines 1050–53, ed. Franco Morenzoni, Corpus christianorum, continuatio mediaevalis 82 (Turnhout, 1988), 88.

51. Delaborde, "Fragments de l'enquête," 57, paragraph 239; 62, paragraph 261; 66, paragraph 281.

52. Ibid., 31, 32, paragraphs 100, 103.

53. Thomas of Chobham, *Summa de arte praedicandi*, chap. 3, lines 1053–57, p. 88.

and provided priests to hear their confessions. Similarly, many of the pilgrims to Saint Louis's tomb made their confessions before setting out on their journeys.[54]

The stigma of begging was even greater when the beggar was a woman, for it exposed her to sexual danger and called her sexual modesty into question. Thus, while some clerics lauded and others criticized men's voluntary begging—begging for penitential purposes—they consistently argued that women should not beg in this way.[55] Saint Elizabeth of Hungary wanted to live by begging, but her confessor, Conrad of Marburg, forbade it. She took up spinning—the quintessential penitential labor for women—instead.[56] Margaret of Ypres begged until her advisors convinced her not to.[57] Clare of Assisi wanted to imitate the mendicant poverty of Saint Francis, but she was compelled to live out her life of poverty as a cloistered nun rather than begging in the streets. She and her fellow nuns at the convent of San Damiano

54. Miri Rubin, *Charity and Community in Medieval Cambridge* (Cambridge, 1987), 148–51. Confession is explicitly linked to the pilgrimage in miracles 5, 7, 11, 20, 28, 39, 43, 45, 48, 51, 58; Delaborde, "Fragments de l'enquête," 32; Guillaume de St.-Pathus, *Les miracles*, 26, 35 (pilgrim confesses while staying in St.- Denis), 69, 87, 123, 135, 138–39, 145, 156, 178.

55. On the controversy surrounding voluntary male mendicancy see Ernest McDonnell, *The Beguines and Beghards in Medieval Culture, with Special Emphasis on the Belgian Scene* (New Brunswick, N.J., 1954), 456–73. On male prohibitions against and critiques of female mendicancy see ibid., pp. 146, 463; Schmitt, *Mort d'une hérésie*, 56–59; Brenda Bolton, " 'Vitae Matrum': A Further Aspect of the Frauenfrage," in *Medieval Women*, ed. Derek Baker (Oxford, 1978), 262; Jo Ann Kay McNamara, *Sisters in Arms: Catholic Nuns through Two Millennia* (Cambridge, Mass., 1996), 250–51; Amy Hollywood, *The Soul as Virgin Wife: Mechthild of Magdeburg, Marguerite Porete, and Meister Eckhart* (Notre Dame, Ind., 1995), 42–44. William of St.-Amour's critique of female religious begging focused not on the issue of female modesty, but on the fact that young women and men who were able-bodied should practice manual labor rather than begging; César Egasse du Boulay, *Historia universitatis Parisiensis*, 5 vols. (Paris, 1665–73; reprint: Frankfort-am-Main, 1966), 3:319.

56. Letter of Conrad of Marburg, ed. Albert Huyskens, *Quellenstudien zur Geschichte der hl. Elizabeth Langräfin von Thüringen* (Marburg, 1908), 158; testimony of Elizabeth's servant Irmengardis, ibid., 130. On spinning as women's quintessential penitential activity see Frances M. Biscoglio, " 'Unspun' Heroes: Iconography of the Spinning Woman in the Middle Ages," *The Journal of Medieval and Renaissance Studies* 25 (1995): 163–76.

57. Thomas de Cantimpré, "Vita Margaretae de Ypris," chap. 22, ed. G. Meerseman in "Les Frères Prêcheurs et le mouvement dévot en Flandres au XIIIe siècle," *Archivum Fratrum Praedicatorum* 18 (1948): 117; trans. Margot H. King, *The Life of Margaret of Ypres* (Toronto, 1990), 57.

in Assisi supported themselves by working—Clare, by spinning and needle-work.[58]

According to Jacques de Vitry, manual labor was central to the peniten-tial spirituality of the Beguine Mary of Oignies, with whom Jacques had a close personal relationship. Indeed, in the preface to his *Life of Mary of Oignies*, Jacques highlighted manual labor—earning "a sparse meal with their hands"—as a central aspect of the voluntary poverty of the Beguine movement in the Low Countries.[59] In his description of early Franciscans in Italy, Jacques wrote of the differing activities of the men and women: the men "go into the cities and villages during the day, so that they convert oth-ers, giving themselves to active work"; the women, by contrast, "live near the cities in various hospices. They accept nothing, but live from the work of their hands."[60]

Jacques's association of manual labor with penitential behavior was natu-ral enough: it was, after all, the punishment that God had imposed on Adam. Indeed, manual labor played a central role in the penitential life of Benedictine monks and the mendicant orders, and the Genesis text describ-ing Adam's punishment was part of the standard liturgy for public penance, which was performed at the beginning of Lent.[61] It is striking, however, that clerics avoided discussing manual labor as a necessary daily activity for women who were members of the involuntarily laboring poor, but then turned around and told women that they should engage in penitential labor. Indeed, clerics like Jacques de Vitry seem to have associated penitential labor especially with women, since they gave men freer rein to engage in ei-ther penitential begging or penitential labor. Robert Grosseteste, a thir-teenth-century bishop of Lincoln who was closely associated with the Fran-

58. John Moorman, *A History of the Franciscan Order from Its Origins to the Year 1517* (Oxford, 1968), 32–39, 207.

59. Jacques de Vitry, *Vita Mariae Oigniacensis*, prologue, in *Acta Sanctorum quotquot tota orbe coluntur*, ed. Joannus Bollandus, 3d ed. (Paris, 1863–), Iunius, 5:547; trans. Margot H. King, *The Life of Marie d'Oignies* (Saskatoon, 1986), 3; on Mary's manual labor, chap. 4, Iunius 5:554, trans. King, 39.

60. R. B. C. Huygens, ed., *Lettres de Jacques de Vitry*, vol. 1 (Leiden, 1960), letter 1, pp. 75–76; trans. Regis J. Armstrong, *Clare of Assisi: Early Documents* (New York, 1988), 246.

61. The Rule of Saint Benedict, chap. 48, in *RB 1980: The Rule of St. Benedict in Latin and English with Notes and Thematic Index*, ed. Timothy Fry, abridged edition (Collegeville, Minn., 1981), 96; Burchard of Worms, *Liber decretorum*, bk. 19, chap. 26, *PL* 140:984; Reimbaldus Leodiensis, *Stromata, seu de uoto reddendo et de paeniten-tia non iteranda*, ed. C. De Clercq, in *Reimbaldi Leodiensis Opera Omnia*, Corpus chris-tianorum, Continuatio mediaevalis 4 (Turnhout, 1966), 110.

ciscans, even drew on the example of female Beguines in order to promote manual labor as a form of voluntary poverty that was superior to begging, even for men.[62]

Jacques de Vitry was so committed to promoting manual labor for religious women that he devoted almost half of a sermon for Benedictine nuns to the topic. In addition to arguing that manual labor was a good aid in fighting temptations and sloth, that it was an excellent instrument of penance, and that it gave one the means to help the poor, Jacques stressed that it was especially important for religious women because it made them financially independent. Nuns who shunned manual labor, he argued, sometimes left their cloisters to seek gifts from relatives, and thus they encountered "many enemies of chastity and corruptors of modesty."[63] As was the case with Robert Grosseteste, Jacques de Vitry seems to have associated penitential manual labor especially with women: he wrote nothing concerning manual labor in his four model sermons for Benedictine and Cistercian monks.[64]

Like Jacques de Vitry, the foundation charter of the *béguinage* of Saint Elizabeth of Gand also stressed manual labor as a central aspect of the Beguines' way of life, and it represented manual labor as a way of protecting

62. Thomas of Eccleston, *Tractatus de adventu Fratrum Minorum in Angliam*, ed. A. G. Little (Manchester, 1951), 99.

63. Jacques de Vitry, "Sermo XXVII, ad moniales nigras," ed. Jean Longère, "Quatre sermons *ad religiosas* de Jacques de Vitry," in *Les religieuses en France au XIIIᵉ siècle*, ed. Michel Parisse (Nancy, 1985), 251; on all the advantages of manual labor, see 249–52. Humbert of Romans made similar comments about the dangers encountered by nuns who left the cloister in order to seek necessities: "they run about to and fro through villages and camps, a practice which is truly unbecoming and dangerous to women." He recommended that nunneries be forbidden to accept new members, unless they were financially stable enough to ensure that their members would not have to resort to mendicancy outside of the cloister: *Opusculum tripartium*, pt. 3, chap. 3, in Ortuin Gratius, *Fasciculus rerum expetendarum et fugiendarum, 2: Appendix ad . . .* (London, 1690), 224; cited and trans. by Edward Tracy Brett, *Humbert of Romans: His Life and Views of Thirteenth-Century Society* (Toronto, 1984), 193. On late twelfth-century precedents for this association of "want and wickedness" in clerics' attitudes to nuns, see Bruce Venarde, *Women's Monasticism and Medieval Society: Nunneries in France and England, 890–1215* (Ithaca, 1997), 168.

64. "Sermo [primus] ad monachos nigros," "Sermo [secundus] ad monachos nigros," "Sermo [primus] ad monachos albos seu grisios," "Sermo [secundus] ad monachos albos seu grisios," Paris, Bibliothèque Nationale de France, ms. lat. 3284, fols. 56v–67v.

religious women's chastity. According to the charter, the countesses of Flanders and Hainault saw many poor women of their area who had to go begging or support themselves by other shameful means. They founded the béguinage so that such women could "support and clothe themselves by suitable work, without shaming themselves or their friends."[65]

Jacques de Vitry's sermon to Benedictine nuns and the foundation charter of Saint Elizabeth of Gand highlight one of the central reasons for male clerics' promotion of penitential manual labor for religious women: they viewed this "productive labor" as a means that would enable religious women to remain off the streets, and, in the case of cloistered nuns, within the domestic sphere of the convent. Strict cloistering was not an issue for religious men, and thus in their case it was not necessary to focus attention on penitential manual labor.

The association of women's penitential manual labor with the private realm of the cloister helps to explain why Guillaume de St.-Pathus—who usually showed very little interest in women's work—went out of his way to point out that Marguerite of la Magdaleine, a sister at the convent of the Filles Dieu in Paris, made silk purses.[66] Most of the Filles Dieu were repentant prostitutes who apparently begged for support for their community.[67] By stressing Marguerite's manual labor Guillaume distinguished her from the other women in the community, for whom begging was not a problem because their sexual purity had already been sullied in their earlier lives as prostitutes. In making this distinction between Marguerite and the others Guillaume lent credence to the claim that Marguerite had entered the Filles Dieu as a young virgin—"pucele et virge."[68]

A second explanation for male clerics' tendency to associate religious women especially with penitential manual labor had to do with their perceptions of women's capacities: even the best among women could not rise as high in the spiritual and intellectual realms as could the best men. As Bonaventure and Jacques de Vitry put it in their discussions of male labor, those men who should engage in manual labor were the "simple" ones, or

65. *Cartulaire du Beguinage de Sainte-Elisabeth à Gand*, ed. Jean Béthune (Bruges, 1883); trans. Emily Amt, *Women's Lives in Medieval Europe: A Sourcebook* (New York, 1993), 264.

66. Guillaume de St.-Pathus, *Les miracles*, miracle 34, p. 101.

67. Their begging is mentioned by Guillaume de la Villeneuve in "Les crieries de Paris," ed. Alfred Franklin, in *Les rues et les cries de Paris au XIIIe siècle* (Paris, 1874; reprint ed., Paris, 1984), 159.

68. Guillaume de St.-Pathus, *Les miracles*, 103.

the "robust poor," who were not capable of fulfilling the responsibilities of higher forms of labor, such as administering the sacraments and preaching.[69] All women—including women religious—were considered unfit for fulfilling these highest spiritual labors, and thus it was appropriate to encourage religious women to engage in penitential manual labor, while exempting some religious men from that activity.

Given clerical views on involuntary begging, women's voluntary begging (an activity which male Franciscans and Dominicans very much claimed for themselves), and female penitential manual labor, it seems plausible that Jehanne of Serris acted in the manner described by Guillaume de St.-Pathus—making a pilgrimage on crutches to St.-Denis, and paying for the trip by selling a bit of yarn that she had produced with her own hands. Thirteenth-century society was willing to support a disabled woman like Jehanne through formal and informal charitable channels, such as the Hôtel Dieu of Paris and almsgiving in the streets, but its clerical elite also taught Jehanne—in the pulpit, the confessional, and perhaps in the hospital—that begging was a doubly questionable activity for a lower-status woman. If she desired divine assistance in the form of a miraculous cure, she should do penance for the sins that undermined her appeals to the saint, and she should choose manual labor, rather than begging, as her penitential activity. Once she was cured of her ailment, Jehanne would rejoin the ranks of the working poor, but the clerics who encouraged her to do penitential labor while she was sick would remain silent about her need to do manual labor once she was well.

What the sources suggest is that two categories of difference complicated the ways in which clerical authors constructed masculine and feminine roles and spheres. First, there was the difference of social status. Clerical authors sometimes elevated the productive and reproductive labors of propertied men and propertied married women, associating both with the intellectual rather than the material realm. By contrast, they associated the productive and reproductive labors of lower-status men and women with the material realm, and they portrayed both men and women of this social level as lasciv-

---

69. Jacques de Vitry, "Sermo XXXV ad Fratres Minores," in Pitra, *Analecta novissima*, 2:400; Bonaventure, "Quaestiones disputatae de perfectione evangelica," quaest. II, art. III, Conclusio, in *Doctoris Seraphici S. Bonaventurae Opera Omnia*, ed. College of St. Bonaventure, 10 vols. (Quaracchi, 1882–1902), 5:161: "inter membra Christi sunt quaedam maxime idonea ad operationes corporales et minime ad spirituales . . . hinc est quod illis pauperibus validis, qui ad opera corporalia maxime sunt idonei et minime ad spiritualia . . . eis est opus manuale in *praecepto*."

ious. However, they placed greater emphasis on the lasciviousness of lower-status women, especially when those women were also single.

The second difference was that between involuntary and voluntary poverty. In their representations of the necessary labors of the involuntary working poor, clerical authors remained so wedded to the exclusive association of men with productive labor and of women with reproductive labor that they ignored, or even erased, the productive labor of women, and especially of married women. By contrast, in their discussions of the penitential activities of the voluntary poor, the clerical elite placed manual labor in a binary opposite with begging, associating women especially with penitential manual labor.

PERSPECTIVES OF THE POOR

Clerical views of women's productive and reproductive labors seem to have had a considerable, though not always decisive, influence on the attitudes of the poor themselves. Some of the evidence—such as the penitential behavior of Jehanne of Serris, as well as of Nicole of Rubercy and Avice of Berneville who were discussed earlier—seems to suggest that lower-status women accepted clerical constructions.[70] Jehanne of Serris's behavior seems to have less to do with female gendering than with clerical constructions of involuntary begging: despite the fact that she had to beg in order to survive, when it came to making a pilgrimage Jehanne acted in conformity with the clerical message that her begging was a tainted activity and that God was more likely to answer her petitions if she paid for a supplicatory pilgrimage with money that she earned with her own hands.

In the cases of Nicole of Rubercy and Avice of Berneville, by contrast, the women acted in ways that were consistent with clerical messages that women—and especially lower status women—were in need of extra assistance in order to overcome the taint of their association with the sexual and reproductive spheres. Nowhere in the *Miracles of Saint Louis* does Guillaume de St.-Pathus ever describe laymen—except for Saint Louis himself—who wore hair shirts and "disciplined" their flesh, details that he includes about Avice of Berneville after her cure, which took place when she was in her sixties and either widowed or single. Nor does Guillaume mention that laymen made special pleas to Saint Louis to overlook their unnamed sins, as he tells us that Nicole did when she was ill, in her forties, and a widow. This gendered asymmetry may be a function of what Guillaume chose to report: be-

70. On Nicole of Rubercy and Avice of Berneville see above, pp. 23–24, 72.

cause of his clerical perception that women—especially lower-status women without men—were more in need of earning God's forgiveness than were men, Guillaume may have remained silent regarding men's penitential behaviors while highlighting those of women, especially those without men. Still, Guillaume did not invent the penances of Nicole and Avice, and the behavior of these two women suggests that they felt a need to earn God's forgiveness, possibly because they had internalized clerical messages about lower-status women.

Even more striking for what they tell us about the impact of clerical messages about women's sexual natures on lower-status women are Guillaume's narratives of Jacqueline of St.-Germain-des-Prés and Ponce of Froitmantel, the one a mature woman, the other a girl on the threshold of puberty. Both Jacqueline and Ponce experienced temporary insanity, apparently because of crises concerning their sexual roles.

In 1283 Jacqueline, who was a forty–year-old sister at the Filles Dieu, and, like many of the sisters there, apparently a former prostitute, fell ill with a fever that took her out of her senses.[71] She began to call the other sisters at the Filles Dieu "ribalds" and "foolish women"—references to their earlier lives in the streets—and to say things that embarrassed the sisters so much that they would not repeat them to the inquisitors at the canonization proceedings. When a priest came to see her during her illness, Jacqueline said that she did not wish to be touched by the hands of a priest, and that she preferred to pray to the devil rather than to Jesus Christ "whom the Jews crucified." Later, she attempted suicide—by attempting to throw herself first into a cesspool then into a well, and by trying to strangle herself. Finally, after several days of this behavior one of the sisters told her to recall "our father Saint Louis who carries you and me and others outside of sin." At that point she calmed down and asked Louis "to return my memory and my senses to me." When the inquisitors saw her the same year she was fine, except that "she was worn out by fasts and vigils and wearing a hair shirt." Jacqueline's illness may have been brought on by a fever, but the form that it took, and the acts of penance that she performed after it was gone, suggest that she bore a heavy emotional and spiritual burden on account of her former life as a prostitute.

We find similar continuities between the behavior of Ponce of Froitmantel—a village near Reims—both during her illness and after she returned to sanity.[72] Sometime around 1272, when she was ten years old, Ponce found a piece of bloody cloth in the fields when she was playing with her friends.

71. Guillaume de St.-Pathus, *Les miracles*, miracle 30.
72. Ibid., miracle 31.

Refusing the advice of her playmates, Ponce kept the cloth, declaring that it was covered with the blood "of our Lord Jesus Christ." From that day until her parents led her to Saint Louis's tomb three years later, Ponce was "crazy and out of her senses." Much of her behavior seems randomly insane—she destroyed things in her house, threw church candles on the floor, and wandered through the fields not knowing where she was. Other behavior, however, suggests that Ponce was trying to escape the role of wife, which she was probably expected to accept upon coming of age. Ponce tore her dress and declared that she was not the daughter of her mother and father but of "a king." In church, moreover, she declared that she was a "gentlewoman" who should be allowed to sit with the priests and sing. After her cure, Ponce again became orderly and lucid, but, Guillaume tells us, "she was so devout that she did not eat flesh on Wednesdays, she fasted on Fridays, ate only bread and water on Saturdays and refused to hear anything about getting married." Ponce's mental crisis between the ages of ten and thirteen looks very much like the emotional breakdown of a young girl who was determined not to accept the sexual role that she was expected to take on as an adult.[73]

Guillaume tells two stories about men who went insane—the first, a knight who went into a state of severe depression when a fellow knight did not go on crusade with him; the second, a canon who became incoherent during a fever.[74] Although homoerotic ties may have been at the center of the knight's attachment to his friend, neither miracle indicates that the men felt any guilt about their sexuality or about their roles as men. The stain of sexuality—and the desire to overcome or escape that stain—seems to have rested much more heavily on women's than on men's consciences; and women without men bore the heaviest emotional burden of all.

While the sources for the *Miracles of Saint Louis* indicate that lower-status women listened to clerical messages about their sexual natures, the same sources indicate that such women—and probably men of the same social level—held views about women's necessary labor that differed from those of lettered men. At the end of each interview with a witness to a miracle, the clerics conducting the Saint Louis inquest asked the witness what he or she was worth. Those who owned real property gave the property's value, while those who did not own real property answered that they "had nothing," and that they were sustained by their own labor or that of another. All of the

73. For discussions of similar patterns in the lives of women saints, see Donald Weinstein and Rudolph Bell, *Saints and Society: The Two Worlds of Western Christendom, 1000–1700* (Chicago, 1982).

74. Guillaume de St.-Pathus, *Les miracles*, miracles 13, 38.

seven women whose testimonies survive were married. Two of the seven had real property, valued at over sixty and over two hundred livres.[75] One of the remaining five answered that she lived on the labor of her husband, who was a dyer.[76] The other four answered that they lived on their own labor and that of their husbands.[77]

At first glance it appears that, like their clerical brothers, men from the laboring poor did not wish to acknowledge that married women worked. All eight of the unpropertied laymen whose interviews survive stated that they lived on their own labor, mentioning nothing about the work of their wives. Two of the eight men also indicated that they supported their families with their own labor. One of those seems to have contradicted his wife in making this claim, since she indicated that she lived on her own labor as well as that of her husband.[78]

While these answers might suggest that some laboring men agreed with the clerical myth about the male breadwinner, there is another plausible reading as well. The differences between the men's and women's answers reflected the economic realities of the high and later Middle Ages: men from the urban laboring classes tended to earn more than what was required to support themselves but not enough to support an entire family. Women, by contrast, frequently earned less than what was required to support an individual.[79] Thus, when men answered that they lived by their own labor, and women that they lived by their own labor and that of their husbands, their answers accurately described their situations.

Working men and women experienced women's work as important and necessary to the household economy. But they also experienced that work as secondary in importance and as an activity that married women often incorporated into or worked around their domestic responsibilities. Thus, in the *Miracles of Saint Louis*, mothers spent more time than did fathers awaiting the cures of their children in St.-Denis. Five mothers stayed at St.-Denis for

75. Delaborde, "Fragments de l'enquête," 62, 69.

76. Ibid., 54.

77. Ibid., 50 (there is a gap after "dicit quod nichil nisi quod lucratur de labore suo . . ."; presumably she went on to say, "et de labore viri sui"; 52, 56, 59.

78. Ibid., 21, 26 (he also has a house), 33, 42 (he says he supports his wife and three daughters, while his wife—50—says she lives on her own labor [and presumably that of her husband—there is a gap in the text]), 44 (he says he supports himself and his family), 61, 67, 71.

79. Bronislaw Geremek, *Le salariat dans l'artisanat parisien au XIIIe–XVe siècles*, trans. from the Polish by Anna Posner and Christiane Klapisch-Zuber (Paris, 1982), 89–91.

between nine and sixteen days, and a sixth stayed a full month. Several of these probably gave up working for the entire period of their stay. Some may not have been working wives. And some, such as Yfame, who worked as a spinner to augment the family income, may have taken their work with them to St.-Denis.[80]

Working people, then, recognized that both married men and married women worked, but they were also more inclined to associate women with domestic responsibilities. There were still male and female realms, but those realms overlapped—physically, in the case of workshops in the home, and economically, in the case of most working households, which relied on the necessary supplement of women's productive labor. Men and women like Jehanne of Serris and her husband experienced women's work as a necessary part of the household economy. While they realized that men earned more and that women mixed productive with reproductive labor, they also understood that their households depended upon the laboring contribution of every adult, including women who had to beg to bring in their share of income. The clerical elite, by contrast, tended to perpetuate a vision of exclusive and separate realms—a productive realm inhabited by men, and a reproductive realm inhabited by women.

80. Guillaume de St.-Pathus, *Les miracles.* Mothers who stayed at the tomb: miracles 6, 11, 16, 23, 41, 49. In miracle 41 the father accompanied the mother to St.-Denis, but then returned to Paris. In four other miracles (10, 53, 54, 56) the mother alone took the child to the tomb. In three additional miracles (22, 31, 36) both parents took the child; and in two—26/27 (this was one narrative about a miracle that benefited two siblings), and 47—the father alone took the child or children but did not stay at the tomb for more than one day. Yfame, the mother who was a spinner, is in miracle 41; Delaborde, "Fragments de l'enquête," 49.

CHAPTER FIVE
WOMEN IN NEED

FIGURE 7. Nicole of Rubercy
On the left Nicole lies in bed, attended by two women and a man. Guillaume de
St.-Pathus tells us that Nicole asked those who came to see her to test her skin to
determine if she could feel anything; they obliged by pricking her with a lancet.
This is what the man appears to be doing. In the center Nicole rides in a cart to
Louis's tomb, which is represented by a statue on the right. Guillaume de Saint-
Pathus, *Les miracles de Saint Louis*, miracle 39. Bibliothèque Nationale de France,
ms. fr. 5716, p. 517. Photo courtesy Bibliothèque Nationale de France, Paris.

WOMEN WITHOUT MEN

On the morning of Good Friday (April 22) in 1272, Nicole
of Rubercy, a forty-two-year-old widowed laundress who
had immigrated to Paris from the diocese of Bayeux in
Normandy a number of years earlier, fell victim to a paralysis. Her head

twisted to one side, her lips trembled, and she lost the senses of touch, taste, and smell. For two days she could neither speak nor eat, and once she started eating again she could handle only soft foods.[1]

Before she fell victim to what appears to have been a stroke, Nicole was one of the many Parisian women without men who lived on the brink of destitution. Deprived of her own laboring capacity and with no family to help her, Nicole was poised to fall over the brink, but close female friends saved her from that fate. One of these was a widow named Contesse, who resided with Nicole in what the *Miracles of Saint* Louis calls a "hostel" on the rue aux Lavandières in the parish of St.-Germain on the Right Bank (map 1).[2] Contesse, who "loved Nicole very much," cared for her friend for the next two months, dressing her, helping her to eat, and taking her to the public baths in the hope that the hot water and air might help her recover. Ten days into the illness the two women traveled to the tomb of Louis IX in St.-Denis. The two women spent nine days at the tomb, retiring each night to a hostel in St.-Denis, but their trip was not successful. Six weeks later, however, when Contesse was taking Nicole to the public baths, they encountered a woman named Mabel of London—a stranger to them—who told them that she had heard a voice commanding her to find the woman who had lost the use of her limbs, and to let that woman know that if she said confession and then visited Saint Louis's tomb she would be relieved of her suffering. So Nicole went to her parish priest, said confession, and then returned to St.-Denis with Contesse, where indeed she was cured.

Contesse, who was probably as poor as her friend, was not the only

1. Guillaume de St.-Pathus, Confesseur de la Reine Marguerite, *Les miracles de Saint Louis*, ed. Percival B. Fay (Paris, 1931), miracle 39.

2. The two women were living in this hostel at the time of the inquest, but they must have been living together in the parish of St.-Nicolas in 1272. We are told that before making her second trip to St.-Denis, Nicole confessed to "Phelipe, the curate of the church of Saint Nicolas, of which she was a parishioner," ibid., 123. At some point between 1272 and 1282 Nicole and Contesse apparently moved from the parish of St.-Nicolas to the rue aux Lavandières in the parish of St.-Germain.

I use the term "hostel" because that is the term employed by Guillaume de St.-Pathus. In miracle 2 (see below, pp. 160–61) he simply indicated that three women sought lodgings in the "house" (*meson*) of another. Probably what is meant in both these cases is a crowded boarding house. How many people inhabited the rooms in such lodgings remains a mystery, but it is reasonable to assume that women like Nicole shared their rooms, and even their beds: see below, p. 161. On the difficulty of determining how many people occupied Parisian lodgings, see Simone Roux, "L'habitat urbain au moyen âge: Le quartier de l'Université de Paris," *Annales: Economies, sociétés, civilisations* 24 (1969): 1196–1219.

woman who helped Nicole. Perronnele the smith, who owned the yard where Nicole had hung her laundry, paid for the cart that carried Nicole to St.-Denis on her two trips, and accompanied Nicole and Contesse on the first day of the first pilgrimage (figure 7). She probably accompanied them on the second trip as well, for we are told that after her cure Nicole walked home with the "women"—presumably Contesse and Perronnele—who had accompanied her to Saint Louis's tomb.[3]

Close friends such as Nicole and Contesse must have been common in late thirteenth- and early fourteenth-century Paris. We glimpse similar relationships in the tax assessments and in court records.[4] Viewed from the perspective of male clerics, however—if they were seen, or imagined at all—such women were very much on the margins of society, for they neither depended upon, nor were they directly subordinate to, men. Their incomes, moreover, placed them at the bottom of the economic ladder, where the necessities of mere survival compelled some of them to turn to prostitution or theft. As indicated in chapter 1, some of the evidence in Nicole's story suggests that she and her friend Contesse may have been former prostitutes: Contesse had the kind of name that prostitutes often gave to themselves, and Nicole was particularly earnest in her pleas for forgiveness at Saint Louis's tomb. We know that other laundresses supplemented their incomes with prostitution. In 1300 Perrenele the laundress was banished from the lands of the abbey of Ste.-Geneviève, on the Left Bank, for pandering and being a prostitute.[5] Prostitutes were sometimes threatened with being put to death if they returned to a given jurisdiction after being banished. The more common threat, and practice, however, was branding with a hot iron.[6]

3. Guillaume de St.-Pathus, *Les miracles*, miracle 39.

4. On women's companionships in Parisian court records see: Dyan Elliott, "Women in Love: Carnal and Spiritual Transgressions in Late Medieval France," paper delivered at symposium on "The Family in the Middle Ages," J. Paul Getty Museum, Los Angeles, Calif., June 1999.

5. "Registre criminel de Ste.-Geneviève," in L. Tanon, *Histoire des justices de Paris* (Paris, 1883), 350 (case from the year 1300). On the discrepancies between men's and women's incomes, see Bronislaw Geremek, *Le salariat dans l'artisanat parisien aux XIIIe–XIVe siècles*, trans. from the Polish by Anna Posner and Christiane Klapisch-Zuber (Paris, 1982), 89–91; and Janice Archer, "Working Women in Thirteenth-Century Paris" (Diss., University of Arizona, 1995), 158, 168–69. For a general discussion of prostitution as a supplement for inadequate wages, see Ruth Karras, *Common Women: Prostitution and Sexuality in Medieval England* (New York, 1996), 48–55.

6. "Registre criminel de Ste.-Geneviève," 347, 348, 350; "Registre criminel de Saint-Germain-des-Prés," ibid., 412. See pp. 29 and 32 for explanations of *brulée* ("branded") and *sus la besche* (the death penalty).

As the behavior of Perrenele the laundress suggests, the low incomes of Parisian women without men meant that even before they fell victim to lasting disability they suffered from dire poverty. Fear of such poverty and of threats to the sexual honor of their daughters may help to explain why rural parents allowed their teenage daughters to remain at home, while sons were pressured to leave home and fend for themselves.[7]

Although dire poverty threatened many of them, the unattached women of Paris and St.-Denis, as Nicole's story indicates, did not always benefit from the forms of charitable assistance that were made available to poor women. This was because people of property tended to view women through the marriage prism, and thus they directed most of their assistance for unattached women to older women—most especially to widows—and to nubile girls, with the sole intention of helping them to marry. In most cases, moreover, help came with strings attached: those who accepted it had to place themselves under male control. As a widow, or possibly a former prostitute, Nicole of Rubercy might have benefited from some of the charities that propertied Parisians directed to unattached women. Nevertheless, we find her before, during, and after her illness attempting to survive without institutional help. Perhaps she did not wish to submit to the yoke that charities for women required. Unquestionably, moreover, Parisian women in need exceeded the capacity of the institutions that attempted to meet their needs.

The evidence from thirteenth- and early fourteenth-century Paris suggests that it had a large population of working women without men, including, in all likelihood, a great number who never married and never joined a formal religious institution. Among the fifteen adult women living in Paris and St.-Denis who were cured by Saint Louis, only four were married at the time of their cure. Three of the remaining eleven belonged to or were associated with religious institutions for unattached women. Only two of the eleven unmarried women were clearly identified as widows; several of the remaining nine were probably lifelong single women.[8]

7. In modern societies that have large numbers of street children, most especially those in Latin America, eastern Europe and Africa, girls are deterred from leaving home by the prospect of falling into prostitution, which is the fate that awaits most girls on the street; Lewis Aptekar, *Street Children of Cali* (Durham, N.C., 1988); Kevin J. Lalor, "Street Children: A Comparative Perspective," *Child Abuse and Neglect* 23 (1999): 760, 761; Thomas J. Scanlon, Andrew Tomkins, Margaret A. Lynch, and Francesca Scanlon, "Street Children in Latin America," *British Medical Journal*, no. 7144 (May 23, 1998): 1597.

8. Guillaume de St.-Pathus, *Les miracles*. Women married at time of cure: miracles 3, 42, 51, 52. Women residing in or affiliated with religious institutions: mir-

Most lifelong single women were of lower status, since noblewomen and women from the merchant elite who did not marry usually found their way into formal religious institutions.[9] Many bourgeois Parisian girls were placed in such institutions at a very young age by parents who had apparently already decided that these daughters would never marry.[10]

For a number of reasons—including elite prejudices against their existence—women who never married are extremely difficult to find in the sources, or to differentiate from other women. The Parisian tax assessments of this period did not list poor wage earners and other people at the bottom of the economic ladder, so that many single women do not appear in these records. Similarly, they do not appear in property records because they lived as boarders in houses owned and rented by people more prosperous than

acles 30, 34, 44. Widows: miracles 4, 39. Other unattached women in Paris and St.-Denis: miracles 2, 5, 35, 37, 43, 58.

9. Bourgeois Parisian families placed their daughters in a variety of religious institutions in and around Paris. Two Cistercian houses—St.-Antoine, which was originally founded just outside of Paris in 1198 and was handed over to the Cistercians in 1204, and Maubuisson, founded near Pontoise by Blanche of Castille in 1236—were among the favorites, as was the Hôtel Dieu of Paris. Others included Jarcy, Gis, Chelles, Yerres, and Longchamp; Anne Terroine, "Recherches sur la bourgeoisie Parisienne au XIIIᵉ siècle," vol. 2 (Unpublished *thèse*, Ecole Nationale des Chartes, 1940), 133–60. On St.-Antoine, see Constance Berman, "Cistercian Nuns and the Development of the Order: The Abbey of Saint-Antoine-des-Champs outside Paris," in *The Joy of Learning: Studies in Honor of Jean Leclercq*, ed. E. Rozanne Elder (Kalamazoo, Mich., 1995), 121–56. On elite practices in Italy, see Stanley Chojnacki, "Measuring Adulthood: Adolescence and Gender in Renaissance Venice," *Journal of Family History* 17 (1992): 371–95. Chojnacki notes that in the fifteenth century a more accepting attitude toward single women living at home began to emerge among Italian urban elites.

10. Terroine, "Recherches," 2:148–51; Adolphe Dutilleux and Joseph Depoin, eds., *Cartulaire de l'abbaye de Maubuisson (Notre-Dame la Royale)*, 2 vols. (Pontoise, 1890–1913), no. 604, 2:164 (Tiphaine Savore was thirteen when she professed at Maubuisson, where she had been raised with a younger sister); A. de Dion, ed., *Cartulaire de l'abbaye de Porrois au diocèse de Paris*, vol. 1 (Paris, 1903), no. 305, pp. 299–301 (Marie and Agnes, daughters of the Parisian goldsmith Jean de Lagny, were less than twelve years old when they were placed in the abbey in 1266; they would decide whether or not to profess when they reached the age of twelve); Auguste Molinier, ed., *Obituaires de la province de Sens*, 4 vols. (Paris, 1902–23), vol. 1, pt. 2, pp. 673, 675, 676 (Blanche des Essarts was seven years old when she was vested at the abbey of Longchamp in 1326; Marguerite la Flamenge was eight when she was vested in 1355; Yolent des Essars was about ten when she was vested in 1349; and Jehanne des Essars was ten when she was vested in 1351).

themselves.[11] Another reason for single women's invisibility has to do with inconsistent naming practices: many married and widowed women were identified in the sources as "so-and-so, the wife of so-and-so," but many other women—both married and single—were identified by place-names, professional names, or descriptive names.[12] Thus, it is often impossible to distinguish single women from widowed or married women. Still, if we look hard enough, we can find some of the single women of Paris. They earned their livings in various sectors of the economy and worked out strategies of survival either on their own or in partnership with other women.

The form of identification that most indisputably points to a single woman is that in which she is identified as someone's daughter, sister, or niece, when the relative in question is clearly irrelevant to the document in question.[13] The problem here, of course, is that we often cannot identify the age of these daughters, sisters, and nieces, so we do not know whether they were nubile girls or older single women. Moreover, there is no way to determine whether or not these women married at some later date.

Paris was one of only three cities in medieval Europe that had gilds that were exclusively or predominantly female, and some of the single women who were identified in the sources as relatives of individuals other than their husbands were members of these gilds. The *Livre des métiers* of Etienne Boileau, which was compiled between 1261 and 1271, included statutes for four gilds in which the nouns and pronouns referring to gild members were

11. On the exclusion of poor wage earners from tax rolls see Archer, "Working Women," 83–84, 152–53. See also her argument on pp. 20 and 56–59 that the terms "chambrière" and "ouvrier/ouvrière" referred to individuals working in the putting-out system rather than domestic servants or wage laborers.

12. On naming patterns in the Parisian tax assessments see Caroline Bourlet, "L'anthroponymie à Paris à la fin du XIIIᵉ siècle d'après les rôles de la taille du règne de Philippe le Bel," in *Genèse médiévale de l'anthroponymie moderne*, ed. Monique Bourin and Pascal Chareille, vol. 2–2 (Tours, 1992), 9–44.

13. Thus, for instance, the statutes of the predominantly female embroiderers' and silk alms purse makers' gilds identified a number of women as the daughters or nieces of men who had nothing to do with the gild. If they had been married, the preferred form of identification would have been "wife of so-in-so" hence it is reasonable to assume that they were single women. On the other hand, one cannot make this assumption in the case of women who were identified as relatives of other women in the gild, for it was natural in the context of the gild statutes to identify them in this way even if they were married; one, in fact, was mentioned both as the sister of another gild member and as someone's wife. G.-B. Depping, ed., *Réglemens sur les arts et métiers de Paris, redigés au XIIIᵉ siècle, et connus sous le nom du Livre des métiers d'Etienne Boileau* (Paris, 1837), 379–86.

exclusively female, as was the case with another gild that was established toward the end of the thirteenth century.[14] There were also a number of other gilds that had a very high percentage of female members.[15] The few membership lists that we have indicate that these gilds included single women. Jehanne the daughter of Giles the mercer, Marie the daughter of Etienne the furrier, Belon the daughter of Michael the convert, Denise the daughter of Jacques the cobbler, and Amelot Marote the daughter of Adam the bathhouse keeper, all members of the embroiderers' gild, were evidently single. Members of the silk alms purse makers' gild who were apparently single included Alice the niece of Brother Richard, Jehannete the daughter of John the physician, and Sedile the daughter of Richard the currier.[16]

14. René de Lespinasse and François Bonnardot, eds., *Le livre des métiers d'Etienne Boileau* (Paris, 1879), nos. 35, 38, 44, 95; pp. 68–70, 74–75, 83–84, 207–8: silk spinners using large spindles, ribbon makers or silk weavers (*ouvriere[s] de tissuz de soie*), weavers of silk head coverings (*tesserandes de queuvrechiers de soie*), and makers of gold embroidered hats and garments (*fesserresse[s] de chappeaux d'or et d'euvres a IIII pertuis*); Depping, *Réglemens*, 382–86: silk alms purse makers. For a general discussion of women in the *Livre des métiers* see E. Dixon, "Craftswomen in the *Livre des métiers*," *Economic Journal* 5, no. 2 (1895): 209–28; Diane Frappier-Bigras, "La famille dans l'artisanat parisien du XIIIᵉ siècle," *Le moyen âge* 95 (1989): 56–62. For broader discussion of women and craft gilds see Maryanne Kowaleski and Judith Bennett, "Crafts, Gilds, and Women in the Middle Ages: Fifty Years after Marian K. Dale," *Signs: Journal of Women in Culture and Society* 14 (1989): 474–88. For background on the *Livre des métiers*, see B. Mahieu, "Le *livre des métiers* d'Etienne Boileau," in *Le siècle de Saint Louis* (Paris, 1970), 64–74. For a general discussion of the occupations of women in the Parisian tax assessments see Archer, "Working Women."

15. The gild of silk spinners using small spindles, the small purse makers' gild (*crespiniers de fil et de soie*) and the linen merchants' gild apparently had a majority of women: Lespinasse and Bonnardot, *Livre des métiers*, nos. 36, 37, 57, pp. 70–73, 117–20; Archer, "Working Women," 259, 254, 172–73. The poulterers', bathhouse keepers', and mercers' gilds were among the gilds with large numbers of women members and no restrictions on their membership: *Livre des métiers*, nos. 70, 73, 75; pp. 147–49, 154–55, 157–59; Archer, "Working Women," 257, 269, 254. The poulterers' gild was explicit about single women's access to full membership rights: Lespinasse and Bonnardot, *Livre des métiers*, no. 70:7, p. 148. Only 16 percent (15 out of 94) of the listed members of the embroiderers' gild were men at the time that its statutes were drawn up. However, men constituted 74 percent (63 out of 85) of the listed taxpayers practicing that craft in the 1297–1300 tax assessments: Depping, *Réglemens*, 379–80; Archer, "Working Women," 258.

16. Depping, *Réglemens*, 379–86.

viduals who were assessed as potential taxpayers on the rue des Frères Mineurs and the rue St.-Côme (see map 1) were women—62 percent of those assessed on these two streets, as against only 13.7 percent of the total number of assessees.[24] Six of the twenty-three were identified as Beguines, and an overlapping six were identified together, as female companions or sisters. A number of these women paid quite substantial taxes, which suggests that a desire for the company of other lay religious women and for the pastoral care of the Franciscans drew them to these two streets.[25] There was a similar relationship between settlements of semireligious women and the local Franciscan convent in Florence as well.[26] Increasingly in the fourteenth century uncloistered semireligious women such as these were persecuted by the church.[27]

Jehanne du Faut—the wealthy benefactor of the spinner Guillemete la Grande—provides an intriguing example of a religious woman who tried living at the Parisian béguinage but then opted for a more independent

24. On the overall percentage of women, see Bourlet, "L'anthroponymie à Paris," 11.

25. The minimum tax in 1292 was one sou. Maheut the Beguine and Dame Aalès des Cordèles each paid 16s.; Jehanne the embroiderer and Martine her companion (later identified as a Beguine) paid 20s. together; Gile the daughter of Jehan de Compiagne paid 36s.; Ermengar the deaf woman paid 12s.; and Marguerite the Beguine and her sister Denise paid 16s. together; Hercule Géraud, *Paris sous Philippe-le-Bel, d'après des documents originaux*, new edition with introduction and index by Lucie Fossier and Caroline Bourlet (Tübingen, 1991), 159, 160. Jehanne and Martine were still together in the 1296, 1297, 1299, and 1300 assessments: Archer, "Working Women," 303.

The 1292 assessment reached further into the ranks of the poor, and assessed more people (fifteen thousand), than did any of the subsequent surviving assessments (which assessed between six and ten thousand individuals). Nevertheless, the 1296 assessment still listed a high proportion of women (six out of thirteen assessed) on the rue des Cordèles (formerly the rue des Frères Mineurs). All six of the women were identified as Beguines; Karl Michaëlsson, *Le livre de la taille de Paris, l'an 1296* (Göteborg, 1958), 232. On the number of individuals assessed in each surviving taille, see Bourlet and Fossier, "Avant propos," in Géraud, *Paris sous Philippe-le-Bel*, ix.

26. Anna Benvenuti Papi, "Mendicant Friars and Female Pinzochere in Tuscany," in *Women and Religion in Medieval and Renaissance Italy*, ed. Daniel Bornstein and Roberto Rusconi, trans. Margery J. Schneider (Chicago, 1996), 91.

27. Robert Lerner, *The Heresy of the Free Spirit in the Later Middle Ages* (Berkeley, Calif., 1972); Elizabeth Makowski, *Canon Law and Cloistered Women: Periculoso and Its Commentators 1298–1545* (Washington, D.C., 1997).

form of religious life. We do not know when Jehanne lived at the béguinage. She shows up in the Parisian tax assessments as an apparently widowed mercer living on the rue Troussevache in the parish of St. Jacques in 1292, 1296, 1297, and 1313; her tax assessments (all relatively high) ranged from forty-eight sous in 1292 to fifteen livres tournois in 1313.[28]

Throughout these years Jehanne's house was next-door to that of Marie Osane, also a wealthy mercer (paying taxes of seven livres ten sous in 1292, and twenty-two livres tournois in 1313), who was sometimes identified as a Beguine. In 1292 and 1296, moreover, a certain "Anés d'Orliens, beguine," who was assessed for relatively high taxes of twenty and thirty-six sous in those years, resided either with Marie or with Jehanne, as did a certain Perrete, at least in 1292. In 1330, when Jehanne made out her will, she was still living on the rue Troussevache, but her neighbor Marie Osane the Beguine was deceased.[29]

We know that Jehanne tried residing at the Parisian béguinage at some point because only residents could own houses there. Moreover, a document concerning the execution of her will identified her as "once a Beguine at [the Paris béguinage]." The document involved the house in the béguinage that Jehanne had passed on to the spinner Guillemete la Grande for the rest of her life: Jehanne had indicated that after Guillemete's death the house was to pass on to Jehanne's daughter Beatrice. However, Jehanne's executors could not carry out this provision because the daughter was not a resident in the béguinage.[30]

The facts that Jehanne had Beguine neighbors, and that she remained a wealthy widow for at least thirty-eight years—in a town where wealthy bourgeois women frequently remarried within a year—suggest that despite her move from the béguinage to the rue Troussevache Jehanne continued to be a semireligious woman. Her unusually long testament corroborates this. In addition to making the usual donations to virtually every religious institution and hospital in Paris, Jehanne made a number of less common bequests: to abandoned children for whom alms were sought at the Cathedral of Nôtre Dame; to poor girls in childbirth at the Hôtel Dieu; to poor prisoners at both the Châtelet and the episcopal prison; to recluses residing at the cemetery of the Innocents and at St.-Quentin near St.-Denis; and to the

28. Michaëlsson, *Le livre de la taille . . . 1296*, 132; Michaëlsson, *Le livre de la taille de Paris, l'an 1297* (Göteborg, 1962), 121; Géraud, *Paris sous Philippe-le-Bel*, 91; Michaëlsson, *Le livre de la taille de Paris, l'an de grace 1313* (Göteborg, 1951), 133.

29. See appendix.

30. AN, X^{ia}7, fol. 89v, quoted by Le Grand, "Les béguines," 328 n. 4. Le Grand was not aware of Jehanne's testament.

béguinage of Rouen. She designated, moreover, that one hundred livres be used to buy cloaks, garments, and shoes for the poor of Paris, and another hundred livres be distributed in small sums to poor households, poor religious, and poor priests. She gave all of her chapel ornaments to a priest named Roland Helloman. Finally, she took the unusual step of naming four women, and no men, as her executors, and made strong statements indicating that her nephews were not to attempt to undermine her testament. She named her daughter Beatrice, who was also her principal heir, as her chief executor.[31]

Thirteenth-century Paris had two institutions that were originally intended to house reformed prostitutes: the convent of St.-Antoine, founded in 1198 by the charismatic preacher Foulques of Neuilly, and the Filles Dieu, founded in the first quarter of the thirteenth century by William of Auvergne.[32] St.-Antoine was handed over to the Cistercian order in 1204 and soon became popular among noble and prosperous bourgeois girls and women who chose or were compelled to enter the monastic life. Thus it seems that the Filles Dieu became the only convent for reformed prostitutes. In both cases, the intent of the original founders was to help prostitutes by getting them off the streets and cloistering them—ushering them, in a sense, into the category of "consecrated widows," loosely defined. St.-Antoine, in its early years, and the Filles Dieu helped single women by turning them into nuns, and thus rendering them "not single." In most cases, women entered institutions such as these when they reached the age of about thirty and had to retire as prostitutes.

While some single women clearly received material assistance from the Filles Dieu and the béguinage of Paris, both institutions fit the Genesis paradigm because they placed unattached women under the authority of male clerics. The same seems to have been true for institutions for widows and older women. The earliest known Parisian shelter for widows, which came to be known as Ste.-Avoye, was founded in 1283 on the rue du Temple by the treasurer of the parish church of St.-Merry, Jean Sequens, and a widow named Constance. The founders specified that the shelter was to house forty poor widows aged fifty or older.[33] In 1306 the wealthy draper Etienne

31. See appendix.

32. On the Filles Dieu see Paul and Marie-Louise Biver, *Abbayes, monastères, couvents de femmes à Paris des origines à la fin du XVIIIe siècle* (Paris, 1975), 67–71. On St.-Antoine, see Berman, "Cistercian Nuns."

33. Gérard Dubois, *Historia ecclesiae parisiensis*, 2 vols. (Paris, 1690–1710), 2:510–11. Dubois gives the date of 1288 in his printed version of the foundation document; however, a fifteenth-century *vidimus* of the same document gives the date

Haudry and his wife Jehanne founded another shelter near the Place de Grève, which was to house thirty-two widows. That shelter came to be known as the Haudriettes.[34] A royal account book from 1342 lists ten shelters for women in Paris, including Ste.-Avoye and the Haudriettes.[35] Additionally, Jean Hubant provided housing for "ten poor aged women" as one of the interlocking charitable institutions that constituted Ave Maria College on the Left Bank.[36]

One of the ten shelters in the account book of 1342, the hospital of Pierre Larrent, benefited from a bequest in the will of a Parisian bourgeois man in 1332. A second, the hospital of Andry Marcel, may have been the same as the shelter that housed fourteen "poor women in the house of Agnes la Martelle on the street called Paradise," which benefited from a bequest by a Parisian bourgeois woman in 1313.[37] These wills referred to St.-Avoye, the Haudriettes, the hospital of Pierre Larrent, and that of Agnes la Martelle as shelters for "poor women" and the 1342 register referred to all

---

of 1283: AN, L 1078, nos. 1 and 2. See also Le Grand, "Les béguines," 334–41, 354–57.

There were similar shelters for widows in Italian towns. See: Richard Trexler, "A Widows' Asylum of the Renaissance: The Orbatello of Florence," in *Old Age in Preindustrial Society*, ed. Peter N. Stearns (New York, 1982), 119–49; F. Semi, *Gli "ospizi" di Venezia* (Venice, 1983), 40–43, 87–95, 161–62; Elizabeth Rothrauff, "Charity in a Medieval Community: Politics, Piety and Poor Relief in Pisa, 1257–1312" (Diss., University of California, Berkeley, 1994), 99.

34. AN, L 1043, nos. 18, 20, 21, 22, 24. Jehanne Haudry's testament (no. 24) specified that the residents should be widows. See also Le Grand, "Les béguines," 354–57, 349–55.

35. They were: Ste.-Avoye ("Bonnes fames de la porte du Temple"), the Haudriettes ("Bonnes fames de lospital Estienne Haudry"), "Bonnes fames de la rue aux Fauconniers," "Bonnes fames du pont parvum [Petit Pont]," "Bonnes fames de lospital Andry Marcel," "Bonnes fames de lospital Jehan Gensan," "Bonnes fames de lospital Denys de St. Just," "Bonnes fames de lospital Gieffroy de Flory," "Bonnes fames de lospital Mestri P. Larrent," and "Bonnes femmes Mestrie Jehanne Mignon," AN, KK 5, fol. 368r–v. The hospice on the rue aux Fauconniers was next to, but distinct from, the béguinage. For locations of the first four shelters listed above, as well as that of Agnes la Martelle, mentioned below, see map 1. See chapter 3, note 43 for discussion of the hospital founded by Ymbert of Lyon, which was not a shelter for women in the early fourteenth century.

36. Astrik Gabriel, *Student Life at Ave Maria College, Medieval Paris: History and Chartulary of the College* (Notre Dame, Ind., 1955), 345.

37. Testament of Jehanne la Fouacière, 1313; testament of Jehan de Troyes, 1332: see appendix.

ten shelters as institutions for "good women." Thus, the evidence does not permit us to determine if the eight institutions other than Ste.-Avoye and the Haudriettes were intended to help only widows, or all poor unattached women. Nevertheless, charitable bequests to Ste.-Avoye and the Haudriettes—which were definitely intended to benefit widows—far outnumbered bequests to the other institutions, and Ste.-Avoye and the Haudriettes were probably the largest, or two of the three largest, of the hospices for women in Paris.[38]

Once they entered a hospice for women, single or widowed women apparently gave up a great deal of their independence. The statutes of the Haudriettes, which were established by the founders, stipulated that women who entered the hospice could never leave it; that they were under the authority of Etienne Haudry and his male heirs; that they could not give away any of their personal property without the permission of the founders and their successors; and that they must designate the hospice and its residents as their heirs. The women were required to pray three times a day for the founders and their successors, and to make confession and receive communion four times a year. Finally, each resident risked expulsion—and the loss of her personal property—if she told a lie, slandered, stole, drank to excess, sinned "with her body," or harbored any outsider, especially a man. Ste.-Avoye had similar rules in the sixteenth century, but we do not know anything about the statutes of that house in the thirteenth and fourteenth centuries.[39] The women of Ave Maria College were required to perform specific

38. In the 1342 register, the largest disbursements to hospices for "bonnes fames" went to the Haudriettes (sixteen livres), Ste. Avoye (eight livres) and the hospice of Andry Marcel (eight livres); AN, KK 5, fol. 368r–v.

Gifts to both Ste.-Avoye and the Haudriettes by testators other than the original founders and their descendants include those of Jehanne la Fouacière, 1313; Margaret, wife of Pierre Loisel, 1330; Jehan de Troyes, 1332; and probably Jehanne de Malaunay, 1311—she gives five sous each to "pauperibus hospitalibus pauperum mulierum viduarum Paris." Testators giving gifts to Ste.-Avoye include Pierre la Pie, 1302; Sédile de Laon, 1316; and Jehanne Haudry, wife of Etienne Haudry (who gave both to the Haudriettes and to Ste.-Avoye), 1309. Testators giving only to the Haudriettes include Guillaume de Mailly, 1327. See appendix.

39. Le Grand, "Les béguines," 349–57. Through extensive work in the archives of the Haudriettes, Michael Connally has found that from the time of its foundation its residents enjoyed private incomes from their own properties, which they sometimes bequeathed to other residents. In most cases, however, it seems that the community eventually gained control of these properties. Michael Connally, "Common Life by the Statutes and in Practice: the Haudriettes," paper delivered to the International Medieval Congress, Leeds, July 2000.

religious duties and were not allowed to admit men of bad morals into their rooms. Nor were they allowed to admit women of any age to their rooms unless they themselves were so old that they needed a servant, who had to be an old woman as well.[40] Although we catch only a passing glimpse of the eight hospices other than St.-Avoye and the Haudriettes that were listed in 1342, it seems reasonable to assume that every hospice for women had a set of rules, that sexual activity was strictly forbidden, and that the women of each institution were subject to a person who had authority over them.

In their testaments, bourgeois Parisians tended to favor charities that defined women through the marriage prism. Eighteen of the thirty-two Parisian bourgeois testators whose wills I have examined gave gifts to shelters for widows, and twelve of those testators provided money for the dowries of poor girls. Additionally, two testators provided money to help poor women in childbirth.[41] Of course, gifts to poor women in childbirth had the potential of helping not only married women but also those who were single. Nevertheless, such gifts defined women in terms of their reproductive functions, as did the more popular act of providing dowries to help poor girls to marry. In the latter case, the express purpose of gifts was to make the girls "not single."[42]

Many testators, both male and female, also gave gifts to their male and female servants.[43] Such gifts were sometimes directly consistent with the

40. Gabriel, *Student Life*, 114, 346–47.

41. See appendix.

42. It is unclear to what extent dowry funds were an attempt to reproduce the bourgeoisie. As Richard Trexler has pointed out, people of any social status could be considered poor if they were unable to live up to the standards that were expected for their social group, hence it was perfectly legitimate for propertied individuals to direct their charities to other members of the elite or even to their own relatives; Trexler, "Charity and the Defense of Urban Elites in the Italian Communes," in *The Rich, the Wellborn, and the Powerful: Elites and Upper Classes in History*, ed. Fredric Cople Jaher (Chicago, 1973), 64–109. In the absence of any other directives, therefore, we cannot really know who ended up receiving the monies that were set aside for dowries. When, however, Etienne Haudry directed in 1312 that his executors were to give five sous to up to eighty marriageable girls, we can expect that the recipients were not of high social status; see appendix.

43. See appendix. A number of these bequests may have been settlements of debts for back wages, but that was not the case with Sédile of Laon, who settled her debts with her servants at the beginning of her will, and went on to give gifts of money and clothing to her own servants, the daughter-in-law of one of her servants, and to servants of two other people. It is also unlikely that the gifts of clothing from Jehanne, the wife of Etienne Haudry, Adam le Panetier, and Jehanne Argence were

marriage prism, since they included provisions for dowries. Moreover, in most cases gifts to female servants were consistent with the idea that women needed to be under male authority, since servants fell under the authority of the heads of the households in which they resided. Such women could be the objects of both the social imagination and the charitable purse. By contrast, single women who lived on their own and worked outside of the elite household structure, as alms purse makers, embroiderers, laundresses, poulterers, hucksters, or whatever—were excluded both from the system of classification that clerics created for women and from the predominant forms of charity that we find in bourgeois wills.

NONELITE SUPPORT FOR POOR WOMEN

How then, did most of the poor women of Paris and St.-Denis really survive? For those suffering from lasting disabilities, the *Miracles of Saint Louis* highlight both the importance and the limitations of nonelite providers of support. Most of those providers were much the same as those that we find in the stories involving men—family, employers, and neighbors. However, unlike men, women like Nicole of Rubercy also found support in their close companions of the same sex. The stories illustrating women's sources of support point to the inadequacies of the clerical perspective, which defined women as both dependent upon and subordinate to men, for the stories reveal nuclear families in which husbands were unable to support their wives through long periods of disability, and they show us female companions who provided the kinds of support that clerics thought women should only get from their husbands. Moreover, the stories indicate that despite clerical messages discouraging female begging, informal alms, especially those given at the door of an individual's parish church, were frequently essential to the survival of women with lasting disabilities.[44]

---

intended to pay off debts. None of these bequests is specifically mentioned as constituting a dowry, but the gifts of bedding from Guillaume Fresnel and Jehan Le Grand were probably intended as dowries.

44. The stories do not tell us anything about consumption loans, although these were also an important aspect of survival for poor people. William C. Jordan, "Jews on Top: Women and the Availability of Consumption Loans in Northern France in the Mid-Thirteenth Century," *Journal of Jewish Studies* 29 (1978): 39–56; Julie Mayade-Claustre, "Le petit peuple en difficulté: La prison pour dettes à Paris à la fin du Moyen âge," unpublished paper delivered to the international congress on "Le petit peuple dans la société de l'occident médiévale," Université de Montréal, October 18–22, 1999.

Among propertyless laborers, as suggested earlier, adults who fell victim to lasting disabilities could not always rely on the support of their families. Three of the stories in the *Miracles of Saint Louis* help to illustrate the role that the nuclear household played when a wife fell ill. In two cases, the wife had to look beyond her immediate family for help. One of these cases, that of Jehanne of Serris, was already discussed in chapter 4. The other case involved Amile of St.-Mathieu, who in 1271 or 1272, some thirty years after she had moved to Paris from Brittany, fell victim to a paralysis when she got up in the middle of the night to give a drink to one of her children. Her entire left side became paralyzed, and a lump appeared in her groin. Eventually, the lump grew into a large, open, malodorous sore.[45]

After Amile had been sick for three or four months, her husband left her, Guillaume de St.-Pathus tells us, "par ennui" (out of frustration, or even irritation). Guillaume continues disapprovingly, "he left Paris, and so he did not assist her at all."[46] Amile was compelled to hobble on a crutch to her parish church, where she begged for alms. This caused her great pain and put her in physical danger as well since she could not feel anything in her left foot, which she had to drag on the ground. On one occasion a piece of glass pierced the foot, but she felt nothing, even when a barber cut into her flesh to remove the glass.

Three-quarters of a year later, Amile finally decided to go to St.-Denis to seek a miraculous cure at Saint Louis's tomb. Her brother accompanied her on the journey, but it seems that her husband was not completely out of the picture: he and his brother visited Amile during her first few days at St.-Denis, and when they heard that she had been cured they went out to see her again. She was already on the road back to Paris when they ran into her, so they all returned to Paris together.

It is perfectly plausible that Amile's husband left home to seek employment.[47] In any case, in view of his visits to her and the availability of Amile's brother, it is clear that the husband's absence did not in fact constitute total abandonment. Nevertheless, as with the case of Jehanne of Serris, we are left with the evidence that a nuclear family was so poor that even the disabled wife was compelled to bring in some income by begging.[48] The nu-

45. Guillaume de St.-Pathus, *Les miracles*, miracle 52.

46. Ibid.

47. On nomadism in search of work among day laborers, see: Geremek, *Le salariat*, 95–97; and Geremek, *The Margins of Society in Late Medieval Paris*, trans. from the French by Jean Birrell (Cambridge, 1987), 253–62.

48. The majority of women receiving alms from the confraternity of Orsanmichele in fourteenth-century Florence were married: Charles de la Roncière,

clear family did not provide Amile and Jehanne with a cushion against beggary. Indeed, it seems that the single woman Nicole of Rubercy was better off in her illness than were Amile and Jehanne.

However, the companionship, and perhaps the material support, of Amile's brother, and the presence of her husband's brother, also suggest that Parisian immigrant workers sometimes maintained important ties with their extended families. In another miracle story, a married women, Marie the Burgundian, who had recently immigrated with her husband to Paris from the diocese of Auxerre was able to rely on her sister. When Marie took her eight-year-old son to St.-Denis to seek a cure for his crippled arm, the sister accompanied her, and it was the sister, in whose care Marie had left the boy, who was with him when he regained the use of his arm.[49] In a third story, the five- or six-year-old brother of Yfame of Lagny, who had migrated to Paris from a village in the same diocese two years earlier, stayed with his sister when her husband went out of town.[50]

The story of Luce, a migrant to St.-Denis from the village of Rémilly-sur-Lozon in Normandy, indicates that in some cases the disabled wives of propertyless workingmen actually could rely on their husbands for long periods. Soon after she gave birth to one of her children, in 1268 or 1269, Luce began to suffer from an eye disease. Within two years, she was completely blind, and she remained in that state for eight years, during which time she gave birth to and nursed another three children.[51]

Because her husband, an immigrant from England, earned enough money to support her and the rest of the family, Luce never had to beg during those eight years.[52] Moreover, her husband did not have to take time off from work to assist his disabled wife because she received assistance from her daughter Emmeline, who was about nine years old when Luce went

---

"Pauvres et pauvreté à Florence au XIVe siècle," in *Etudes sur l'histoire de la pauvreté (moyen âge–XVIe siècle)*, ed. Michel Mollat, 2 vols. (Paris, 1974), 2:694. On wives of working men who begged in eighteenth-century France, see Olwen Hufton, "Women and the Family Economy in Eighteenth-Century France," *French Historical Studies* 9 (1975): 20–21.

49. Guillaume de St.-Pathus, *Les miracles*, miracle 49. The fact that Marie's second husband was a mason suggests that she and her first husband were immigrant workers.

50. H.-François Delaborde, ed., "Fragments de l'enquête faite à Saint-Denis en 1282 en vue de la canonisation de Saint Louis," *Mémoires de la Société de l'Histoire de Paris et de l'Ile-de-France* 23 (1896): 46–47.

51. Ibid., 56–57, 59.

52. Ibid., 57, 59, 62, 66.

blind, and from a male servant who had been with Luce since her previous marriage, to another Englishman.[53] Emmeline's role in looking after her younger siblings fits a broader pattern in medieval miracle stories, a pattern that, along with the fear of prostitution and poverty, may well help to explain why girls remained at home with their rural families longer than boys.[54]

We do not know what Luce's husband did for a living, but we do know that he was propertyless and that he supported his family by his own labor.[55] We also know that Luce was too poor to hire a wet nurse, and that she went to work peddling pickled fish and petty merchandise after she regained her eyesight.[56] Nevertheless, the presence of a household servant, and the fact that for eight years her husband was able to support a household of at least six without any financial assistance from his wife, suggest that this family was more prosperous than were the families of Amile of St.-Mathieu and Jehanne of Serris.

The *Miracles of Saint Louis* do not include any stories about Parisian single women who received assistance from their parents or siblings when illness or disability prevented them from working. We can surmise from the stories about Amile, Jehanne, and Moriset the swineherd why such assistance might have been rare: nuclear families that barely managed to stay afloat could not afford to support additional adults. We do find one blind woman in Pontoise who relied on her sister as her guide when she had to beg. In that case, however, the sister may well have profited from her role, since the guides of blind people also received alms.[57]

Many immigrant women would not have had nearby relatives to turn to

53. Ibid., 56–57, 59, 64.

54. Poor families in modern societies where street children are common also keep daughters at home longer than sons because the daughters care for younger siblings; see above, note 7. On the broader pattern of older sisters as caretakers in medieval miracle stories see: Didier Lett, *L'enfant des miracles: Enfance et société au Moyen Age (XIIᵉ–XIIIᵉ siècle)* (Paris, 1997), 188–92; and Lett, "La sorella maggiore 'madre sostituta' nei 'Miracoli di San Luigi,' " *Quaderni storici* 83 (1993): 341–53. On differences between boys' and women's ages of migration in the Middle Ages see above, pp. 30–32

55. Delaborde, "Fragments de l'enquête," 56, 61. When asked what his property was worth, Luce's husband answered that he had very little, and that he lived by his own labor. Luce answered that she had nothing, and that she lived by her own labor and that of her husband.

56. Guillaume de Saint-Pathus, *Les miracles*, miracle 51; Delaborde, "Fragments de l'enquête," 70.

57. Guillaume de Saint-Pathus, *Les miracles*, miracle 59.

when they needed help. Nevertheless, we should not completely discount the importance of blood connections for single women, including single immigrant women. The inquest concerning the forty-first miracle of Saint Louis indicates that Yfame of Lagny, the wife of the dyer Herbert of Fontenay, immigrated to Paris a year before she married her husband. She had an aunt who apparently already resided in Paris and was married to a dyer, and it is possible that the aunt helped her to find housing or employment, or that she introduced Yfame to her future husband.[58] Moreover, the presence of five sets of mothers and daughters and two sets of sisters in the embroiderers' gild of Paris, and of one set each of mother and daughter, aunt and niece, and sisters in the silk alms purse makers' gild, indicates that single women frequently relied on their relatives when they entered the employment market.[59]

Some of the unattached poor women of Paris were able to turn to their work affiliations for help when they were in trouble. Such help did not come, however, from the gilds. The statutes for the gilds with large numbers of women made no mention of special arrangements for indigent members and their families.[60] Conversely, the six gilds in the *Livre des métiers* that did mention special arrangements for needy members or their families were overwhelmingly male in their membership. Among these, the tailors', glovers', roasters', and cobblers' gilds designated certain fines for the support of poor members.[61] We find no female tailors or roasters in the Parisian tax lists of 1297–1300, an average of 2 female and 48 male glovers for each of those years, and an average of 6 female and 328 male cobblers for each of those years.[62] The statutes of the iron buckle makers' and strap makers' gilds

58. Delaborde, "Fragments de l'enquête," 42, 46.

59. Depping, *Réglemens*, 379–86.

60. The word "confrarie," which could refer to a religious or charitable organization, is used in the statutes of the ribbon makers or silk weavers, but as Gustave Fagniez pointed out, that word frequently meant "the gild" in the *Livre des métiers*. Lespinasse and Bonnardot, *Le livre des métiers*, no. 37, art. 5, p. 72; Gustave Fagniez, *Etudes sur l'industrie et la classe industrielle à Paris au XIIIe et au XIVe siècle* (Paris, 1877; reprint ed., New York, 1970), 33. See ibid., 31–42 for a general discussion of Parisian confraternities. See also the references in Catherine Vincent, *Les confréries médiévales dans le royaume de France: XIIIe–XVe siècle* (Paris, 1994).

61. Lespinasse and Bonnardot, *Le livre des métiers*, no. 56, art. 5; no. 69, art. 14; no. 84, art. 12; no. 88, art. 13; pp. 116, 146, 184, 195.

62. Archer, "Working Women," 258, 264, 266, 267. Similarly, the gild of curriers of squirrel garments (*conreurs de robe vaire*) instituted mutual aid for members in 1319. There were no female curriers (*corroyeurs*) in the tax lists of 1297–1300: Fagniez, *Études*, 290–91; Archer, "Working Women," 267.

indicated that the gild would pay the entrance or apprenticeship fees of orphaned or poor children of members.[63] There were no female makers of iron buckles in the tax lists of 1297–1300, and women strap makers were outnumbered by a ratio of ten to one (an average of 17 women and 179 men per year).[64] It seems, then, that very few women in thirteenth-century Paris benefited from the mutual aid that some gilds provided for members.

Even in Paris, moreover, most working women were engaged in types of work—domestic service, wool spinning, wool carding, laundering—that fell outside of the gild structure. For these women, the most likely sources of aid in times of need would have been their families (if they were married), private alms, or their own employers, with whom many of them lived. Such was the case with the wool carder Orenge of Fontenay. In 1272 Orenge had been living for twenty years in the house of her employer Maurice the weaver.[65] In that year, Orenge's right arm and elbow became so inflamed that she could not work, dress herself, or tie a knot. She remained in that condition for four years, apparently continuing to reside in Maurice's home. A woman identified as Orenge's hostess—probably Maurice's wife—as well as a neighbor named Hodierne of Fontenay, perhaps an immigrant from Orenge's home village, assisted Orenge when she needed to get dressed. Apparently, though, their assistance did not include regular bathing: because she could no longer wash her own hair, Orenge had her head shorn.

Sometime around 1276 Orenge made a pilgrimage to Saint Louis's tomb and was cured. Guillaume de St.-Pathus's narrative leaves us with the impression that she returned to Maurice's house and went to work for him once again. Throughout the four-year hiatus in her service, Maurice the weaver apparently remained constant in his support of Orenge the wool carder.

63. Lespinasse and Bonnardot, *Le livre des métiers*, no. 21, arts. 5–6; no. 87, art. 7; pp. 49, 189.

64. Archer, "Working Women," 263, 264. Among those listed in the tax assessments as buckle maker (*bouclier*) rather than iron buckle maker (*bouclier de fer*), there was an average of 7 women and 88 men per year—or 7.4 percent women. Women constituted 13.8 percent of the taxpayers in the tax assessments of 1297–1300. Thus 7.4 percent and 10 percent were less than the average; Archer, "Working Women," p. 110.

65. Guillaume de St.-Pathus, *Les miracles*, miracle 58. Guillaume stated that Orenge had been living there thirty years, but he was probably referring to the length of time she had been there in 1282, the time of the inquest, rather than in 1272.

Of course, not all employers were as generous as Maurice the weaver. Agnes of Pontoise had worked as a domestic servant in the houses of several bourgeois of Pontoise, but when she went blind she had to resort to begging in the streets for her bread. Amelot of Chaumont worked for two years as a servant in the house of one of the prominent bourgeois of St.-Denis, but in her final illness she was moved to the Hôtel Dieu of St.-Denis, where she died.[66]

Amelot of Chambly—the woman bent double, most likely by spinal tuberculosis, whose story was discussed in chapter 4—benefited from a third source of nonelite support for Parisian women: the neighborhood or parish.[67] Everyone in St.-Denis knew Amelot by sight—children fled when they saw her coming[68]—but even those who saw her almost every day at the Basilica of St.-Denis might not know much about her. Eleven years later, in 1282, Jehan Augier, one of the prominent bourgeois of St.-Denis, recalled helping Amelot negotiate the stairs of the basilica.[69] He recalled the day she was cured as well, and he remembered that she remained healthy for about a year after that. But he knew nothing about her background, and he had no idea what had become of her. Jehan's recollections concerning Amelot were typical of the witnesses from St.-Denis who had not lived near her. By contrast, Robert of Cantarage, a smith who had immigrated to St.-Denis from the diocese of Evreux, and who lived on her street, knew that she was from the village of Chambly le Haubergier near Senlis, that she was buried at the parish church of St.-Marcel in St.-Denis, and that her affliction had not been congenital.[70]

Another smith named Ace provided lodging for Amelot, "for the love of God," and when the streets were too muddy for her to go out begging, he gave her bread. Moreover, when she asked for it, he gave her advice: after she had made several unsuccessful visits to Louis's tomb, for instance, it was Ace who suggested that she confess her sins and try again. It was good advice—for on the next visit, she was cured: her back straightened out to such a degree that she subsequently carried laundry on her head and buckets of water on a pole that rested on her shoulders, "just like other women."[71]

66. Ibid., miracles 2, 59.
67. Ibid., miracle 5; Delaborde, "Fragments de l'enquête," 18–39.
68. Delaborde, "Fragments de l'enquête," 31.
69. On Jehan's family, see Anne Terroine, *Un bourgeois parisien du XIII* siècle: Geoffroy de Saint-Laurent, 1245?–1290*, ed. Lucie Fossier (Paris, 1992), 35–36.
70. Delaborde, "Fragments de l'enquête," 24–26.
71. Ibid., 26, 32.

Ace's role in helping Amelot is significant. Studies of neighborly care for the poor in nineteenth- and twentieth-century Europe and the Americas stress the predominance of networks dominated by women.[72] In thirteenth-century Paris and St.-Denis, by contrast, men like Ace and Herbert the Englishman, who provided lodging for Guillot of Caux, were also important in neighborhood networks of support.[73] In all likelihood, men's integration into poor people's neighborhood networks in medieval Paris derived from the greater integration of the physical spaces of work and residence in the preindustrial age.

Amelot of Chambly's story also illustrates the ways in which news traveled among neighbors and the interest that they took in each other's well-being. Before Amelot even left the church of St.-Denis on the day that she was cured, news of her cure reached Ace the smith. Ace's work prevented him from going out to greet Amelot, but his wife went to the church, and accompanied her back to their house.[74] Robert of Cantarage was somewhere else in St.-Denis when Amelot was cured, but he too heard the news and went to the church to greet her and walk home with her.

News also traveled quickly between St.-Denis and the Right Bank neighborhoods of Paris. When the news reached Nicole of Rubercy's parish priest that she had been cured, he walked to the hospital of St.-Lazare, beyond the walls of Paris, to greet her on her return home. And when Amile of St.-Mathieu was cured, a woman returning to Paris from St.-Denis told Amile's husband, who went out from Paris to greet her.[75] In two miracle stories involving cures of children, we are told that after they and their parents returned to Paris their neighbors came over to rejoice in their good fortune. In one of those cases, moreover, the neighbors held a feast for the cured girl and her parents.[76]

72. E. Ross, "Survival Networks: Women's Neighborhood Sharing in London before World War I," *History Workshop Journal* 15 (1983): 4–27; M. Young and P. Willmott, *Family and Kinship in East London* (London, 1957); Larissa A. Lomnitz, *Networks and Marginality: Life in a Mexican Shantytown* (New York, 1977); Carol B. Stack, *All Our Kin: Strategies for Survival in a Black Community* (New York, 1974). For an excellent survey of the literature on networks of care, see Peregrine Horden, "Household Care and Informal Networks: Comparisons and Continuities from Antiquity to the Present," in *The Locus of Care: Families, Communities, Institutions, and the Provision of Welfare since Antiquity*, ed. Peregrine Horden and Richard Smith (New York, 1998), 21–67.

73. See above, p. 103.

74. Delaborde, "Fragments de l'enquête," 32.

75. Guillaume de Saint-Pathus, *Les miracles*, miracles 39, 52.

76. Ibid., miracle 36; Delaborde, "Fragments de l'enquête," 49.

The *Miracles of Saint Louis* and the sources related to it thus suggest that some immigrant workers in Paris formed meaningful bonds with their neighbors. We know that in some cases those bonds were reinforced by craft ties as well. The Parisian dyer Herbert of Fontenay, for instance, married Yfame, the niece of a woman who was married to another dyer, and when he and Yfame took their daughter to St.-Denis to seek a cure they lodged in the house of a fellow dyer from Herbert's home village in the diocese of Paris.[77]

One story in the Saint Louis sources suggests that the church's efforts to strengthen pastoral care in the thirteenth century could also work to strengthen bonds among neighbors: before Jehanne, a hunchbacked woman who lived in the parish of St.-Merri, set out for St.-Denis to seek a cure, she confessed her sins and asked her neighbors to pardon her if she had vexed them in any way.[78] Seeking reconciliation was often part of the ritual for penitential pilgrimages, and confessors' manuals advised priests to recommend that penitents seek reconciliation with their neighbors.[79] Rarely, however, do the sources enable us to see this advice put to work.

Of course, not all neighbors got along with each other, and certain categories of people—old unattached women, for instance—may have been more subject to isolation and mistrust than others. When an elderly neighbor entered the Parisian home of Yfame of Lagny to warm herself by the fire one morning, Yfame began to suspect that the woman was responsible for the onset of her daughter's illness. The night before, Yfame had been awakened by the sounds of someone moving about her home; in the morning she discovered that her daughter was ill. It seems that Yfame connected the two events, and she thought it significant that her neighbor failed to say "God bless her!" when she told the neighbor that her daughter was ill.[80] Proximity, then, could lead not only to mutual care, but also to mistrust.

77. Delaborde, "Fragments de l'enquête," 42, 44.

78. Guillaume de St.-Pathus, *Les miracles*, miracle 43.

79. Letter of Hugh of Amiens, Archbishop of Rouen, to Thierry, Bishop of Amiens, ed. and trans. Teresa G. Frisch, *Gothic Art 1140–c. 1450*, Medieval Academy Reprints (Toronto, 1987), 25; Thomas of Chobham, *Summa confessorum*, art. 6, dist. 5, quest. 6, ed. F. Broomfield, Analecta mediaevalia namurcensia 25 (Louvain, 1968), 320. For a broader discussion of Thomas of Chobham's concern with relations among neighbors see Mary Mansfield, *The Humiliation of Sinners: Public Penance in Thirteenth-Century France* (Ithaca, 1995), 45–48.

80. Delaborde, "Fragments de l'enquête," 47. On stereotypes of old women and their association with sorcery, see Joel Agrimi and Chiara Crisciani, "Savoir médical et anthropologie religieuse: Les représentations et les fonctions de la *vetula* (XIIIᵉ–XVᵉ siècles)," *Annales: Economies, sociétés, civilisations* (1993): 1281–1308.

While the assistance that Ace the smith gave to Amelot of Chambly was not gender-specific—we know that neighbors sometimes took care of disabled men as well[81]—the kind of bond that we observe in the relationship between Nicole of Rubercy and her friend Contesse seems to have been more typical of women than of men. The *Miracles of Saint Louis* includes two stories about unrelated single or widowed women who took care of each other, but none about unrelated single or widowed men who took care of each other. In part, this gendered difference resulted from women's greater economic and physical vulnerability: women needed to band together more than men did. In part, the difference reflected the gendered role that women played as nursemaids for the sick.[82]

Amelot of Chaumont was the second unattached woman who received care from female companions. In January or February 1277, when Amelot was about twenty-eight years old, she and two other women moved from Chaumont in the Vexin (the region of the Ile-de-France that borders on Normandy) to St.-Denis.[83] The three women went first to the house of Marguerite of Rocigny, with whom, it seems, they had some prior connection.[84] Marguerite could not accommodate the women, but she recom-

81. Guillaume de St.-Pathus, *Les miracles*, miracle 9.

82. Didier Lett did not consider the role that women played as nurses to the sick in his analysis of the predominant role that older sisters played in assisting their siblings in the *Miracles of Saint Louis*. "La sorella maggiore"; *L'enfant des miracles*, 188–92.

83. Guillaume de St.-Pathus, *Les miracles*, miracle 2.

84. This hypothesis is based on the role that Marguerite plays in the narrative: the three women went first to Marguerite's hostel, Amelot later moved to her hostel, and Marguerite was with Amelot on the day that she was cured. If indeed the immigrant women had a contact in the town, they fit a broader pattern of women's migration from the countryside to the metropolis. P. J. P. Goldberg, *Women, Work, and Life Cycle in a Medieval Economy* (Oxford, 1992), 301–2; Vivien Brodsky Elliott, "Single Women in the London Marriage Market: Age, Status, and Mobility, 1598–1619," in *Marriage and Society: Studies in the Social History of Marriage*, ed. R. B. Outhwaite (London, 1981), 94–95; Olwen Hufton, "Women and the Family," 5; Cissie Fairchilds, *Domestic Enemies: Servants and Their Masters in Old Regime France* (Baltimore, 1984), 66–67.

Claude Gauvard's discussion of links between city and countryside indirectly supports the idea that migrants to the city often had contacts there: "Violence citadine et réseaux de solidarité: L'exemple française au XIVe et XVe siècles," *Annales: Economies, sociétés, civilisations* 48 (1993): 1113–26. The concentration of people from certain regions of France in certain streets and parishes of Paris also points to a pattern of migration through contacts. See above, p. 37.

mended the house of her neighbor, Emmeline, where the three women took up lodging and where Amelot shared a bed with one of her two companions from Chaumont. Several nights after Amelot arrived in St.-Denis, one of her legs became paralyzed. The next day, Emmeline carried Amelot on a stretcher to Saint Louis's tomb. She was assisted by three women, including one, or possibly two, of Amelot's companions from Chaumont.

Amelot was not cured on that first day, but she did receive a pair of crutches, which enabled her to return to Emmeline's hostel by her own power. During the next two months she visited the tomb often, and in the meantime, she apparently moved to Marguerite of Rocigny's house.[85] Marguerite was with Amelot at Louis's tomb on the day she was finally cured, and she comforted her when sharp pains signaled the beginning of the end of her paralysis.

Nicole the laundress and Amelot the immigrant from Chaumont provide us with important glimpses into the lives of single women immigrants in Paris and St.-Denis. Apparently these two women had no family members to turn to, but they could rely on their female companions. Moreover, it is clear that in Amelot's case her solidarities with other women began to take shape even before she left her hometown.

The trio of women who immigrated from Chaumont fit into a gendered pattern of migration that P. J. P. Goldberg has observed for late medieval England: women were more inclined to migrate in small clusters than were men.[86] Unfortunately, Amelot's case is the only one in the Saint Louis sources that spells out the circumstances of a woman's migration, and I know of no other sources that could tell us how women immigrated to Paris in this period. However, the Saint Louis sources also describe the circumstances under which two young men traveled from the provinces to Paris, and both of these cases fit the gendered pattern in the English sources. Each of the two men in the Saint Louis miracles attached himself to one or several groups along the way, but neither of them had a permanent traveling companion.[87]

In addition to finding that women in late medieval England tended to migrate to towns in small clusters, Goldberg and several early modern historians have observed that single women in late medieval England and early modern France and England tended to settle near one another in certain

85. Louis Carolus-Barré, ed., "Consultation du Cardinal Pietro Colonna sur le IIe miracle de Saint Louis," *Bibliothèque de l'Ecole des Chartes* 117 (1959): 72; Guillaume de St.-Pathus, *Les miracles*, miracle 2, 11.

86. Goldberg, *Women, Work, and Life Cycle*, 300.

87. Guillaume de St.-Pathus, *Les miracles*, miracle 15, 18.

neighborhoods and houses.[88] Since most of the Parisian poor do not show up in the city's late thirteenth- and early fourteenth-century tax assessments, our picture of medieval spinster clustering there is incomplete. We will never know, for instance, how many laundresses actually resided on the rue aux Lavandières. Nevertheless, it is clear that women did cluster in certain parts of the city, such as the two streets around the Franciscan convent. Perhaps more important for our purposes than this visible pattern of noneconomically motivated female clustering is the fact that the Parisian tax assessments are sprinkled with references to female companions—women who formed business partnerships together, and who probably lived together as well. Some of them did so for considerable lengths of time: Ameline Agace and her companion Marie, for instance, were assessed together in 1292, 1296, and 1297; Aalis of St.-Joce (who was identified in various years as a Beguine, a silk worker and a maker of alms purses) was assessed together with a companion named Philippote in 1296 and 1297 and with an unnamed companion, quite possibly Philippote, in 1313.[89]

The Parisian tax lists thus suggest that thirteenth-century Paris was also a site of medieval spinster clustering, and the sources for the miracles of Saint Louis provide two striking qualitative descriptions of medieval women's informal, nonfamilial solidarities. In Amelot's case the solidarity may have been very strong or very weak: it did not require a great deal of commitment to carry a woman a few blocks on a stretcher, and there is no way of knowing if Marguerite's presence on the day Amelot was cured was merely coincidental or part of a regular pattern of caretaking.

In Nicole's case, however, the bonds were quite impressive. We know that Contesse looked after Nicole for two months, and that their more prosperous neighbor paid for two journeys to St.-Denis (a round trip of about

88. Goldberg, *Women, Work and Life Cycle*, 305–24; Olwen Hufton, "Women without Men: Widows and Spinsters in Britain and France in the Eighteenth Century," *Journal of Family History* 9 (1984): 355–76; Pamela Sharpe, "Literally Spinsters: A New Interpretation of Local Economy and Demography in Coylton in the Seventeenth and Eighteenth Centuries," *Economic History Review* 44 (1991): 46–65.

89. In 1296 Aalis of Saint-Joce and Philippote jointly paid an above average tax of 18s. In 1313 Aaliz de Saint-Joce and her unnamed companion paid a tax of 30s. tournois: Michaëlsson, *Le livre de la taille . . . 1296*, 20, 167; Michaëlsson, *Le livre de la taille . . . 1297*, 151; Géraud, *Paris sous Philippe-le-Bel*, 130; Michaëlsson, *Le livre de la taille . . . 1313*, 11; Archer, "Working Women," 299, 300. Only the assessments of 1292, 1296, 1297, and 1313 have been published. The assessments of 1296 to 1300 are in AN, register KK283. Those of 1292 and 1313 are in the Bibliothèque Nationale: ms. fr. 6220 and 6736.

ten miles) and accompanied Nicole on at least one of the journeys. Unfortunately, Guillaume de St.-Pathus does not tell us how Nicole and Contesse supported themselves during the two months of Nicole's illness. It is unlikely that they had any savings to draw on, given the lodgings they inhabited.[90] Thus, I would surmise either that Contesse took Nicole out begging, or that Perronnele supported them during that time.

The sources for the miracles of Saint Louis indicate that in late thirteenth-century Paris poor women survived lasting disabilities with varying combinations of assistance from family members, employers, neighbors, close companions, and informal alms. A few also benefited from their affiliations with institutions for unattached women; and some stayed for short periods of time in the charitable hospitals. However, the most important support came from informal, noninstitutional sources. The Saint Louis sources also indicate that many immigrants—even very recent ones—managed to maintain and acquire meaningful social networks in their new environment. Some people who migrated to Paris and St.-Denis—like Amelot of Chaumont and Yfame of Lagny, both from the Ile-de-France—seem to have had contacts when they reached the metropolis. Once in Paris or St.-Denis, moreover, they maintained meaningful contacts with friends and relations from home. Thirty years after she moved to Paris from Brittany, Amile of St.-Mathieu turned to her brother when she needed help. Ten years after Herbert of Fontenay moved to Paris from a village in the diocese of Paris, and five years after his friend from the same village had moved to St.-Denis, probably after apprenticing in Paris with him, he sought lodging in his friend's house. Two years after Yfame of Lagny moved to Paris, and a year after she married, she took her young brother into her home. Soon after Marie the Burgundian moved to Paris from Burgundy, she and her husband turned to her sister for help with her sick child.

People maintained meaningful relations with friends and relatives from home, but they also formed new relationships, often with immigrants from other regions. The crippled woman Amelot, who came to St.-Denis from near Senlis, got help and solace from two smiths who were immigrants from two different dioceses in Normandy. Herbert of Fontenay decided to take his crippled daughter to Saint Louis's tomb after consulting with a friend—a neighbor and fellow dyer who had immigrated to Paris from En-

90. Some women who were paired together had very uneven incomes: in 1292, for instance, Agnes the Beguine, a spinner, was assessed for a tax of 36s., and her companion was assessed for 3s.: Géraud, *Paris sous Philippe-le-Bel*, 21.

gland.[91] Herbert and his wife Yfame were from two different villages in the diocese of Paris, but they asked a woman from the diocese of Beauvais and a woman from Brittany to serve as godmothers to their daughter.[92]

Along with other sources from thirteenth-century Paris, the Saint Louis sources indicate that the marriage paradigm created obstacles to defining and solving poor women's dilemmas. Women suffering from lengthy disabilities did not always receive adequate support from their husbands; female companions, however, sometimes provided such support. The Saint Louis sources thus suggest that we need to refine our assumptions about the advantages of marriage for women in high and late medieval cities.[93] While it is reasonable to assume that women who married master craftsmen or merchants were much better off than were single women, distinctions between the married and the unmarried begin to blur when we look at the working and nonworking poor. To be sure, men's wages were better than women's, but the wages of a workingman and his wife often supported more than two people, and the man's wages alone were often insufficient for supporting a family. Thus, some married women had to beg, at times, in order to enhance their husbands' incomes. Because women's wages were often insufficient to support even one person, single women with children were at a special disadvantage. Those without children, however, could pool their resources and provide support for each other in times of need, thus sometimes becoming better off than disabled women with men.

The sources from Paris also suggest that elite charities for women were either too few or too restrictive to meet the needs of most of the unattached women in Paris. The support that women provided for each other and that they found among their neighbors was, in the end, more important to their survival than was elite charity. Indeed, the evidence for both poor men and poor women indicates that poor people were active agents in the survival of their fellows. Poor people were not, as the histories of medieval charity might lead us to believe, mere passive recipients of assistance from the wealthy and powerful.[94]

91. Delaborde, "Fragments de l'enquête," 40, 42.

92. Ibid., 50, 52.

93. Martha Howell argues for such advantages in *Women, Production, and Patriarchy in Late Medieval Cities* (Chicago, 1986).

94. Judith Bennett also makes this point: "Conviviality and Charity in Medieval and Early Modern England," *Past and Present*, no. 134 (1992): 19–41.

CONCLUSION

The *Miracles of Saint Louis* provide us with a photograph, so to speak, of poor people in Paris and St.-Denis at the end of the thirteenth century. The photograph is both remarkably sharp in its detailed depiction of daily life and dangerously deceptive in its evocation of stability. To be sure, Amelot of Chambly, Nicole of Rubercy, Gilbert of Sens, and the other men and women discussed in these pages really did work and beg in the neighborhoods of Paris and St.-Denis, and a number of them were remembered in their neighborhoods long after they died. But it is doubtful that neighbors continued to share such collective memories after the second decade of the fourteenth century. Death began to sweep across the landscape too ferociously; neighbors and neighborhoods began to change too quickly.

The famines of 1315–23 were followed by others in 1328, 1334, and 1340–41. Then, in August of 1348, the Black Death arrived. Within eighteen months, half of the population of Paris had died. Hardest hit were children and the poor.[1] As if natural disasters were not enough, the lives of laboring Parisians were disrupted by the Hundred Years' War, which lasted from 1337 to 1453. Even periods of truce were dangerous, since marauding armed companies continued to ravage the countryside. In the 1350s, peasants from the region around Paris took refuge inside the city. Between 1358 and 1360 the Parisian suburbs were abandoned; the Filles Dieu were compelled to move from their original location to the hospital that had been founded by Ymbert of Lyon.[2] Until the English occupation of 1420–36, im-

---

1. Raymond Cazelles, *Nouvelle histoire de Paris: De la fin du règne de Philippe Auguste à la mort de Charles V, 1223–1380* (Paris, 1972), 148–50; Cazelles, "La peste de 1348–1349, épidémie prolétarienne et enfantine," *Bulletin philologique et historique (jusqu'à 1600) du Comité des travaux historiques et scientifiques* (1962): 293–305; Michel Mollat, "Notes sur la mortalité à Paris, d'après les comptes de l'oeuvre de Saint-Germain-l'Auxerrois," *Le moyen âge* 69 (1963): 505–27.

2. Guy Fourquin, *Les campagnes de la région parisienne à la fin du moyen âge: Du milieu du XIIIe au debut du XVIe siècle* (Paris, 1964), 230, 248–50; Cazelles, *Nouvelle histoire*, 155; on the Filles Dieu, see chap. 3, note 43.

migration and relocation continued to replenish the working population of Paris. We know that in 1375, for instance, a group of wool carders who had moved to Paris because of the war founded a confraternity at the hospital of Saint-Esprit in the Place de Grève.[3] Despite migration, however, the population of Paris remained considerably smaller than in the late thirteenth and early fourteenth centuries.[4]

Unlike the poor, Parisians of property were remarkably successful in assuring that they would be remembered by future generations. Indeed, given the ravages of war and disease, and the continuous obsession on the part of French ruling elites with leaving their mark on the city of Paris by erecting new buildings, the lasting footprints left by the charitable institutions that were founded by elite Parisians of the thirteenth and early fourteenth centuries is somewhat remarkable. Louis IX's hospital for the blind, the Quinze-Vingts, persisted until the 1780s, when it was transferred from the area west of the Louvre to the faubourg St.-Antoine.[5] Under its historic name, the eighteenth-century hospital remains a major institution for the blind. Its archives, which are housed in dusty rooms above the director's office, contain records reaching back to the time of the founder. The Parisian béguinage, also one of King Louis IX's foundations, persisted only into the 1460s, when King Louis XI gave it over to women of the Third Order of Saint Francis, who renamed it the Convent of Ave Maria. In the 1480s the religious order of the Clarisses took over Ave Maria and remained there until the Revolution.[6] The rue Ave Maria in the Fourth Arrondissement marks the area where the béguinage once stood. The "good women" of Ste.-Avoye and their property on the rue du Temple were folded into the Ursuline Order in 1620, but the house retained its original name. The nuns of Ste.-Avoye were dispersed during the Revolution and the convent was demolished in 1838 in order to make room for the rue Rambuteau.[7] The passage Ste.-Avoye, which runs from the rue Rambuteau to the rue du Temple

3. Bronislaw Geremek, *Le Salariat dans l'artisanat parisien aux XIIIᵉ–XVᵉ siècles*, translated from the Polish by Anna Posner and Christiane Klapisch-Zuber (Paris, 1982), 120.

4. Ibid.; Cazelles, *Nouvelle histoire*, 153–56.

5. Léon Le Grand, "Les Quinze-Vingts depuis leur fondation jusqu'à leur translation au faubourg Saint-Antoine, XIIIᵉ–XVIIIᵉ siècles," *Mémoires de la Société de l'Histoire de Paris et de l'Ile-de-France* 13 (1886): 189.

6. Léon Le Grand, "Les béguines de Paris," *Mémoires de la Société de l'Histoire de Paris et de l'Ile-de-France* 20 (1983): 334.

7. Paul Biver and Marie-Louise Biver, *Abbayes, monastères, couvents de femmes à Paris des origines à la fin du XVIIIᵉ siècle* (Paris, 1975), 103–7.

in the Third Arrondissement, marks the approximate location where the convent once stood. The house of the Haudriettes persisted until 1622, when the name was suppressed and the few remaining residents were moved to a convent in the faubourg St.-Honoré, which was handed over to Augustinian nuns and named the Assumption of Our Lady.[8] The memory of the earlier institution has been kept alive by the rue des Haudriettes in the Third Arrondissement. Jean Hubant's Ave Maria College lasted until 1769, when it was merged with the College of Louis-le-Grand. Even in the 1780s, however, annual commemorative celebrations for Hubant continued to be held in the chapel of Louis-le-Grand.[9] The colleges of St.-Victor and St.-Honoré continued to lodge students until the seventeenth century.[10]

The influential clerics who controlled the written word in the thirteenth century also left enduring legacies. Thomas of Chobham's manual for confessors was copied into over one hundred manuscripts in the thirteenth through fifteenth centuries. Surviving manuscripts of the sermon materials of Gilbert of Tournai and Humbert of Romans indicate that those two authors also remained extremely influential. Indeed, Gilbert's and Humbert's sermon materials also went through numerous printings between the fifteenth and eighteenth centuries, apparently because parish priests continued to draw on them for their sermons.[11]

Most enduring of all have been the stereotypes about and disapproval of poor and disabled men and poor women without men. In the early modern

8. Ibid., 23.

9. Astrik Gabriel, *Student Life in Ave Maria College, Medieval Paris* (Notre Dame, Ind., 1955), 241–42.

10. J. M. Reitzel, "The Medieval Houses of Bon-Enfants," *Viator: Medieval and Renaissance Studies* 11 (1980): 205.

11. On Thomas of Chobham, see John Baldwin, *Masters, Princes and Merchants: The Social Views of Peter the Chanter and His Circle*, 2 vols. (Princeton, N.J., 1970), 2:26 n. 216. On Gilbert of Tournai, see J. B. Schneyer, *Repertorium der lateinischen Sermones des Mittelalters für die Zeit von 1150–1350*, Beiträge zur Geschichte der Philosophie und Theologie des Mittelalters, Texte und Untersuchungen 43, 11 vols. (Munich, 1969–80), Heft 2, 306–7; and P. Glorieux, *Répertoire des maîtres en théologie de Paris au XIIIᵉ siècle*, vol. 2 (Paris, 1933), 56–59. On Humbert of Romans, see Thomas Kaeppeli, *Scriptores Ordinis Praedicatorum Medii Aevii*, 3 vols. (Rome, 1970–80), 2:287–88. Schneyer lists sixty manuscripts of Gilbert's *ad status* sermons and five printed editions from 1473–1511. Kaeppeli lists twenty manuscripts of parts of Humbert's *De eruditione praedicatorum*, and five editions before the nineteenth century (1508, 1603, 1607, 1677, 1739). He lists twenty-one manuscripts of other sermons and sermon materials by Humbert, and one fifteenth-century printed edition.

period, town officials in England extended financial assistance and favored status to widows, while denying these privileges to women who had never married. Such women, who were considered sexually dangerous, were sometimes even driven from their towns.[12] In the early part of this century, psychiatrists in the United States defined a category of female psychopath which seemed to encompass all working-class women who lived on their own and were sexually active. Like clerics of the thirteenth century, psychiatrists blamed these women for the sexual downfall of men, often placing them in institutions for the insane.[13] In the 1950s and 1960s poor mothers without men were blamed for perpetuating in their children the psychological conditions that gave rise to "the culture of poverty."[14] In contemporary Latin America, Africa, and eastern Europe, boys predominate among street children in part because parents are more protective of the sexual honor of their daughters and in part because there is a greater expectation that boys should fend for themselves.[15] Disabled men continue to suffer from a stigma which marks them as not masculine.[16]

It is the poor themselves, whose perspectives might challenge these stereotypes, who leave behind the least enduring legacies. To be sure, the renown of Saint Louis rubbed off on those whom he cured. Thus, the neighbors of Amelot of Chambly and Gilbert of Sens still recounted their stories close to a decade after they had died, and Guillaume de St.-Pathus saw fit to fashion a written account of those stories. Guillaume's narratives were preserved in a mere handful of medieval manuscripts that were accessible to a very narrow circle of members of the elite. Only in the eighteenth century, when their stories were reproduced in printed editions, would as-

12. Amy M. Froide, "Marital Status as a Category of Difference: Singlewomen and Widows in Early Modern England," in *Singlewomen in the European Past*, ed. Judith M. Bennett and Amy M. Froide (Philadelphia, 1999), 236–69.

13. Elizabeth Lunbeck, *The Psychiatric Persuasion: Knowledge, Gender, and Power in Modern America* (Princeton, N.J., 1994), chap. 7.

14. Alice O'Connor, *Poverty Knowledge: Social Science, Social Policy and the Poor in Twentieth-Century U.S. History* (Princeton, N.J., 2001), chaps. 4, 6.

15. See chapter 5, note 7.

16. Robert Murphy, "Encounters: The Body Silent in America," in *Disability and Culture*, ed. Benedicte Ingstad and Susan Reynolds Whyte (Berkeley, Calif., 1995), 140–58; Thomas J. Gerschick and Adam S. Miller, "Coming to Terms: Masculinity and Physical Disability," in *Men's Health and Illness: Gender, Power and the Body*, ed. Donald Sabo and David Frederick Gordon (Thousand Oaks, Calif., 1995), 183–204; Kathy Charmaz, "Identity Dilemmas of Chronically Ill Men," in Sabo and Gordon, *Men's Health and Illness*, 266–91.

pects of these people's lives become accessible again to nonelite audiences.[17] But Guillaume and the other members of the elite who controlled the written word had already determined which aspects of these people's lives would be passed on to posterity. Many of the things that we would like to know about the poor of medieval Paris were buried with them when they died.

17. Percival B. Fay, "Introduction," Guillaume de St.-Pathus, Confesseur de la reine Marguerite, *Les miracles de Saint Louis*, ed. Fay (Paris, 1931), iii–xi.

APPENDIX
PARISIAN WILLS, 1200-1348

Following is a list of the thirty-two bourgeois Parisian wills for the period 1200–1348 that I have been able to locate. This is a modest list compared with those for other towns, largely because there was no central repository for Parisian private documents. We are dependent on the record-keeping whims of individual religious institutions, which often chose to make authenticated copies of extracted clauses from original documents rather than copying the entire documents. As a result, we know of the existence of many Parisian wills that are no longer extant; but only complete originals or complete copies of originals provide the information that is useful for this book.

Initials in parentheses after the date of each testator's will indicate that the testator left bequests to the following:

C   *Collège/s* for boys
D   Dowries for poor girls
L   Poor women in labor
S   Servants
W   Shelter/s for women

Adam Le Panetier, 1271 (**SW**): AN, LL 387, fols. 73r–74r.
Arnoul le Cervoisier, 1286: Léon Brièle, ed., *Archives de l'Hôtel Dieu de Paris* (Paris, 1894), 433–34.
Emeline, wife of Nicolas, minister of the Quinze-Vingts, 1303: Archives des Quinze-Vingts, ms. 5848 (henceforth Quinze-Vingts 5848), fols. 192r–192v.
Etienne Haudry, 1312 (**CDW**): AN, L 1043, no. 25.
Gervais Ruffus, 1260 (**CDW**): AN, S 6213, no. 149.
Girart de Troyes, 1298 (**D**): Quinze Vingts 5848, fols. 236v–238v.
Guillaume au Long Nez, 1327: Archives de l'Assistance Publique (henceforth AAP), Fonds St.-Jacques, no. 11.
Guillaume de Mailly, 1327 (**CW**): AN, L 938, no. 61.
Guillaume Fresnel, 1293 (**S**): AN, S 896, no. 17.
Jacqueline, widow of Theobald de Morise, 1273: AN, L 859, no. 2610.
Jehan de Fontenoi and Bauteut his wife, 1227 (**CDW**): AN, L 547, no. 1.

Jehan de Troyes, 1332 (**CSW**): AAP, Fonds St.-Jacques, no. 17.

Jehan Langlais, 1316 (**W**): Quinze Vingts 5848, fols. 293r–294v.

Jehan le Grand, 1310 (**DS**): Quinze Vingts 5848, fols. 213r–216r.

Jehanne Argence, 1273 (**CS**): J. Depoin, ed., *Recueil de chartes et documents de Saint-Martin-des-Champs*, 5 vols. (Paris, 1912–21), 5:97–98.

Jehanne de Malaunay, 1310 (**CDW**): Arthur Goldmann, ed., "Inventaire de Galeran le Breton et testament de Jeanne de Malaunay, bourgeois de Paris (1299–1311)," *Bulletin de la Société de l'Histoire de Paris et de l'Ile-de-France* 19 (1892): 167–70.

Jehanne du Faut, 1330 (**CLW**): AAP, Fonds St.-Jacques, no. 14.

Jehanne Grinell, wife of Jehan Grinell, 1305 (**W**): AN, L 554A, no. 53.

Jehanne Haudry, wife of Etienne Haudry, 1309 (**CSW**): AN, L 1043, no. 24.

Jehanne la Fouacière, 1313 (**CDLW**): AN, L 938, no. 46.

Jehanne la Patrice, 1303: AAP, Fonds Hôtel-Dieu, Liasse 132, no. 765.

Margaret, wife of Pierre Loisel, 1330 (**CW**): AN, L 938, no. 58.

Marie, widow of Robert Evrout, 1307 (**CDSW**): AN, L 849, no. 100. Anne Terroine, "Recherches sur la bourgeoisie parisienne au XIIIe siècle," 4 vols. (Unpublished *thèse*, École Nationale des Chartes, 1940), 4:130–36.

Philippe de Cormeilles, 1329: AAP, Fonds St.-Jacques, no. 13.

Pierre la Pie, 1302 (**CW**): Anne Terroine and Lucie Fossier, eds., *Chartes et documents de l'Abbaye de Saint-Magloire*, 3 vols. (Paris, 1966–), 2:148.

Robert Evrout, 1306 (**CDSW**): AN, L 840, no. 99; Terroine, "Recherches," 4:122–29.

Robert le Vinetier, 1311 (**D**): AN, L 1021, no. 18; Terroine, "Recherches," 4:159–71.

Roger du Four du Temple, 1281: Brièle, *Archives de l'Hôtel-Dieu de Paris*, 419–20.

Sédile de Laon, 1316 (**SW**): Léon Le Grand, ed., "Testament d'une bourgeoise de Paris," *Bulletin de la Société de l'Histoire de Paris et de l'Ile-de-France* 14 (1887): 42–47.

Simon Piz-d'Oue, canon of St.-Germain-l'Auxerrois, 1307 (**CDW**): Henri Martin, ed., "Testament de Simon Piz-d'Oue, chanoine de Saint-Germain-l'Auxerrois (3 octobre, 1307)," *Bulletin de la Société de l'Histoire de Paris et de l'Ile-de-France* 31 (1909): 33–39.

Thomas le Tailleur, 1307: Quinze Vingts 5848, fols. 49v–50v.

Thiphaine la Commine, 1295 (**D**): Brièle, *Archives de l'Hôtel- Dieu de Paris*, 550–53.

BIBLIOGRAPHY

ARCHIVAL AND MANUSCRIPT SOURCES

Paris, Archives de l'Assistance Publique
    Fonds Hôtel-Dieu, Liasse 132.
    Fonds St.-Jacques.
Paris, Archives des Quinze-Vingts
    MS. 5848.
Paris, Archives Nationales
    KK 5
    L 547
    L 554A
    L 840
    L 849
    L 859
    L 938
    L 1021
    L 1043
    L 1053
    L 1078
    LL 7
    LL 387
    S 896
    S 5073b
    S 6213
Paris, Bibliothèque Nationale de France
    MS. fr. 4976.
    MS. fr. 5716.
    MS. lat. 3284.
    MS. lat. 15943.

PUBLISHED SOURCES

Akehurst, R. P., ed. *The Etablissements de Saint Louis: Thirteenth-Century Law Texts from Tours, Orléans, and Paris.* Philadelphia, 1996.
Albertus Magnus. *Quaestiones super de animalibus.* Edited by Ephrem Filthaut. In *Al-*

berti Magni Opera Omnia, edited by Bernhard Geyer et al., 12:77–309. vols. 1–Cologne, 1951–.

Amt, Emily, ed. *Women's Lives in Medieval Europe: A Sourcebook*. New York, 1993.

Armstrong, Regis J., ed. and trans. *Clare of Assisi: Early Documents*. New York, 1988.

Augustine. *Sancti Aurelii Augustini Enarrationes in Psalmos LI-C*. Edited by Eligius Dekkers and Johannes Fraipont. Corpus christianorum, Series latina 39. Turnhout, 1956.

Azo. *Summa Azonis: Summa perutilis excellentissimi iuris monarche domini Azonis superrime maxima diligentia castigata*. Lyon, 1530.

Béthune, Jean, ed. *Cartulaire du Béguinage de Sainte-Elisabeth à Gand*. Bruges, 1883.

Bonaventure. *Apologia pauperum contra calumniatorem*. Edited by the College of Saint Bonaventure. In *Doctoris Seraphici S. Bonaventurae Opera Omnia*, 8:223–330. 10 vols. Quaracchi, 1882–1902.

———. *Quaestiones disputatae de perfectione evangelica*. Edited by the College of Saint Bonaventure. In *Doctoris Seraphici S. Bonaventurae Opera Omnia*, 5:117–98. 10 vols. Quaracchi, 1882–1902.

——— (attributed). *Expositio super regulam Fratrum Minorum*. Edited by the College of Saint Bonaventure. In *Doctoris Seraphici S. Bonaventurae Opera Omnia*, 8:391–437. 10 vols. Quaracchi, 1882–1902.

Brièle, Léon, ed. *Archives de l'Hôtel Dieu de Paris (1157–1300)*. Paris, 1894.

Burchard of Worms. *Liber decretorum. PL* 140:557–1058.

Carolus-Barré, Louis, ed. "Consultation du Cardinal Pietro Colonna sur le IIe miracle de Saint Louis." *Bibliothèque de l'Ecole des Chartres* 117 (1959): 57–71.

Casagrande, Carla, ed. *Prediche alle donne del secolo XIII*. Milan, 1978.

Clark, Elizabeth, and Herbert Richardson, ed. and trans. *Women and Religion: A Feminist Sourcebook of Christian Thought*. New York, 1977.

Delaborde, H.-François, ed. "Fragments de l'enquête faite à Saint-Denis en 1282 en vue de la canonisation de Saint Louis." *Mémoires de la Société de l'Histoire de Paris et de l'Ile-de-France* 23 (1896): 1–71.

Denifle, Henricus, ed. *Chartularium universitatis Parisiensis*. 4 vols. Paris, 1889–97.

Depoin, J., ed. *Recueil de chartes et documents de Saint-Martin-des-Champs*. 5 vols. Paris, 1912–21.

Depping, G.-B., ed. *Réglemens sur les arts et métiers de Paris, redigés au XIIIe siècle, et connus sous le nom du Livre des métiers d'Etienne Boileau*. Paris, 1837.

Digestum vetus seu Pandectarum Iuris civilis tomus primus. Venice, 1584.

Dion, A. de, ed. *Cartulaire de l'abbaye de Porrois au diocèse de Paris*. Paris, 1903.

Dutilleux, Adolphe, and Joseph Depoin, eds. *Cartulaire de l'abbaye de Maubuisson (Notre-Dame la Royale)*. 2 vols. Pontoise, 1890–1913.

Fry, Timothy, ed. *RB 1980: The Rule of Saint Benedict in Latin and English with Notes and Thematic Index*. Abridged Edition. Collegeville, Minn., 1981.

Gabriel, Astrik, ed. "Statutes of Ave Maria College." In *Student Life in Ave Maria College, Medieval Paris: History and Chartulary of the College*, 319–83. Notre Dame, Ind., 1955.

Géraud, Hercule. *Paris sous Philippe-le-Bel, d'après des documents originaux et notamment d'après un manuscrit contenant "Le Rôle de la Taille" imposée sur les habitants de Paris en 1292.* 1837. Reprint, with introduction and index by Caroline Bourlet and Lucie Fossier. Tübingen, 1991.

Goldberg, P. J. P., ed. and trans. *Women in England c. 1275–1525.* Manchester, 1995.

Goldmann, Arthur, ed. "Inventaire de Galeran le Breton et testament de Jeanne de Malaunay, bourgeois de Paris (1299–1311)." *Bulletin de la Société de l'Histoire de Paris et de l'Ile-de-France* 19 (1892): 163–70.

Gout, Raoul, ed. and trans. *La vie de Sainte Douceline: Texte Provençal du XIVe siècle.* Paris, 1927.

Gratian. *Decretum Gratiani emendatum, et notationibus illustratum, una cum glossis Gregorii xiii. pont. max.* Rome, 1588.

Guibert of Nogent. *De vita sua sive monodiarum suarum libri tres.* Translated by C. C. Swinton Bland, with introduction and notes by John F. Benton. In *Self and Society in Medieval France.* New York, 1970.

Guillaume de Chartres. *De vita et actibus regis Francorum Ludovici et de miraculis.* RHGF 20:27–47.

Guillaume de la Villeneuve. "Les crieries de Paris." Edited by Alfred Franklin. In *Les rues et les cries de Paris au XIIIe siècle: Pièces historiques publiées d'après les manuscrits de la Bibliothèque nationale, et précédées d'une étude sur les rues de Paris au XIIIe siècle,* 153–64. Paris, 1874. Reprint, Paris, 1984.

Guillaume de Nangis. *Vie de Saint Louis.* RHGF 20:314–465.

Guillaume de St.-Pathus, Confesseur de la reine Marguerite. *Les miracles de Saint Louis.* Edited by Percival B. Fay. Paris, 1931.

Guillaume le Clerc de Normandie. *Le Besant de Dieu.* Edited by Pierre Ruelle. Brussels, 1973.

Hellot, A., ed. "Chronique Parisienne anonyme de 1316 à 1339, précédée d'additions à la chronique française dite de Guillaume de Nangis." *Mémoires de la Société de l'Histoire de Paris et de l'Ile-de-France* 11(1884): 1–207.

Hermensart, Pagart d', ed. "Documents inédits contenus dans les archives de Saint Omer." *Bulletin historique et philologique du Comité des travaux historiques et scientifiques* (1900): 71–78.

Honorius of Autun. *Sermo generalis.* PL 172:861–870.

Hugh of Amiens, archbishop of Rouen. "Letter to Thierry, Bishop of Amiens." Edited and translated by Teresa G. Frisch. In *Gothic Art, 1140–c. 1450,* Medieval Academy Reprints for Teaching 25. Toronto, 1987.

Hugh of St.-Victor. *Adnotationes Elucidatoriae in Pentateuchon.* PL 175:29–80.

Humbert of Romans. *De eruditione religiosorum praedicatorum.* Bk. 2, tractatus 1. Edited by Marguerin de la Bigne. In *Maxima bibliotheca veterum patrum et antiquorum scriptorum ecclesiasticorum,* 25:456–506. 27 vols. Lyon, 1677.

Huyskens, Albert, ed. *Quellenstudien zur Geschichte der hl. Elizabeth Landgräfin von Thüringen.* Marburg, 1908.

Ivo of Chartres. *Decretum.* PL 161:47–1036.

Jacobus de Voragine. *Legenda aurea.* Edited by Th. Graesse. Dresden, 1846.

Jacobus de Voragine. *The Golden Legend*. Translated and adapted from the Latin by Granger Ryan and Helmut Ripperger. New York, 1941.

Jacques de Vitry. "Deux sermons de Jacques de Vitry (+1240) *Ad Servos et Ancillas*." Edited by Jean Longère. In *La femme au moyen âge*, edited by Michel Rouche and Jean Heuclin, 261–96. Maubeuge, 1990.

——. *The Exempla or Illustrative Stories for the Sermones Vulgares of Jacques de Vitry*. Edited by Thomas Frederick Crane. Reprint, New York, 1971.

——. *Lettres de Jacques de Vitry*. Edited by R. B. C. Huygens. Leiden, 1960.

——. *The Life of Marie d'Oignies*. Translated by Margot H. King. Saskatoon, 1986.

——. "Quatre sermons *ad religiosas* de Jacques de Vitry." Edited by Jean Longère. In *Les religieuses en France au XIIIe siècle*, edited by Michel Parisse, 215–300. Nancy, 1985.

——. *Sermones vulgares*. Edited by Joannes Baptista Cardinalis Pitra. In *Analecta novissima spicilegii Solesmensis, altera continuatio*, 2:344–442. 2 vols. Reprint, Farnborough, 1967.

——. *Vita Mariae Oigniacensis*. In *Acta Sanctorum quotquot toto orbe coluntur*. Edited by Joannus Bollandus et al. 3rd ed. Iunius 5, pp. 547–72. Vols. 1– . Paris, 1863– .

Jean de Jandun. *Eloge de Paris, composé en 1323 par un habitant de Senlis, Jean de Jandun*. Edited by Taranne and Leroux de Lincy. Paris, 1856.

Jean of St.-Victor. *Excerpta e memoriali Historiarum, auctore Johanne Parisiensi, Sancti Victoris Parisiensis canonico regulari*. *RHGF* 21:630–76.

Jean, sire de Joinville. *Histoire de Saint Louis*. Edited by Natalis de Wailly. Paris, 1868.

——. *The Life of St. Louis*. Translated by René Hague. New York, 1955.

Jehan le Marchant. *Le livre des miracles de Notre-Dame de Chartres*. Edited by M. G. Duplessis. Chartres, 1855.

Jerome. "Against Vigilantius." Translated by W. H. Freemantle. In *The Principle Works of St. Jerome*, 417–23. The Nicene and Post-Nicene Fathers, vol. 6. Grand Rapids, Mich., 1954.

——. *De perpetua Virginitate B. Mariae*. *PL* 23:193–216.

——. *Liber Contra Vigilantium*. *PL* 23:339–52.

Johannes de Erfordia. *Die Summa confessorum des Johannes von Erfurt*. Edited by Norbert Brieskorn. 3 vols. Frankfurt-am-Main, 1980–81.

John of Freiburg. *Summa confessorum reverendi patris Joannis de Friburgo*. Lyon, 1518.

Langfors, Arthur, ed. *Roman de Fauvel*. Société des Anciens Textes Français. Paris, 1914.

Le Grand, Léon, èd. "Reglèment donné auz Quinze-Vingts par Michel de Brache, aumônier du roi Jean (1351–1355)." In "Les Quinze-Vingts," part 2, *Mémoires de la Société de l'histoire de Paris et de l'Ile-de-France* 14 (1887): 154–64.

——. "Testament d'une bourgeoise de Paris." *Bulletin de la Société de l'Histoire de Paris et de l'Ile-de-France* 14 (1887): 42–47.

Lespinasse, Réné de. *Les métiers et corporations de la ville de Paris XIVe–XVIIIe siècle*. 3 vols. Paris, 1886–97.

Lespinasse, René de, and François Bonnardot, eds. *Le livre des métiers d'Etienne Boileau*. Paris, 1879.

Mansi, J. D., ed. *Sacrorum conciliorum nova et amplissima collectio.* 53 vols. Florence, 1759–98. Reprint, Graz, 1960–61.

Martin, Henri, ed. "Testament de Simon Piz-d'Oue, chanoine de Saint-Germaine-l'Auxerrois (3 octobre, 1307)." *Bulletin de la Société de l'Histoire de Paris et de l'Ile-de-France* 31 (1909): 32–39.

Michaëlsson, Karl, ed. *Le livre de la taille de Paris, l'an de grace 1313.* Göteborg, 1951.

——. *Le livre de la taille de Paris, l'an 1296.* Göteborg, 1958.

——. *Le livre de la taille de Paris, l'an 1297.* Göteborg, 1962.

Molinier, Auguste. *Obituaires de la province de Sens.* 4 vols. Paris, 1902–23.

Peter the Chanter. *Summa de sacramentis et animae consiliis.* Edited by Jean-Albert Dugauquier. 5 vols. Analecta mediaevalia Namurcensia 4, 7, 11, 16, 21. Louvain, 1954–67.

——. *Verbum abbreviatum.* PL 205:21–554.

Prosper of Aquitaine. *Liber sententiarum ex Augustino delibatarum.* PL 51:427–534.

Reimbaldus Leodiensis. *Stromata, seu de uoto reddendo et de paenitentia non iteranda.* Edited by C. De Clerq. In *Reimbaldi Leodiensis Opera Omnia.* Corpus christianorum, Continuatio mediaevalis 4. Turnhout, 1966.

Roques, Mario, ed. *Le garçon et l'aveugle: Jeu du XIIIᵉ siècle.* Translated into modern French by Jean Dufournet. Paris, 1989.

Rutebeuf. *Oeuvres complètes.* Edited by Michel Zink. 2 vols. Paris, 1989.

Salmon, André, ed. *De reversione beati Martini a burgundia tractatus.* In *Supplément aux chroniques de Touraine,* 14–34. Tours, 1856.

Schwalm, Jacob, ed. "Relatio de statu ecclesiae in regno Alemanniae (1273)." In *Monumenta Germaniae Historica, Legum, sectio IV,* 3:589–94. Vols. 1– . Hanover, 1893– , Reprint, 1980.

Stephen of Bourbon. *Tractatus de diversis materiis praedicabilibus.* Edited by A. Lecoy de la Marche. In *Anecdotes historiques, légendes et apologues tirés du recueil inédit d'Etienne de Bourbon Dominicain du XIIIᵉ siècle.* Paris, 1877.

Tanon, L., ed. *Histoire des justices de Paris.* Paris, 1883.

Terroine, Anne, and Lucie Fossier, eds. *Chartes et documents de l'Abbaye de Saint-Magloire.* vols. 1– Paris, 1966– .

Tertullian. "On the Veiling of Virgins." Edited by A. Cleveland Coxe. In *Fathers of the Third Century,* 27–38. Ante Nicene Fathers, vol. 4. Reprint, Grand Rapids, Mich., 1976.

Thomas Aquinas. *Contra impugnantes dei cultum et religionem.* In *Sancti Thomae Aquinatis Doctoris Angelici Ordinis Praedicatorum Opera Omnia,* 15:1–75. 25 vols. Parma, 1852–73. Reprint, New York, 1948–50.

——. *In quattuor libros sententiarum.* Edited by Robert Busa. In *S. Thomae Aquinatis Opera omnia,* vol 1. 7 vols. Stuttgart, 1980.

——. *Summa theologiae.* Latin text and English translation by the Blackfriars. 61 vols. New York, 1964–81.

Thomas of Cantimpré. *Bonum universale de apibus.* Douai, 1627.

——. *The Life of Margaret of Ypres.* Translated by Margot H. King. Toronto, 1990.

——. *Vita Margaretae de Ypris.* Edited by G. Meerseman. In "Les Frères Prêcheurs et le mouvement dévot en Flandres au XIIIe siècle." *Archivum Fratrum Praedicatorum* 18 (1948): 106–30.

Thomas of Chobham. *Summa de arte praedicandi*. Edited by Franco Morenzoni. Corpus christianorum, continuatio mediaevalis 82. Turnhout, 1988.

——. *Thomae de Chobham Summa confessorum*. Edited by F. Broomfield. Analecta mediaevalia Namurcensia 25. Louvain, 1968.

Thomas of Eccleston. *Tractatus de adventu Fratrum Minorum in Angliam*. Edited by A. G. Little. Manchester, 1951.

Viollet, Paul, ed. *Les établissements de Saint Louis*. 4 vols. Société de l'histoire de France. Paris, 1881–86.

Volumen legum parvum, quod vocant, in quo haec insunt: tres posteriores libri Codicis D. Iustiniani. Venice, 1583.

William of Canterbury. *Miracula Gloriosi Martyris Thomae, Cantuariensis Archiepiscopi*. In *Materials for the History of Thomas Becket*, edited by James Craigie Robertson, 1:137–546. 7 vols. London: 1875–85.

SECONDARY SOURCES

Agrimi, Joel, and Chiara Crisciani. "Savoir médical et anthropologie religieuse: Les représentations et les fonctions de la *vetula* (XIIIe–XVe siècles)." *Annales: Economies, sociétés, civilisations* 48 (1993): 1281–1308.

Alarcón, Norma. "The Theoretical Subject(s) of This Bridge Called My Back." In *Making Face, Making Soul/Haciendo Caras: Creative and Critical Perspectives by Feminists of Color*, edited by Gloria Anzaldúa, 356–69. San Francisco, 1990.

Allen, Prudence. *The Concept of Woman: The Aristotelian Revolution 750 B.C.–A.D. 1250*. Montreal, 1985.

Aptekar, Lewis. *Street Children of Cali*. Durham, N.C., 1988.

Archer, Janice. "Working Women in Thirteenth-Century Paris." Ph.D. diss., University of Arizona, 1995.

Baldwin, John. *Masters, Princes and Merchants: The Social Views of Peter the Chanter and His Circle*. 2 vols. Princeton, N.J., 1970.

Batany, Jean. "Les pauvres et la pauvreté dans les revues des 'Estats du monde.'" In *Etudes sur l'histoire de la pauvreté*, edited by Michel Mollat, 2:469–86. 2 vols. Paris, 1974.

Bavoux, Paule. "Enfants trouvés et orphelins du XIVe au XVIe siècles à Paris." In *Assistance et assistés jusqu'à 1610*. Actes du 97e Congrès National des Sociétés Savantes, Nantes, 1972, 359–70. Paris, 1979.

Beattie, Cordelia. "The Problem of Women's Work Identities in Post Black Death England." In *The Problem of Labour in Fourteenth-Century England*. Edited by James Bothwell, P. J. P. Goldberg, and W. M. Ormrod. York, Eng., 2000. 1–19.

Bennett, Judith. *Ale, Beer, and Brewsters in England: Women's Work in a Changing World, 1300–1600*. New York, 1996.

——. "Conviviality and Charity in Medieval and Early Modern England." *Past and Present*, no. 134 (1992): 19–41.

Bennett, Judith, and Amy Froide, eds. *Singlewomen in the European Past, 1250–1800*. Philadelphia, 1999.

Bent, Margaret, and Andrew Wathey, eds. *Fauvel Studies: Allegory, Chronicle, Music, and Image in Paris, Bibliothèque Nationale, ms. français 146*. Oxford, 1998.

Berman, Constance. "Cistercian Nuns and the Development of the Order: The Abbey of Saint-Antoine-des-Champs outside Paris." In *The Joy of Learning: Studies in Honor of Jean Leclerq*, edited by E. Rozanne Elder, 121–56. Kalamazoo, Mich., 1995.

Berthelé, Joseph. "La vie interieure d'un hospice du XIVe au XVIe siècle: l'Hôpital du Saint-Esprit-en-Grève à Paris." *L'hôpital et l'aide sociale à Paris*, no. 7 (January–February 1961): 81–91; no. 8 (March–April 1961): 225–35; no. 9 (May–June 1961): 375–83; no. 10 (July–August 1961): 537–41; no. 11 (September–October 1961): 687–703; no. 12 (November–December 1961): 847–52.

Biscoglio, Frances M. " 'Unspun' heroes: Iconography of the Spinning Woman in the Middle Ages." *The Journal of Medieval and Renaissance Studies* 25 (1995): 163–76.

Biver, Paul, and Marie-Louise Biver. *Abbayes, monastères, couvents de femmes à Paris des origines à la fin du XVIIIe siècle*. Paris, 1975.

Bloch, R. Howard. *Medieval Misogyny and the Invention of Western Romantic Love*. Chicago, 1991.

Bolton, Brenda. " 'Vitae Matrum': A Further Aspect of the Frauenfrage." In *Medieval Women*, edited by Derek Baker, 253–74. Oxford, 1978.

Bornstein, Daniel. "Violenza al corpo di una santa: Fra agiografia e pornografia." *Quaderni medievali* 39 (1995): 31–46.

Børresen, Kari Elisabeth. *Subordination and Equivalence: The Nature and Role of Women in Augustine and Thomas Aquinas*. Translated by Charles H. Talbot. Washington, D.C., 1981.

Boswell, John. *The Kindness of Strangers: The Abandonment of Children from Late Antiquity to the Renaissance*. New York, 1988.

Bourlet, Caroline. "L'anthroponymie à Paris à la fin du XIIIe siècle d'après les rôles de la taille du règne de Philippe le Bel." In *Genèse médiévale de l'anthroponymie moderne*, edited by Monique Bourin and Pascal Chareille, 2–2: 9–44. Tours, 1992.

Boyarin, Daniel. *Carnal Israel: Reading Sex in Talmudic Culture*. Berkeley, Calif., 1993.

Branner, Robert. *Manuscript Painting in Paris during the Reign of Saint Louis*. Berkeley, Calif., 1977.

Brett, Edward Tracy. *Humbert of Romans: His Life and Views of Thirteenth-Century Society*. Toronto, 1984.

Brown, Elizabeth A. R., and Nancy Freeman Regalado. "*La grant feste*: Philip the Fair's Celebration of the Knighting of His Sons in Paris at Pentecost in 1313." In *City and Spectacle in Medieval Europe*, edited by Barbara Hanawalt and Kathryn L. Reyerson, 56–86. Minneapolis, 1994.

Brunel, Ghislain, and Elisabeth Lalou, eds. *Sources d'histoire médiévale IXe–milieu du XIVe siècle*. Paris, 1992.

Buc, Philippe. *L'ambiguïté du livre: Prince, pouvoir, et peuple dans les commentaires de la Bible au moyen âge*. Paris, 1994.

Bynum, Caroline Walker. *Fragmentation and Redemption: Essays on Gender and the Human Body in Medieval Religion*. New York, 1991.

Carolus-Barré, Louis. *Le procès de canonisation de Saint Louis (1272–1297): Essai de reconstitution*. Rome, 1994.

Carozzi, Claude. "Douceline et les autres." In *La religion populaire en Languedoc du XIIIᵉ siècle à la moitié du XIVᵉ siècle*, 251–67. Cahiers de Fanjeaux, 11. Toulouse, 1976.

Casagrande, Carla. "The Protected Woman." Translated by Clarissa Botsford. In *A History of Women in the West*, vol. 2: *Silences of the Middle Ages*, edited by Christiane Klapisch-Zuber, 70–104. Cambridge, Mass., 1992.

Castelli, Elizabeth. "Virginity and Its Meaning for Women's Sexuality in Early Christianity." *Journal of Feminist Studies in Religion* 2 (1986): 61–88.

Cazelles, Brigitte. "Introduction." In *The Lady as Saint: A Collection of French Hagiographic Romances of the Thirteenth Century*. Philadelphia, 1991.

Cazelles, Raymond. *Nouvelle histoire de Paris, de la fin du règne de Philippe Auguste à la mort de Charles V, 1223–1380*. Paris, 1972.

——. "Le parisien au temps de Saint Louis." In *Septième centenaire de la mort de Saint Louis, Actes des Colloques de Royaumont et de Paris (21–27 mai 1970)*, 97–104. Paris, 1976.

——. "La peste de 1348–1349, épidémie prolétarienne et enfantine." *Bulletin philologique et historique (jusqu'à 1610) du Comité des Travaux Historiques et Scientifiques*, 1962, 293–305. Paris, 1965.

——. "La population de Paris avant la peste noire." In *Académie des Inscriptions et Belles Lettres: Comptes rendus*, 539–54. Paris, 1966.

——. "Quelques reflexions à propos des mutations de la monnaie royale française (1260–1360)." *Le moyen âge* 72 (1966): 83–105, 251–78.

Chabot, Isabelle. "La reconnaissance du travail des femmes dans la Florence du bas Moyen Age: Context idéologique et réalité." In *La donna nell'economia secc. XIII–XVIII*, edited by Simonetta Cavaciocchi, 563–76. Florence, 1990.

——. "Widowhood and Poverty in Late Medieval Florence." In *Charity and the Poor in Medieval and Renaissance Europe*, edited by John Henderson. *Continuity and Change* 3, no. 2 (1988): 299–311.

Charmaz, Kathy. "Identity Dilemmas of Chronically Ill Men." In *Men's Health and Illness: Gender, Power, and the Body*, edited by Donald Sabo and David Frederick Gordon, 266–91. Thousand Oaks, Calif., 1995.

Chennaf, Sharaf, and Odile Redon. "Les miracles de Saint Louis." In *Les miracles: Miroirs des corps*, edited by Jacques Gelis and Odile Redon, 53–86. Paris, 1983.

Chiffoleau, Jacques. *La comptabilité de l'au-delà: Les hommes, la mort et la religion dans la région d'Avignon à la fin du moyen âge (vers 1320–vers 1480)*. Rome, 1980.

Chojnacki, Stanley. "Measuring Adulthood: Adolescence and Gender in Renaissance Venice." *Journal of Family History* 17 (1992): 371–95.

Clark, Elaine. "Social Welfare and Mutual Aid in the Medieval Countryside." *Journal of British Studies* 33 (1984): 381–406.

Cohen, Esther. " 'To Die A Criminal for the Public Good': The Execution Ritual in Late Medieval Paris." In *Law, Custom, and the Social Fabric in Medieval Europe: Essays in Honor of Bryce Lyon*, edited by Bernard S. Bacharach and David Nicholas, 285–304. Studies in Medieval Culture 28. Kalamazoo, Mich., 1990.

Cohen, Gustave. "Le thème de l'aveugle et du paralytique dans la littérature française." In *Mélanges offerts à Emile Picot par ses amis et ses élèves*, 2:393–404. 2 vols. Paris, 1913. Reprint, Geneva, 1969.

Colish, Marcia. "Cosmetic Theology: The Transformation of a Stoic Theme." In *Assays: Critical Approaches to Medieval and Renaissance Texts*, edited by Peggy A. Knapp and Michael A. Stugrin, 3–14. Pittsburgh, 1981.

Collins, Patricia Hill. *Black Feminist Thought: Knowledge, Consciousness, and the Politics of Empowerment*. Boston, 1990.

Connally, Michael. "Common Life by the Statutes and in Practice: The Haudriettes." Paper presented at the International Medieval Congress, Leeds, July 2000.

Corzo, Luis Revest. *Hospitales y pobres en el Castellón de otros tiempos*. Castellón de la Plana, 1947.

Coyecque, E. *L'Hôtel-Dieu de Paris au moyen âge: Histoire et documents*. 2 vols. Paris, 1891.

Davis, Michael T. "Desespoir, Esperance, et Douce France: The New Palace, Paris, and the Royal State." In *Fauvel Studies: Allegory, Chronicle, Music, and Image in Paris, Bibliothèque Nationale de France, ms. français 146*, edited by Margaret Bent and Andrew Wathey, 187–214. Oxford, 1998.

D'Avray, D., and M. Tausche. "Marriage Sermons in *ad status* Collections of the Central Middle Ages." *Archives d'histoire doctrinale et littéraire du moyen âge* 47 (1980): 71–119.

Desportes, Pierre. "La population de Reims au XVe siècle d'après un denombrement de 1422." *Le moyen âge* 72 (1966): 463–509.

Didier, Philippe. "Le contrat d'apprentissage en Bourgogne aux XIVe et XVe siècles." *Revue historique de droit français et étranger* 54 (1976): 35–57.

Dillard, Heath. *Daughters of the Reconquest: Women in Castilian Town Society, 1100–1300*. Cambridge, 1984.

Dixon, E. "Craftswomen in the *Livre des métiers*." *Economic Journal* 5, no. 2(1895): 209–28.

Douie, D. L. *The Conflict between the Seculars and the Mendicants at the University of Paris in the Thirteenth Century*. The Aquinas Society of London, Aquinas Paper 23. London, 1954.

Dubois, Gérard. *Historia ecclesiae parisiensis*. 2 vols. Paris, 1690–1710.

Dubois, Henri. "Les feux féminins à Dijon aux XIVe et XVe siècles (1394–1407)." In *La femme au moyen âge*, edited by Michel Rouche and Jean Heuclin, 395–405. Maubeuge, 1990.

——. "La pauvreté dans les premières 'cherches de feux' bourguignonnes." In *Hori-*

zons marins, itinéraires spirituels (V^e–XVIIIe siècles), edited by Henri Dubois, Jean-Claude Hocquet, and Andre Vauchez, 1:291–301. 2 vols. Paris, 1987.

Du Boulay, César Egasse. *Historia universitatis Parisiensis.* 5 vols. Paris, 1665–73. Reprint, Frankfurt-am-Main, 1966.

Du Breul, Jacques. *Le théâtre des antiquitez de Paris.* Paris, 1639.

Duby, Georges. *Le temps des cathédrales: L'art et la société, 980–1420.* Paris, 1976.

——. *The Three Orders: Feudal Society Imagined.* Translated by Arthur Goldhammer. Chicago, 1980.

Dufeil, Michel-Marie. *Guillaume de St.-Amour et la polémique universitaire parisienne, 1250–1259.* Paris, 1972.

Dyer, Christopher. *Standards of Living in the Later Middle Ages: Social Change in England c. 1200–1520.* Cambridge, 1989.

Edin, Kathryn. *The Myths of Dependence and Self-Sufficiency: Women, Welfare, and Low-Wage Work.* Piscataway, N.J., 1994.

——. *There's a Lot of Month Left at the End of the Money: How Welfare Recipients Make Ends Meet in Chicago.* New York, 1993.

Edin, Kathryn, and Laura Lein. *Making Ends Meet: How Single Mothers Survive Welfare and Low-Wage Work.* New York, 1997.

Elliott, Dyan. "Dress as Mediator Between Inner and Outer Self: The Pious Matron of the High Middle Ages." *Mediaeval Studies* 53 (1991): 279–308.

——. *Fallen Bodies: Pollution, Sexuality, and Demonology in the Middle Ages.* Philadelphia, 1999.

——. *Spiritual Marriage: Sexual Abstinence in Medieval Wedlock.* Princeton, N.J., 1993.

——. "Women in Love: Carnal and Spiritual Transgressions in Late Medieval France." Unpublished paper delivered at symposium on "The Family in the Middle Ages," J. Paul Getty Museum, Los Angeles, Calif., June 1999.

Elliott, Vivien Brodsky. "Single Women in the London Marriage Market: Age, Status, and Mobility, 1598–1619." In *Marriage and Society: Studies in the Social History of Marriage*, edited by R. B. Outhwaite, 81–100. London, 1981.

Epstein, Steven A. *Wage Labor and Guilds in Medieval Europe.* Chapel Hill, 1991.

——. *Wills and Wealth in Medieval Genoa, 1150–1250.* Cambridge, Mass., 1984.

Fagniez, Gustave. *Etudes sur l'industrie et la classe industrielle à Paris au XIIIe et au XIVe siècle.* Paris, 1877. Reprint, New York, 1970.

Fairchilds, Cissie. *Domestic Enemies: Servants and Their Masters in Old Regime France.* Baltimore, 1984.

Farmer, Sharon. *Communities of Saint Martin: Legend and Ritual in Medieval Tours.* Ithaca, 1991.

——. "Down and Out and Female in Thirteenth-Century Paris." *American Historical Review* 103 (1998): 345–72.

——. "Gender and Migration in Thirteenth-Century Paris." Paper presented to the annual meeting of the American Historical Association, Washington, D.C., January 1999.

——. "It Is Not Good that [Wo]man Should Be Alone: Elite Responses to Singlewomen in High Medieval Paris." In *Singlewomen in the European Past, 1250–1800*, edited by Judith Bennett and Amy Froide, 82–105. Philadelphia, 1999.

Farmer, Sharon, and Carol Braun Pasternack, eds. *Genders and Other Identities in the Middle Ages: The Interplay of Differences*. Minneapolis, 2002.

Favier, J. "L'hôtel royal de Philippe le Bel." *L'histoire* no. 4 (1978): 31–40.

Fawtier, R., and F. Lot. *Histoire des institutions françaises au moyen âge*. Vol. 2, *Institutions royales*. Paris, 1958.

Finucane, Ronald C. *Miracles and Pilgrims: Popular Beliefs in Medieval England*. Totowa, N.J., 1977.

———. *The Rescue of the Innocents: Endangered Children in Medieval Miracles*. New York, 1997.

Foreville, Raymonde. "Les 'Miracula S. Thomae Cantuariensis.' " In *Assistance et assisté jusqu'à 1610, Actes du 97ᵉ Congrès National des Sociétés Savantes, Nantes, 1972*, 452. Paris, 1979.

Fourquin, Guy. *Les campagnes de la région parisienne à la fin du moyen âge: Du milieu du XIIIᵉ au debut du XVIᵉ siècle*. Paris, 1964.

Frappier-Bigras, Diane. "La famille dans l'artisanat parisien du XIIIᵉ siècle." *Le moyen âge* 95 (1989): 47–74.

Freedman, Paul. *The Image of the Medieval Peasant as Alien and Exemplary*. Stanford, Calif., 1999.

Friedman, Albert. " 'When Adam Delved . . . ': Contexts of an Historical Proverb." In *The Learned and the Lewed: Studies in Chaucer and Medieval Literature*, edited by Larry D. Benson, 213–30. Cambridge, Mass., 1974.

Froide, Amy M. "Marital Status as a Category of Difference: Singlewomen and Widows in Early Modern England." In *Singlewomen in the European Past, 1250–1800*, edited by Judith Bennett and Froide, 236–69. Philadelphia, 1999.

Gabriel, Astrik L. "The College System in the Fourteenth-Century Universities." In *The Forward Movement of the Fourteenth Century*, edited by Francis Lee Utley, 79–123. Columbus, Ohio, 1961.

———. *Student Life in Ave Maria College, Medieval Paris: History and Chartulary of the College*. Notre Dame, Ind., 1955.

Gauvard, Claude. *"De Grace Especial": Crime, état et société en France à la fin du moyen âge*. Paris, 1991.

———. "Violence citadine et réseaux de solidarité: L'example française au XIVᵉ et XVᵉ siècles." *Annales: Economies, Sociétés, Civilisations* 48 (1993): 1113–26.

Geremek, Bronislaw. "La lutte contre le vagabondage à Paris aux XIVᵉ et XVᵉ siècles." In *Ricerche storiche ed economiche in memoria di Corrado Barbagallo*, edited by Luigi di Rosa, 213–36. Naples, 1970.

———. *The Margins of Society in Late Medieval Paris*. Translated from the French by Jean Birrell. Cambridge, 1987.

———. *La potence ou la pitié: L'Europe et les pauvres du moyen age à nos jours*. Paris, 1987.

———. *Poverty: A History*. Translated by Agnieszka Kolakowska. Oxford, 1994.

———. *Le salariat dans l'artisanat parisien aux XIIIᵉ–XVᵉ siècles*. Translated from the Polish by Anna Posner and Christiane Klapisch-Zuber. Paris, 1982.

Gerschick, Thomas J., and Adam S. Miller. "Coming to Terms: Masculinity and Physical Disability." In *Men's Health and Illness: Gender, Power and the Body*, edited by Donald Sabo and David Frederick Gordon, 183–204. Thousand Oaks, Calif., 1995.

Glorieux, P. *Répertoire des maîtres en théologie de Paris au XIIIᵉ siècle*. 2 vols. Etudes de philosophie médiévale 17, 18. Paris, 1933.

Godding, P. "La pratique testamentaire en Flandre au XIIIᵉ siècle." *Tijdschrift voor Rechtgeschiedenis* 58 (1990): 281–300.

Goldberg, P. J. P. "Marriage, Migration, and Servanthood: The York Cause Paper Evidence." In *Woman Is a Worthy Wight: Women in English Society c. 1200–1500*, edited by Goldberg, 1–15. Wolfboro Falls, N.H., 1992.

———. *Women, Work and Life Cycle in a Medieval Economy*. Oxford, 1992.

Gonthier, Nicole. *Lyon et ses pauvres au moyen âge (1350–1500)*. Lyon, 1978.

Goodich, Michael. *Violence and Miracle in the Fourteenth Century: Private Grief and Public Salvation*. Chicago, 1995.

Gravdal, Kathryn. *Ravishing Maidens: Writing Rape in Medieval French Literature and Law*. Philadelphia, 1991.

Guerout, Jean. "Le palais de la Cité à Paris des origines à 1417: Essai topographique et archéologique." In *Mémoires de la Fédération des Sociétés Historiques et Archéologiques de Paris et de l'Ile-de-France* 2 (1950): 23–44.

Guest, Gerald B. "A Discourse on the Poor: The Hours of Jeanne d'Evreux." *Viator: Medieval and Renaissance Studies* 26 (1995): 153–80.

Hajnal, J. "European Marriage Patterns in Perspective." In *Population in History*, edited by D. V. Glass and D. E. C. Eversley, 101–43. London, 1965.

Hallam, Elizabeth. *Capetian France, 987–1328*. New York, 1980.

Hanawalt, Barbara. *Growing Up in Medieval London: The Experience of Childhood in History*. New York, 1993.

———. *The Ties That Bound: Peasant Families in Medieval England*. New York, 1986.

Hasenohr, Geneviève. "La vie quotidienne de la femme vue par l'église: L'enseignement des 'Journées chrétiennes' de la fin du moyen-âge." In *Frau und spätmittelalterlicher Alltag*, 19–101. Vienna, 1986.

Helmholz, R. H. *Marriage Litigation in Medieval England*. London, 1974.

Henderson, John. "The Parish and the Poor in Florence at the Time of the Black Death: The Case of S. Frediano." In *Charity and the Poor in Medieval and Renaissance Europe*, edited by Henderson. *Continuity and Change* 3, no. 2 (1988): 247–72.

———. *Piety and Charity in Late Medieval Florence*. Oxford, 1994.

———, ed. *Charity and the Poor in Medieval and Renaissance Europe. Continuity and Change* 3, no. 2 (1988).

Henderson, John, and Richard Wall, eds. *Poor Women and Children in the European Past*. London, 1994.

Herlihy, David. "Demography." In *Dictionary of the Middle Ages*, edited by Joseph Strayer, 4:136–48. 13 vols. New York: 1982–89.

———. *Opera Muliebra: Women and Work in Medieval Europe*. New York, 1990.

Hohenberg, Paul M., and Lynn Hollen Lees. *The Making of Urban Europe.* Cambridge, Mass., 1988.

Hollywood, Amy. *The Soul as Virgin Wife: Mechthild of Magdeburg, Marguerite Porete, and Meister Eckhart.* Notre Dame, Ind., 1995.

hooks, bell. *Feminist Theory: From Margin to Center.* Boston, 1984.

Horden, Peregrine. "Household Care and Informal Networks: Comparisons and Continuities from Antiquity to the Present." In *The Locus of Care: Families, Communities, Institutions, and the Provision of Welfare since Antiquity,* edited by Peregrine Horden and Richard Smith, 21–67. New York, 1998.

Howell, Martha. "Fixing Movables: Gifts by Testament in Late Medieval Douai." *Past and Present,* no. 150 (February, 1996): 3–45.

——. *The Marriage Exchange: Property, Social Place, and Gender in Cities of the Low Countries, 1300–1550.* Chicago, 1998.

——. "Women, the Family Economy, and the Structures of Market Production during the Late Middle Ages." In *Women and Work in Preindustrial Europe,* edited by Barbara Hannawalt, 198–222. Bloomington, Ind., 1986.

——. *Women, Production, and Patriarchy in Late Medieval Cities.* Chicago, 1986.

Hufton, Olwen. "Women and the Family Economy in Eighteenth-Century France." *French Historical Studies* 9 (1975): 1–22.

——. "Women without Men: Widows and Spinsters in Britain and France in the Eighteenth Century." *Journal of Family History* 9 (winter 1984): 355–76.

Hughes, Diane Owen. "Distinguishing Signs: Ear-Rings, Jews and Franciscan Rhetoric in the Italian Renaissance City." *Past and Present,* no. 112 (1986): 3–59.

Jaillot, Jean Baptiste Michel. *Recherches critiques, historiques et topographiques sur la ville de Paris depuis ses commencemens connus jusqu'à présent.* 6 vols. Paris, 1775.

Jordan, William Chester. *The French Monarchy and the Jews: From Philip Augustus to the Last Capetians.* Philadelphia, 1989.

——. *The Great Famine: Northern Europe in the Early Fourteenth Century.* Princeton, 1996.

——. "Jews on Top: Women and the Availability of Consumption Loans in Northern France in the Mid-Thirteenth Century." *Journal of Jewish Studies* 29 (1978): 39–56.

Kaeppeli, Thomas. *Scriptores Ordinis Praedicatorum Medii Aevii.* 3 vols. Rome, 1970–80.

Karras, Ruth. *Common Women: Prostitution and Sexuality in Medieval England.* New York, 1996.

Kertzer, David, and Caroline Brettell. "Advances in Italian and Iberian Family History." *Journal of Family History* 12 (1987): 87–120.

Klapisch-Zuber, Christiane. "Women Servants in Florence During the Fourteenth and Fifteenth Centuries." In *Women and Work in Preindustrial Europe,* edited by Barbara Hannawalt, 56–80. Bloomington, Ind., 1986.

Kowaleski, Maryanne. "The History of Urban Families in Medieval England." *Journal of Medieval History* 14 (1988): 47–63.

——. "Singlewomen in Medieval and Early Modern Europe: The Demographic Perspective." In *Singlewomen in the European Past, 1250–1800*, edited by Judith Bennett and Amy Froide, 38–81, 325–344. Philadelphia, 1999.

Kowaleski, Maryanne, and Judith Bennett. "Crafts, Gilds, and Women in the Middle Ages: Fifty Years after Marian K. Dale." *Signs: Journal of Women in Culture and Society* 14 (1989): 474–88.

Kraemer, Ross Shepard. *Her Share of the Blessings: Women's Religions among Pagans, Jews, and Christians in the Greco-Roman World*. New York, 1992.

Krötzl, Christian. *Pilger, Mirakel und Alltag: Formen des Verhaltens im skandinavischen Mittelalter*. Helsinki, 1994.

Kruger, Steven. "Becoming Christian, Becoming Male?" In *Becoming Male in the Middle Ages*, edited by Jeffrey Jerome Cohen and Bonnie Wheeler, 21–41. New York, 1997.

——. "Medieval Christian (Dis)identifications: Muslims and Jews in Guibert of Nogent." *New Literary History* 28 (1997): 185–203.

Labande, Edmond-René. "Eléments d'une enquête sur les conditions de déplacement du pèlerin aux Xe et XIe siècles." In *Pellegrinaggi e culto dei santi in Europa fino alla prima crociata*, 95–111. Convegni del Centro di studi sulla spiritualità medievale 5. Todi, 1963.

Lalor, Kevin J. "Street Children: A Comparative Perspective." *Child Abuse and Neglect* 23 (1999): 759–70.

Lalou, E. "Les révoltes contre le pouvoir à la fin du XIIIe siècle et au début du XIVe." In *Violence et contestation du Moyen Age*, 159–84. Paris, 1989.

La Roncière, Charles de. "Pauvres et pauvreté à Florence au XIVe siècle." In *Etudes sur l'histoire de la pauvreté*, edited by Michel Mollat, 2:661–745. 2 vols. Paris, 1974.

——. *Prix et salaires à Florence au XIVe siècle, 1280–1380*. Rome, 1982.

Laslett, Peter. "Family, Kinship, and Collectivity as Systems of Support in Pre-Industrial Europe: A Consideration of the 'Nuclear-Hardship' Hypothesis." *Continuity and Change* 3 (1988): 153–75.

Lebeuf, L'Abbé. *Histoire de la ville et de tout le diocèse de Paris, Rectifications et additions, ville de Paris et ancienne banlieue, par Fernand Bournon*. Paris, 1890.

Le Goff, Jacques. "Saint de l'église et saint du peuple: Les miracles officiels de Saint Louis entre sa mort et sa canonisation." In *Histoire sociale, sensibilités collectives et mentalités: Mélanges Robert Mandrou*, 169–80. Paris, 1985.

——. *Saint Louis*. Paris, 1996.

Le Grand, Léon. "Les béguines de Paris." *Mémoires de la Société de l'Histoire de Paris et de l'Ile-de-France* 20 (1893): 295–357.

——. "Les maisons-Dieu et léproseries du diocèse de Paris au milieu du XIVe siècle." *Mémoires de la Société de l'histoire de Paris et de l'Ile-de-France* 25 (1898): 47–175.

——. "Les Quinze-Vingts: Depuis leur fondation jusqu'à leur translation au faubourg Saint-Antoine, XIIIe–XVIIIe siècles." *Mémoires de la Société de l'Histoire de Paris et de l'Ile-de-France* 13 (1886): 107–260; 14 (1887):1–208.

Lerner, Robert. *The Heresy of the Free Spirit in the Later Middle Ages*. Berkeley, Calif., 1972.

Le Roy Ladurie, Emmanuel. *Montaillou: The Promised Land of Error*. Translated by Barbara Bray. New York, 1978.

Lett, Didier. "La sorella maggiore 'madre sostituta' nei 'Miracoli di San Luigi.' " *Quaderni storici* 83 (1993): 341–53.

———. *L'enfant des miracles: Enfance et société au moyen âge (XIIᵉ–XIIIᵉ siècle)*. Paris, 1997.

Leyser, Henrietta. *Medieval Women: A Social History of Women in England, 450–1500*. London, 1996.

Little, Lester K. *Religious Poverty and the Profit Economy in Medieval Europe*. Ithaca, 1978.

Loats, Carol L. "Gender, Guilds, and Work Identity: Perspectives from Sixteenth-Century Paris." *French Historical Studies* 20 (1997): 15–30.

Lomnitz, Larissa A. *Networks and Marginality: Life in a Mexican Shantytown*. New York, 1977.

Lunbeck, Elizabeth. *The Psychiatric Persuasion: Knowledge, Gender, and Power in Modern America*. Princeton, N.J., 1994.

Mahieu, B. "Le *Livre des metiers* d'Etienne Boileau." In *Le siècle de Saint Louis*, 64–74. Paris, 1970.

Maillard, François. "Tarifs des 'Coutumes' pour la vente du poisson de mer à Paris au début du XIVᵉ siècle." *Bulletin philologique et historique* (1966): 247–58.

Makowski, Elizabeth. *Canon Law and Cloistered Women: Periculoso and Its Commentators, 1298–1545*. Washington, D.C., 1997.

Mansfield, Mary. *The Humiliation of Sinners: Public Penance in Thirteenth-Century France*. Ithaca, 1995.

Mayade-Claustre, Julie. "Le petit peuple en difficulté: La prison pour dettes à Paris à la fin du moyen âge." Paper presented at the international congress on "Le petit peuple dans la société de l'occident médiévale." Université de Montréal, October 18–22, 1999.

McDonnell, Ernest. *The Beguines and Beghards in Medieval Culture, with Special Emphasis on the Belgian Scene*. New Brunswick, N.J., 1954.

McNamara, Jo Ann Kay. *A New Song: Celibate Women in the First Three Christian Centuries*. Women and History, 6/7. New York, 1983.

———. *Sisters in Arms: Catholic Nuns through Two Millennia*. Cambridge, Mass., 1996.

Michaëlsson, Karl. *Etudes sur les noms de personnes français d'après les rôles de la taille parisiens*. Uppsala, 1927.

———. "Les noms d'origine dans le rôle de la taille parisien de 1313." *Symbolae Philologicae Gotoburgenses*, Acta universitatis Gotoburgensis, 56, no. 3(1950): 357–400.

Michaud-Frejaville, Françoise. "Bons et loyaux services: Les contrats d'apprentissage en Orléanais (1380–1480)." In *Les entrées dans la vie: Initiations et apprentissages*, 183–208. Congrès de la Société des Historiens Médiévistes de l'Enseignement Superieur Public. Nancy, 1982.

Mirrer, Louise. *Women, Jews, and Muslims in the Texts of Reconquest Castile*. Ann Arbor, 1996.

Moisà, Maria, and Judith Bennett. "Debate: Conviviality and Charity in Medieval and Early Modern England." *Past and Present*, no. 154 (February 1997): 223–42.

Mollat, Michel. "Notes sur la mortalité à Paris, d'après les comptes de l'oeuvre de Saint-Germaine-l'Auxerrois." *Le moyen âge* 69 (1963): 505–27.

——. *The Poor in the Middle Ages: An Essay in Social History.* Translated by Arthur Goldhammer. New Haven, Conn., 1986.

Mollat, Michel, ed. *Etudes sur l'histoire de la pauvreté.* 2 vols. Paris, 1974.

Mols, Roger. *Introduction à la démographie historique des villes d'Europe du XIVe au XVIIIe siècle.* 3 vols. Gembloux, 1954–56.

Moorman, John. *A History of the Franciscan Order from Its Origins to the Year 1517.* Oxford, 1968.

Murphy, Robert. "Encounters: The Body Silent in America." In *Disability and Culture*, edited by Benedicte Ingstad and Susan Reynolds Whyte, 140–58. Berkeley, Calif., 1995.

Murray, Alexander. "Religion among the Poor in Thirteenth-Century France: The Testimony of Humbert de Romans." *Traditio: Studies in Ancient and Medieval History, Thought and Religion* 30 (1974): 285–323.

Nahon, Géraud. "La communauté juive de Paris au XIIIe siècle: Problèmes topographiques, démographiques et institutionnels." In *Etudes sur l'histoire de Paris et de l'Ile de France: Actes du 100e Congrès National des Sociétés Savantes, Paris, 1975, Section de philologie et d'histoire jusqu'à 1610*, 2:143–58. Paris, 1978.

Nicholas, David. "Child and Adolescent Labour in the Late Medieval City: A Flemish Model in Regional Perspective." *English Historical Review* 110 (1995): 1103–31.

——. *The Domestic Life of a Medieval City: Women, Children, and the Family in Fourteenth-Century Ghent.* Lincoln, Neb., 1985.

O'Connor, Alice. *Poverty Knowledge: Social Science, Social Policy, and the Poor in Twentieth-Century U.S. History.* Princeton, N.J., 2001.

Ong, Walter. "Latin Language Study as a Renaissance Puberty Rite." In *Rhetoric, Romance, and Technology: Studies in the Interaction of Expression and Culture.* Ithaca, 1971.

Opitz, Claudia. *Frauenalltag im Mittelalter: Biographien des 13. und 14. Jahrhunderts.* Weinheim, 1985.

Paden, William D. "The Figure of the Shepherdess in the Medieval Pastourelle." *Medievalia et humanistica* 25 (1998): 1–14.

Papi, Anna Benvenuti. "Mendicant Friars and Female Pinzochere in Tuscany." Translated by Margery J. Schneider. In *Women and Religion in Medieval and Renaissance Italy*, edited by Daniel Bornstein and Roberto Rusconi, 84–103. Chicago, 1996.

Pasztor, Edith. "I Papi del Duecento e Trecento di fronte alla vita religiosa femminile." In *Il movimento religioso femminile in Umbria nei secoli XIII–XIV*, edited by Roberto Rusconi, 29–67. Citta di Castello, 1984.

Patten, J. "Patterns of Migration and Movement of Labor to Three Pre-Industrial East Anglian Towns." *Journal of Historical Geography* 2 (1976): 111–29.

Perrenoud, Alfred. *La population de Genève du seizième au debut du dix-neuvième siècle: Etude démographique.* Geneva, 1979.

Persram, Nalini. "Politicizing the *Féminine* Globalizing the Feminist." *Alternatives* 19 (1994): 275–313.

Phythian-Adams, Charles. *Desolation of a City: Coventry and the Urban Crisis of the Late Middle Ages.* Cambridge, 1979.

Pinker, Steven. *The Language Instinct.* New York, 1994.

Poussou, Jean-Pierre. "Mobilité et migrations." In *Histoire de la population française,* edited by Jacques Dupâquier et al., 2:99–143. 4 vols. Paris, 1988.

Prevenier, Walter. "Violence against Women in a Medieval Metropolis: Paris around 1400." In *Law, Custom, and the Social Fabric in Medieval Europe: Essays in Honor of Bryce Lyon,* edited by Bernard S. Bachrach and David Nicholas, 263–84. Studies in Medieval Culture 28. Kalamazoo, Mich., 1990.

Reitzel, J. M. "Medieval Houses of Bons-Enfants." *Viator: Medieval and Renaissance Studies* 11 (1980): 179–207.

Reyerson, Kathryn L. "The Adolescent Apprentice/Worker in Medieval Montpellier." *Journal of Family History* 17 (1992): 353–70.

——. "Urbanism, Western European." In *Dictionary of the Middle Ages,* edited by Joseph Strayer, 12:311–20. 13 volumes. New York: 1982–89.

Richard, Jules-Marie. *Une petite-nièce de Saint Louis: Mahaut, Comtesse d'Artois et de Bourgogne.* Paris, 1887.

Roch, Jean-Louis. "Le jeu de l'aumône au moyen âge." *Annales: Economies, sociétés, civilisations* 44 (1989): 505–27.

Romano, Dennis. "Charity and Community in Early Renaissance Venice." *Journal of Urban History* 11 (1984): 63–82.

Ross, E. "Survival Networks: Women's Neighborhood Sharing in London before World War I." *History Workshop Journal* 15 (1983): 4–27.

Rossiaud, Jacques. *Medieval Prostitution.* Translated by Lydia G. Cochrane. Oxford, 1988.

Rothrauff, Elizabeth. "Charity in a Medieval Community: Politics, Piety, and Poor Relief in Pisa, 1257–1312." Ph.D. diss., University of California, Berkeley, 1994.

Roux, Simone. "L'habitat urbain au moyen âge: Le quartier de l'Université de Paris." *Annales: Economies, sociétés, civilisations* 24 (1969): 1196–1219.

Rubin, Miri. *Charity and Community in Medieval Cambridge.* Cambridge, 1987.

Ruggiero, Guido. *Violence in Renaissance Venice.* New Brunswick, N.J., 1980.

Ruiz, Teofilo. "The Business of Salvation: Castilian Wills in the Late Middle Ages." In *On the Social Origins of Medieval Institutions: Essays in Honor of Joseph F. O'-Callaghan,* edited by Donald J. Kagay and Theresa M. Vann, 63–89. Leiden, 1998.

Saint-Denis, Alain. *L'Hôtel-Dieu de Laon, 1150–1300.* Nancy, 1983.

Salisbury, Joyce. *Church Fathers, Independent Virgins.* London, 1991.

Sandoval, Chela. "U.S. Third World Feminism: The Theory and Method of Oppositional Consciousness in the Postmodern World." *Genders* 10 (spring 1991): 1–24.

Saunier, Annie. *"Le pauvre malade" dans le cadre hospitalier médiéval: France du nord, vers 1300–1500.* Paris, 1993.

Scanlon, Thomas J., Andrew Tomkins, Margaret A. Lynch, and Francesca Scanlon.

"Street Children in Latin America." *British Medical Journal*, no. 7144 (23 May, 1998): 1596–1600.

Schmitt, Jean-Claude. *Mort d'une heresie: L'église et les clercs face aux béguines et béghards du Rhin supérieure du XIVe au XVe siècle*. Paris, 1978.

Schneyer, J. B. *Repertorium der lateinischen Sermones des Mittelalters für die Zeit von 1150–1350*. 11 vols. Beiträge zur Geschichte der Philosophie und Theologie des Mittelalters, Texte und Untersuchungen, vol. 43, nos. 1–11. Munich, 1969–90.

Semi, F. *Gli "ospizi" di Venezia*. Venice, 1983.

Semmler, Josef. "Die Residenzen der Fürsten und Prälaten im mittelalterlichen Paris (12.–14. Jahrhundert)." In *Mélanges offerts à René Crozet*, ed. Pierre Gallais and Yves-Jean Riou, 2:1217–1236. 2 vols. Poitiers, 1966.

Sharpe, Pamela. "Literally Spinsters: A New Interpretation of Local Economy and Demography in Coylton in the Seventeenth and Eighteenth Centuries." *Economic History Review* 44 (1991): 46–65.

Simons, Walter. "Reading a Saint's Body: Rapture and Bodily Movement in the *Vitae* of Thirteenth-Century Beguines." In *Framing Medieval Bodies*, edited by Sarah Kay and Miri Rubin, 10–23. Manchester, 1994.

Sivéry, Gérard. *L'économie du royaume de France au siècle de Saint Louis (vers 1180–vers 1315)*. Lille, 1984.

Smith, Richard. "Geographical Diversity in the Resort to Marriage in Late Medieval Europe: Work, Reputation, and Unmarried Females in the Household Formation Systems of Northern and Southern Europe." In *Woman Is a Worthy Wight: Women in English Society c. 1200–1500*, edited by P. J. P. Goldberg, 16–59. Wolfboro Falls, N.H., 1992.

Spelman, Elizabeth. *Inessential Woman: Problems of Exclusion in Feminist Thought*. Boston, 1988.

Stack, Carol B. *All Our Kin: Strategies for Survival in a Black Community*. New York, 1974. Reprint, 1997.

Stella, Alessandro. *La révolte des Ciompi: Les hommes, les lieux, le travail*. Paris, 1993.

Stuard, Susan Mosher. "Ancillary Evidence for the Decline of Medieval Slavery." *Past and Present*, no. 149 (November 1995): 3–28.

Swanson, Heather. "The Illusion of Economic Structure: Craft Guilds in Late Medieval English Towns." *Past and Present*, no. 121 (1988): 29–48.

Swanson, Jenny. *John of Wales: A Study of the Works and Ideas of a Thirteenth-Century Friar*. Cambridge, 1989.

Szittya, Penn R. *The Antifraternal Tradition in Medieval Literature*. Princeton, N.J., 1986.

Terroine, Anne. *Un bourgeois Parisien du XIIIe siècle: Geoffroy de Saint-Laurent, 1245?–1290*. Edited by Lucie Fossier. Paris, 1992.

———. "Études sur la bourgeoisie parisienne: Gandoufle d'Arcelles et les compagnies placentines à Paris (fin du XIIIe siècle)." *Annales d'histoire sociale* 7 (1945): 54–71; 8 (1945): 53–74.

———. "Recherches sur la bourgeoisie Parisienne au XIIIe siècle." 4 vols. Unpublished *thèse*, Ecole Nationale des Chartres, 1940.

Thompson, E. P. "The Moral Economy of the English Crowd in the Eighteenth Century." *Past and Present*, no. 50 (1971): 76–136.

Tierney, Brian. "The Decretists and the 'Deserving Poor.'" *Comparative Studies in Society and History* 1 (1958–59): 360–73.

———. *Medieval Poor Law: A Sketch of Canonical Theory and Its Application in England*. Berkeley, Calif., 1959.

Tits-Dieuaide, M. J. "Les tables des pauvres dans les anciennes principautés belges au moyen âge." *Tijdschrift voor Geschiedenis* 88 (1975): 562–83.

Trexler, Richard. "Charity and the Defense of Urban Elites in the Italian Communes." In *The Rich, the Well Born, and the Powerful: Elites and Upper Classes in History*, edited by Frederic Cople Jaher, 64–109. Urbana, Ill., 1973.

———. "Neighbors and Comrades: The Revolutionaries of Florence, 1378." *Social Analysis: Journal of Cultural and Social Practice* 14 (December 1983): 53–106.

———. "A Widows' Asylum of the Renaissance: The Orbatello of Florence." In *Old Age in Preindustrial Society*, ed. Peter N. Stearns, 119–49. New York, 1982.

Van den Hoven, Birgit. *Work in Ancient and Medieval Thought*. Amsterdam, 1996.

Vauchez, André. *La sainteté en occident aux derniers siècles du moyen âge: D'après les procès de canonisation et les documents hagiographiques*. Rome, 1981.

Vecchio, Silvana. "The Good Wife." Translated by Clarissa Botsford. In *A History of Women in the West*, vol. 2: *Silences of the Middle Ages*, ed. Christiane Klapisch-Zuber, 105–35. Cambridge, Mass., 1992.

Venarde, Bruce. *Women's Monasticism and Medieval Society: Nunneries in France and England, 890–1215*. Ithaca, 1997.

Vincent, Catherine. *Les confréries médiévales dans la royaume de France: XIIIᵉ–XVᵉ siècle*. Paris, 1994.

Vincent-Cassy, Mireille. "Quand les femmes deviennent paresseuses." In *Femmes, mariages, lignages, XIIᵉ–XIVᵉ siècles: Mélanges offerts à Georges Duby*, 431–47. Brussels, 1992.

Weinstein, Donald, and Rudolph Bell. *Saints and Society: The Two Worlds of Western Christendom, 1000–1700*. Chicago, 1982.

Wilkins, Nigel. *Nicolas Flamel: Des livres et de l'or*. Paris, 1993.

Young, M., and P. Willmott. *Family and Kinship in East London*. London, 1957.

Zinn, Maxine Baca, and Bonnie Thornton Dill. "Theorizing Difference from Multiracial Feminism." *Feminist Studies* 22 (1996): 321–31.

INDEX

Abandoned children, 79, 146
Adam and Eve, 39, 70–71, 105–6, 113. *See also* Eve
Adam le Panetier, 150, 171
Agnes of Pontoise, 27, 100, 157
Agrimi, Joel, 159
Alarcón, Norma, 41
Albertus Magnus, 105
Allen, Prudence, 106
Amelot of Chambly, 56–57, 64, 72, 125, 157–58, 163, 168
Amelot of Chaumont, 23, 26–27, 30, 36, 100, 157, 160–63
Amile of St.-Mathieu, 152–54, 158, 163
Apprentices, 19, 21, 79–80, 94–98, 143, 155
Aptekar, Lewis, 139
Archer, Janice, 13, 19, 23, 29, 32, 93–94, 122, 138, 141–42, 145, 155–56, 162
Artisans, ties among, 155, 159, 163
Augustine, Saint, 44, 61, 113
Avarice of poor, 49–50, 62–63, 89
Ave Maria College, 15, 81, 83–85, 148–50, 167
Avice of Berneville, 72, 131–32
Azo, 66

Baldwin, John, 167
Batany, Jean, 64
Bavoux, Paule, 78–79, 81, 83
Beattie, Cordelia, 40, 50
Beggars
    female, attitudes toward, 90, 122, 124–25
    male, attitudes toward, 60–70
    number of, 33
Begging, gendered patterns of, 90
Beguines, 127–29
    of Paris, 14, 114, 143–47, 162, 166
Bell, Rudolph, 133
Bennett, Judith, 7, 29, 33, 142, 164

Bent, Margaret, 71
Berman, Constance, 140, 147
Berthelé, Joseph, 78
Biscoglio, Frances M., 126
Biver, Paul and Marie Louise, 87, 147, 166
Black Death, 7, 24–27, 88, 165
Blind persons, 27, 34, 60, 62–63, 83, 88–89, 100, 118–19, 125, 153–54, 157. *See also* Quinze-Vingts
Bloch, R. Howard, 106
Body
    and femininity, 39–42
    and lower status men, 40, 43, 44–60
Bolton, Brenda, 126
Bonaventure, 44–46, 65–66, 71, 129–30
Bornstein, Daniel, 42
Borresen, Kari Elisabeth, 113
Boswell, John, 61, 79
Bourlet, Caroline, 24, 40, 103, 141, 145
Boyarin, Daniel, 113
Branner, Robert, 17
Brett, Edward Tracy, 128
Brettell, Caroline, 26
Brittany, immigrants from, 19–22, 37, 152, 163–64
Brown, Elizabeth A. R., 12
Brunel, Ghislain, 16
Buc, Philippe, 46, 113
Burchard of Worms, 127
Butchers, 27, 52
Bynum, Caroline, 41

Canonization process, 7–8, 50–51
Carolus-Barré, Louis, 7, 9–10, 161
Carozzi, Claude, 42
Casagrande, Carla, 107, 115, 117
Castelli, Elizabeth, 114
Cazelles, Brigitte, 42
Cazelles, Raymond, 9, 17–19, 35–36, 165–66
Chabot, Isabelle, 6, 40

Charity
of elites, 3–4, 33, 75, 80–90, 143–51, 164
of the working poor, 80, 90–104, 125,
151–64
Charmaz, Kathy, 168
Chartularium universitatis Parisiensis, 84
Chennaf, Sharaf, 8
Chiffoleau, Jacques, 4
Chojnacki, Stanley, 140
"Chronique Parisienne anonyme de 1316 à
1339," 35–36
Clare of Assisi, 126
Cloth workers. *See* Dyers; Fullers; Spinners;
Weavers; Wool combers and carders
Cohen, Esther, 37–38
Cohen, Gustave, 60
Colish, Marcia, 43
Colleges for school boys, 14–15, 81–85, 167
Collins, Patricia Hill, 41
Companions
female, 6–7, 90, 103, 137–38, 145,
160–63
male, 103
Confession, 99, 124, 126, 137, 159
Connally, Michael, 149
Consumption loans, 151
Corpus juris civilis, 66
Corzo, Luis Revest, 65
Cosmetics
of false beggars, 65–69
of women, 43, 67–69
Court records, gendered patterns in, 40, 118
Coyecque, E., 88
Crisciani, Chiara, 159

Davis, Michael T., 11
D'Avray, D., 3, 109
Deaf persons, 32, 34, 74–81, 83, 99–100
Debauchery of poor, 50
Depping, G. P., 141
Deserving poor, 3, 34, 124
Desportes, Pierre, 28, 31
Didier, Philippe, 95
*Digestum vetus seu Pandectarum Iuris civilis
tomus primus*, 68
Dill, Bonnie Thornton, 41
Dillard, Heath, 40
Dishonesty of poor, 50–51, 59, 61, 64–67, 69
Dixon, E., 142
Dominican order, 3, 44, 61, 130. *See also* Al-
bertus Magnus; Humbert of Romans;
Stephen of Bourbon; Thomas Aquinas;
Thomas of Cantimpré

Douceline of Digne, 42
Douie, D. L., 44
Dowries for poor girls, 34, 81–82, 139, 143,
150–51
Drunkenness, of poor, 47, 61
Dubois, Gérard, 147
Dubois, Henry, 5, 24, 29
Du Boulay, César Egasse, 126
Du Breul, Jacques, 87
Duby, Georges, 1, 46
Dufeil, Michel-Marie, 44
Dyer, Christopher, 5–6
Dyers, 21, 23, 27, 35, 155, 159, 163

Edin, Kathryn, 2
Elite attitudes toward poor, 3–4, 6, 10,
124–25, 167–68
Elite definitions of poor, 3, 6
Elizabeth of Hungary, 126
Elliott, Dyan, 3, 43, 114, 138
Elliott, Vivien Brodsky, 160
Emeline, wife of Nicolas, minister of the
Quinze-Vingts, 26, 89, 171
Employers, care by, 94–100, 156–57
England, immigrants from, 19–23, 28, 103,
153–54, 157, 163
Epstein, Steven A., 4, 95–97
Etablissements de Saint Louis, 64
Etienne Haudry, 13, 16, 84, 147–48, 150,
171. *See also* Haudriettes; Jehanne
Haudry
Eve, 111, 113. *See also* Adam and Eve

Fagniez, Gustave, 81, 96, 98, 101, 155
Fairchilds, Cissie, 160
False beggars, 64–69, 86, 111, 124–25
Family, support of, 6, 27, 90–94, 152–55, 163
Farmer, Sharon, 41, 60, 63, 95
Favier, J., 16
Fawtier, R., 16
Fay, Percival B., 7, 169
Feminine labors, hierarchies of. *See* Femi-
ninities, hierarchies of
Femininities, hierarchies of, 10, 40–41,
106–13, 130
Filles Dieu, Parisian convent of, 14, 87, 129,
132, 147, 165
Finucane, Ronald C., 8, 51
Fiscal poor, 5, 24
Foreville, Raymonde, 123
Fossier, Lucie, 145
Fourquin, Guy, 165
Fourth Lateran Council, 67

Franciscans, 3, 9, 44, 61, 114, 127, 130, 144–45. *See also* Bonaventure; Gilbert of Tournai

Frappier-Bigras, Diane, 142

Freedman, Paul, 46, 70–71

Friedman, Albert, 70–71

Froide, Amy, 29, 168

Fullers, 35, 98

Gabriel, Astrik, 84–86, 148, 167

Le garcon et l'aveugle, 61–62, 89

Gauvard, Claude, 37, 160

Gender categories, multiplicity of, 1, 2, 41. *See also* Femininities, hierarchies of; Masculinities, hierarchies of

Genesis, 39, 46, 74, 105, 117, 147

Geremek, Bronislaw, 4, 6, 13, 23, 32–35, 64–66, 85, 88, 95, 101, 134, 138, 152, 166

Gerschick, Thomas J., 168

Gervais Ruffus, 84, 171

Gilbert of Sens, 102–3, 168

Gilbert of Tournai, 2–3, 48–49, 66, 70, 97, 109, 111–13, 115–17, 167

Gilds, 100–102, 122
     women and, 7, 29, 141–42, 155–56

Girart de Troyes, 89, 171

Glorieux, P., 167

Godding, P., 4

Goldberg, P. J. P., 6–7, 19–20, 23, 25–26, 29, 31–32, 50, 160–62

Gonthier, Nicole, 4–6, 24

Goodich, Michael, 8

Gratian, 50, 61

Gravdal, Kathryn, 107

Great Famine, 33, 35–36, 165

Guerout, Jean, 11

Guest, Gerald B., 64

Guibert of Nogent, 78

Guillaume au Long Nez, 89, 171

Guillaume de Chartres, 18

Guillaume de la Villeneuve, 129

Guillaume de Nangis, 18, 35–36

Guillaume Fresnel, 151, 171

Guillaume le Clerc de Normandie, 49–50

Guillot of Caux, 72, 83, 88, 103, 158

Guillot the Cripple, 98–100

Hajnal, John, 25–26, 29

Hallam, Elizabeth, 35

Hanawalt, Barbara, 37, 80, 97

Hasenohr, Geneviève, 107

Haudriettes, 14, 148–49, 167

Helmholz, R. H., 50

Henderson, John, 4, 6, 34

Herbert of Fontenay, 21, 155, 159, 163–64. *See also* Yfame of Lagny

Herlihy, David, 18, 19, 21, 98

Historiography
     of medieval gender categories, 41–43
     of medieval poor, 3–7

Hohenberg, Paul M., 20

Hollywood, Amy, 42, 126

Honorius of Autun, 49

hooks, bell, 41

Horden, Peregrine, 26–27, 158

Hospitals, 3, 4, 14–15, 85–92, 100, 146, 157. *See also* Hôtel Dieu of Paris; Quinze-Vingts; St.-Esprit-en-Grève; Ymbert of Lyon

Hôtel Dieu of Paris, 15, 87–88, 120–23, 125, 130, 140, 146

Household pattern, northwest European, 25–29

Housing for the poor, 85–86, 103, 137, 140, 160–61

Howell, Martha, 7, 29, 164

Hufton, Olwen, 123, 153, 160, 162

Hugh of Amiens, 159

Hugh of St.-Victor, 106

Hughes, Diane Owen, 67

Huguccio, 49

Humbert of Romans, 2–3, 38, 45–49, 66, 69–71, 106, 108–11, 115, 117, 128, 167

Hundred Years' War, 165

Idleness
     of poor, 60
     of women, 118

Italians, in Paris, 12, 13, 16, 24

Ivo of Chartres, 68

Jacob of Voragine, 60, 62

Jacqueline of St.-Germain-des-Prés, 132

Jacques de Vitry, 2–3, 45, 48–49, 65, 69–71, 97, 105, 109, 111–13, 115–17, 127–30

Jaillot, Jean Baptiste Michel, 101

Jean, sire de Joinville, 67

Jean de Jandun, 11–12

Jean of St.-Victor, 35, 68

Jehan de Fontenoi, and Bauteut, his wife, 34, 171

Jehan de Troyes, 33, 79, 84, 89, 148–49, 172

Jehan Langlais, 33, 89, 172

Jehan le Grand, currier, 33, 97, 151, 171

Jehan le Grand, deceased husband of Jehanne de Malaunay, 26

Jehan le Grand, wholesaler of ocean fish, 16
Jehan le Marchant, 61
Jehanne Argence, 150, 172
Jehanne de Malaunay, 26, 85, 149, 172
Jehanne du Faut, 79, 85, 143–47, 172
Jehanne Haudry, wife of Etienne Haudry,
    16, 79, 84, 148–50, 172
Jehanne la Fouacière, 84–85, 87, 148–49, 172
Jehanne of Serris, 88, 119–24, 130–31, 135,
    152–54
Jehan of La Haye, 36, 83
Jerome, 61–62
Jews
    gendering of, 40–41
    of Paris, 16, 24
Johannes de Erfordia, 50
John, Count of Chalon, 75
John of Freiburg, 61, 66
John of Wales, 49
Jordan, William Chester, 16, 18, 36, 68, 151

Kaeppeli, Thomas, 167
Karras, Ruth, 23, 37, 67, 138
Kertzer, David, 26
Klapisch-Zuber, Christiane, 7
Knights, 44, 46
Kowaleski, Maryanne, 7, 27, 29, 82, 142
Kraemer, Ross Shepard, 114
Krötzl, Christian, 8
Kruger, Steven, 40

Labande, E. R., 124
Labor
    penitential, 119, 122–23, 127–31
    productive, men and, 39, 44–50,
        118–19, 121, 123, 131, 134
    productive, women and, 23, 117–19,
        121, 127, 130, 133–35
    reproductive, women and, 39, 121, 131
    See also Femininities, hierarchies of;
        Masculinities, hierarchies of
Lalor, Kevin J., 139
Lalou, Elisabeth, 16, 36
La Roncière, Charles de, 5–6, 152
Lasciviousness
    of poor persons, 47–48, 61, 69–70, 89,
        116, 130–31
    of poor women, 106, 108, 110, 116, 131
    of women, 105
Laslett, Peter, 25–26
Laundresses, 23–24, 123, 136, 138–39, 143,
    156, 161–62
Lebeuf, L'Abbé, 87

Lees, Lynn Hollen, 20
Le Goff, Jacques, 8
Le Grand, Léon, 87, 89, 143–44, 148–49,
    166
Lein, Laura, 2
Lerner, Robert, 145
Le Roy Ladurie, Emmanuel, 8
Lett, Didier, 8, 154, 160
Little, Lester K., 44–45
Livre des métiers, 35, 93, 101, 141, 142, 155
Lomnitz, Larissa A., 158
Lot, F., 16
Louis IX, 7, 11–12, 35, 89, 143–44, 166
    inquest concerning his miracles, 7, 9,
        24, 51, 56–59, 77, 118, 132
Louis the deaf-mute, 32, 36, 74–81, 83,
    99–100
Luce of Rémilly-sur-Lozon, 23, 26, 28,
    118–19, 125, 153–54
Lunbeck, Elizabeth, 168
Lynch, Margaret A., 139

Mahieu, B., 142
Maillard, François, 17
Makowski, Elizabeth, 145
Mansfield, Mary, 159
Margaret, wife of Pierre Loisel, 84–85, 87,
    149, 172
Marguerite of La Magdaleine, 129
Marguerite, wife of Louis IX, 9, 79, 87
Marie, widow of Robert Evrout, 26, 34, 84,
    172
Marriage, age at, 25–27
Married men, sick or disabled, 94
Married women, sick or disabled, 88,
    119–24, 130–31, 135, 152–54, 164
Martin, Saint, 60, 62
Masculinities, hierarchies of, 10, 40–41,
    44–50, 130
Maubuisson, abbey of, 140
Mayade-Claustre, Julie, 151
McNamara, Jo Ann Kay, 114, 126
Menstrual rags, 62
Michaëlsson, Karl, 19–20
Michaud-Frejaville, Françoise, 80, 95–96
Migrants, networks among, 36–37, 155–56,
    159–60, 163
Migration, 25, 28–29, 93–94
    gendered patterns of, 10, 20–21, 26,
        28–32, 95, 139, 154, 161
    to Paris and St.-Denis, 9–10, 17–22,
        26–27, 30, 36–37, 92–93, 98, 120,
        136, 152–53, 155–56, 159–60, 165–66

Miller, Adam S., 168
Miracles, location of, 52–56
Mirrer, Louise, 41
Mollat, Michel, 4, 64
Mols, Roger, 82
Moorman, John, 127
Moriset of Ranton, 32, 57–58, 76, 83, 154
Murphy, Robert, 168
Murray, Alexander, 38

Nahon, Géraud, 16
Neighbors
    charity of, 6, 90, 102–3, 157–58, 160,
        164
    memory of, 165
    ties among, 158–59
Nicholas, David, 28, 37
Nicolas Flamel, 86
Nicole of Rubercy, 23–24, 131–32, 136–39,
    153, 158, 160–63

O'Connor, Alice, 2, 168
Old persons, 101
    hospices for, 14–15, 81, 86, 101, 143,
        147–50
    men, 82, 102–3
    women, 67, 82, 139, 159
Ong, Walter, 78
Opitz, Claudia, 8
Orenge of Fontenay, 23, 26, 28, 98, 100, 143,
    156
Orphans, 78, 81, 83, 85, 101, 143, 155

Paden, William D., 107
Papi, Anna Benvenuti, 145
Parish church, beggars at, 34, 121, 123, 152
Parish networks, 34
Pasternack, Carol Braun, 41
Pasztor, Edith, 114
Patten, J., 20
Peasant women, 110–11, 115
Perrenoud, Alfred, 20
Persram, Nalini, 41
Peter the Chanter, 65, 67–68, 125
Philippe de Cormeilles, 85, 172
Philip the Fair, 11–12, 35
Physicians, consultation of, 54–55
Phythian-Adams, Charles, 82
Pierre la Pie, 84, 89, 149, 172
Pinker, Steven, 77
Ponce of Froitmantel, 132–33
Poor, self perceptions of, 10, 70–73, 131–35
Population, of Paris, 17–18

Porrois, abbey of, 140
Poussou, Jean-Pierre, 20
Prevenier, Walter, 37–38
Prostitutes, 23–24, 68–69, 108, 110–11, 115,
    129, 132, 138–39, 143, 147, 154

Quinze-Vingts, hospital of, 14, 88–90, 166

Raou the Cobbler, 34, 58, 83
Rape, of poor women, 37–38, 107
Rebellion, in Paris, 35, 71
Redon, Odile, 8
Regalado, Nancy Freeman, 12
Reimbaldus Leodiensis, 127
Reitzel, J. M., 83–84, 167
Reyerson, Kathryn L., 18, 95–96
Richard, Jules-Marie, 16, 80
Richard of Briqueville, 23, 93–94
Richard Vaudien, 23
Rich matrons, responsibilities of, 108–10,
    112–13
Robert Evrout, 16, 84, 172. See also Marie
Robert le Vinetier, 89, 172
Robert of Cantarage, 72–73, 157–58
Roch, Jean-Louis, 4, 64
Roman de Fauvel, 71
Romano, Dennis, 4
Ross, E., 158
Rossiaud, Jacques, 37
Rothrauff, Elizabeth, 148
Roux, Simone, 137
Rubin, Miri, 4, 6, 126
Ruggiero, Guido, 37–38
Ruiz, Teofilo, 65
Rule of Saint Benedict, 127
Rutebeuf, 11, 33, 89, 144

St.-Antoine, convent of, 15, 140, 147
Saint-Denis, Alain, 4
Ste.-Avoye, hospice of, 14, 147–49, 166
St.-Esprit-en-Grève, hospital of, 78, 81, 83,
    85, 143, 166
Salisbury, Joyce, 114
Sandoval, Chela, 41
Sarah, wife of Tobias, 109, 112
Saunier, Annie, 88
Scanlon, Francesca, 139
Scanlon, Thomas J., 139
Schmitt, Jean-Claude, 115, 126
Schneyer, J. B., 167
Sédile of Laon, 89, 149–50, 172
Semi, F., 148
Semmler, Josef, 12

Sermon literature, 37–38, 42, 107. *See also*
    Gilbert of Tournai; Humbert of Romans;
    Jacques de Vitry; Stephen of Bourbon;
    Thomas of Chobham
Servants, 7, 16, 27–31, 37, 95–97, 100, 103,
    143, 150–51, 154, 156–57
    sermons about, 47–48, 70, 108–9,
        111–17
Sexuality, 132–33
Sharpe, Pamela, 162
Siblings, support of, 91, 93, 152–54, 160,
    163
Simon Piz-d'Oue, 33, 84, 172
Simons, Walter, 42
Single men, 25, 27–29, 82, 119
Single women, 23–29, 37, 82–83, 106,
    114–15, 117, 119, 132, 139–44, 147, 149,
    151, 155, 160, 164, 168
Sivéry, Gérard, 5, 13, 17, 35
Smith, Richard, 25–26, 29, 31
Smiths, 72, 75, 125, 138, 157
Spelman, Elizabeth, 41
Spinners, 27, 119, 123, 126–27, 135,
    142–43, 146, 156
Spinster clustering. *See* Companions: fe-
    male
Spouses, support of, 94, 153–54
Stack, Carol B., 2, 158
Standards of living, 5
Stella, Alessandro, 5–6, 23–24
Stephen of Bourbon, 63, 67
Stuard, Susan Mosher, 112
Swanson, Heather, 122
Swanson, Jenny, 49
Szittya, Penn R., 44

Tailors, 23, 52, 93, 101–2, 155
Tanon, L., 138
Tausche, M., 3, 109
Tax assessments, 5, 6, 40
    Parisian, 13, 16–17, 19–20, 24, 32, 37,
        40, 94, 98, 101–3, 122, 138, 140–42,
        145–46, 155–56, 162
Terroine, Anne, 12–13, 16, 37, 52, 100, 140,
    157
Tertullian, 114
Thomas Aquinas, 45, 49–50, 61–62, 68,
    113
Thomas le Tailleur, 89, 172
Thomas of Cantimpré, 45, 126
Thomas of Chobham, 40, 61, 63, 65–69,
    125, 159, 167

Thomas of Eccleston, 128
Thomas of Voudai, 83
Thompson, E. P., 71
Tierney, Brian, 6, 49, 91, 124
Tits-Dieuaide, M. J., 4
Tomkins, Andrew, 139
Trexler, Richard, 4, 6, 85, 91, 148, 150

Unemployment, 35, 65

Vagrancy, laws against, 64–65
Van den Hoven, Birgit, 44, 68
Vauchez, André, 8, 53
Vecchio, Silvana, 112
Venarde, Bruce, 128
Vincent, Catherine, 4, 155
Vincent-Cassy, Mireille, 112, 117
Voluntary poverty, 3, 44, 49, 61, 124, 126,
    130–31

Wages, inadequacy of, 5, 23, 34, 63, 123,
    134, 139, 164
Wall, Richard, 5
Wathey, Andrew, 71
Wealth in Paris, 11–17
Weavers, 28, 35, 100, 143, 156
Weinstein, Donald, 133
Widows, 6, 13, 23–24, 26, 28–30, 81–82,
    91–92, 111, 131, 136, 139–40, 146–49,
    160, 168
    remarriage of, 25–26
    See also Old persons: hospices for
Wilkins, Nigel, 86
William of Canterbury, 51
Willmott, P., 158
Witnesses in court
    character of, 24
    poor as, 50–51
Wool carders and combers, 23, 28, 100,
    143–44, 156, 166

Yfame of Lagny, 26–27, 135, 153, 155, 159,
    163–64
Ymbert of Lyon, hospital of, 14, 87, 148,
    165
Young, M., 158
Youths
    female, 92
    male, 25, 30–32, 78, 82–84, 91–93,
        98–100, 103

Zinn, Maxine Baca, 41